We dedicate this book to all educators who have the courage and passion to be innovative.

We also dedicate this book to our respective families who are our daily inspirations: Howie, Benjamin, and Jake; Barry, Jeffrey, Lauren, and Matthew.

Breaking the Mold of School Instruction and Organization

Breaking the Mold of School Instruction and Organization

Innovative and Successful Practices for the Twenty-First Century

Edited by Andrea Honigsfeld
and Audrey Cohan

ROWMAN & LITTLEFIELD EDUCATION

A division of

ROWMAN & LITTLEFIELD PUBLISHERS, INC.
Lanham • New York • Toronto • Plymouth, UK

Published by Rowman & Littlefield Education
A division of Rowman & Littlefield Publishers, Inc.
A wholly owned subsidiary of The Rowman & Littlefield Publishing Group, Inc.
4501 Forbes Boulevard, Suite 200, Lanham, Maryland 20706
http://www.rowmaneducation.com

Estover Road
Plymouth PL6 7PY
United Kingdom

British Library Cataloguing in Publication Information Available

Library of Congress Cataloging-in-Publication Data

Honigsfeld, Andrea, 1965–
    Breaking the mold of school instruction and organization : innovative and successful
    practices for the twenty-first century / Andrea Honigsfeld and Audrey Cohan.
        p. cm.
    Includes bibliographical references.
    ISBN 978-1-60709-400-5 (cloth : alk. paper)—ISBN 978-1-60709-401-2 (pbk. : alk.
paper)—ISBN 978-1-60709-402-9 (electronic)
    1. School improvement programs.   2. Learning, Psychology of.   3. Effective
teaching.   4. Educational innovations.
    I. Cohan, Audrey.   II. Title.
    LB2822.8.H66 2009
    371.2'07—dc22   2009028602

Printed in the United States of America

⊗™ The paper used in this publication meets the minimum requirements of American
National Standard for Information Sciences—Permanence of Paper for Printed Library
Materials, ANSI/NISO Z39.48-1992.

Contents

Foreword

Breaking the mold of instruction and organization requires innovation. Innovation requires leadership. Leadership requires a human engine that can "inspire, charm, cajole, persuade and, when necessary, coerce" (Meacham, 2008, p. 188).

Innovation by way of positive leadership is recognizable, but interpreted differently by many. It is concrete and productive, but subject to multiple perceptions, interchangeable views, and often leads to definitive setbacks and stalemates. Educational leaders, as change agents, must be prepared for both progress and frustration.

Leadership has been defined by hundreds—but no two definitions are essentially similar and most are theoretical and analytic—when the act of leading is practical and often is a global response to what one human acutely senses is necessary. Leadership is the cause of substantial disagreement among some and blind allegiance by others. It is impossible to train for leadership because it emerges in different formats and styles with every venture. Nevertheless, professors futilely attempt to develop leadership skills among those who either intuitively adopt the stature or who never would—and never could.

Leadership toward innovation emerges from a deep fountain of commitment, conscience, devotion to concept, passion, and a willingness to endure the scorn of those who do not and cannot understand. Adults teach youth not to be seen or heard and to know their place. We then wonder why so many become followers. The most compelling success stories recognize the important role of the students, the teachers, the parents, and the community in the process of growth and change. Sometimes this process takes place though renewal or redesign and sometimes the innovation begins from a grassroots effort in response to an overwhelming challenge.

We choose teachers who are required to adhere to administrative mandates and state-, or government-selected curriculum or programs, and then chide them for not exerting creativity and innovation. We offer tenure to those who seek safety and do as they are told and, when their careers advance, we alter expectations and require unique behaviors—from adults who have never been permitted to engage in self-selected innovative behaviors.

We choose administrators who are expected to provide leadership after years of demonstrating good followership, and then fail to protect them from the envy that status invariably engenders. We encourage marching to the beat of the drummers individuals hear, but rarely defend those who enable or promote other-than-traditional approaches. Unfortunately, we encourage innovation with the full knowledge that many colleagues will criticize any ideas reflective of diversity. In reality, we are a profession of replicators. We repackage the old so that it looks new; we distort the new so that people feel comfortable with the not-too-different approach.

Thus, it is wondrous that so many outstanding educators responded to this book's call for chapters on innovation and ways to improve schooling. As you read these entries, soberly consider the energy, creativity, intelligence, and time each contributed to the project described. Consider your own reaction. Would you have been willing to devote the same amount of effort to something that unique, or would you have dismissed it as not quite worthy? How receptive are you personally to change, particularly when that concept is someone else's idea? What do you like very much, what do you believe has promise for your own educational environment, and what causes no positive reaction at all and may be dismissed easily?

As you read the enclosed compelling stories of innovations and success, you will enter unique classrooms, meet visionary educators and leaders, walk down the corridors of redesigned or newly constructed schools, and visit communities where change impacts positively on student learning. You will find yourself in schools that value and respond to each child's unique cultural, academic, linguistic, and learning-styles needs. You will also observe schools that have forged close partnerships with a local institution. You will visit classrooms, schools, and communities in the United States and overseas where children succeed and educators experience the highest levels of professional accomplishments.

When educators can no longer look away, and change is demanded in struggling and failing schools, innovative school instruction and organization will become a reality. When readers like you decide that a specific program or idea has proven itself sufficiently well researched and exciting to earn your earnest participation, the momentum for change will spread.

—Professor Rita Dunn

REFERENCES

Meacham, J. (2008). *American lion: Andrew Jackson in the White House.* New York: Random House.

Preface

Andrea Honigsfeld and Audrey Cohan

EDUCATING CHILDREN IN THE TWENTY-FIRST CENTURY

The date was: 01/01/01: the beginning of a much anticipated new era, the twenty-first century. Long before that date though, readers of both scholarly and popular books started to see a surge of publications addressing the twenty-first century (see Tonkin & Edwards, 1981). As early as 2005 (and now in its 3rd edition published in 2007), Friedman was ready to describe the brief history of the twenty-first century in his best seller *The World is Flat*. His ultimate purpose was to help make sense of the "quantum leap" or globalization we have all been experiencing, as well as to explore the extent to which changes and advances in technology and communication created a new economic and political context.

Martin (2006) went as far as trying to define *The Meaning of the Twenty-first Century,* whereas many others provided advice to political and business leaders on how to prepare for the new global/digital age. In 2000, PBS broadcast a television program and then released a videotape on creating *The Twenty-first Century CEO*. Steffen (2006) offered guidance on creating an economically and environmentally sustainable future for the next generation, with Al Gore writing an insightful foreword. Curry, Jiobu, and Schwirian (2007) explored social inequalities that continue into the twenty-first century, as well as new trends in social transformation and their implications for global citizenship.

Many publications strive to identify the essential knowledge and skills needed for the twenty-first century in an extensive range of subject matters from world politics (Duncan, Jancar-Webster, & Switky, 2005) and the United Nations (Mingst & Karns, 2006), to criminal justice technology (Moriarty, 2006), to non-government organization management (Quelch & Laidler-Kylander, 2005).

The field of education is certainly no exception to this trend: books on twenty-first-century issues abound. Authors of numerous recent books addressed the changing local and global circumstances as they simultaneously discussed their selected instructional topics: whether it be higher education (Kezar, 2001), environmental education (Palmer, 1998), multicultural education (Diaz, 2000), urban education (Obiakor & Beachum, 2005), inclusive education (Sands, Kozleski, & French, 2000), literacy (Tompkins, 2005), reading instruction (Graves, Juel, & Graves, 2006), mathematics (Huetinck & Munshin, 2008), school leadership (Hoyle, 1998), childcare and family support (Finn-Stevenson & Ziegler, 1999), and so forth. We know the list could go on and will go on!

Simplicio (2007) described the twenty-first-century students or "millennial" students as ones who attend better-equipped schools with ample resources and classes taught by well-qualified teachers. On the whole, this might be the case. He cautiously acknowledged that "although millennial students are better informed, more technologically savvy, and worldlier, they are also more diverse, more demanding, needier, and harder to teach than any other students in the past" (p. 2). He also depicted a new educational environment in which:

> Gone are the days of quiet straight rows of attentive students. Gone are lessons taught through pure lectures that provided little time nor desire for dialogue. Gone are the classroom drill and practice skill exercise. Gone are examinations that measure academic success based upon a student's ability to memorize facts and statistics. (p. 1)

Are they really gone? Are all students' needs responded to in every classroom in the United States? Are all students engaged actively and successfully in the learning process? In a local and global context, we support Simplicio's (2007) optimism, and with our selection of success stories we offer answers to some previously unanswered questions raised by this plethora of recent publications.

OUR PURPOSE

The purpose of this book is to offer a collection of innovative ideas representing best practices from authors of diverse experiences and backgrounds. Each chapter in its own context is about how educators successfully break the traditional mold of education, create innovative and successful opportunities for learning, and address their students' diverse needs. Well-established, world renowned authors tell their stories of authentic accomplishments alongside first-time writers who share lesser known, but equally compelling stories of success.

From classroom innovations, through examples of positive unconventional leadership, to school and disctrictwide initiatives, we present unique narratives of innovations that will motivate and inspire both novice and experienced teachers and administrators. Chapters written by or about practicing teachers demonstrate how they leave the constraints of their classroom behind and successfully reach all students.

Several chapters are dedicated to exploring leadership practices and initiatives about school leaders who innovatively create new learning spaces and opportunities. Other chapters examine school districts that work with 20th-century resources, yet meet the demands of the twenty-first century. Their examples reveal how to accomplish uncommon successes with nontraditional initiatives.

To broaden the perspective, we showcase examples of successful community involvement and support where the boundary of the school and the community are blurred. When school and community become one, this translates into enhanced learning. School buildings welcome the community, and classrooms move out into the community for the benefit of students and neighbors. When facility designers, educators, and community members join together they produce exemplars of learning spaces that span across multiple generations and accommodate differentiated instruction and learning styles. These chapters will represent unique educational practices from less commonly featured world locales, such as Hungary, Iceland, New Zealand, and Zambia.

As you visit classrooms, districts, renovated historic buildings, science centers, concert halls, and more, we hope you enjoy this journey as much as we did.

REFERENCES

CEO exchange: Creating the CEO of the twenty-first Century. (2000). New York: PBS.

Curry, T., Jiobu, R., & Schwirian, K. (2007). *Sociology for the twenty-first century.* Upper Saddle River, NJ: Prentice Hall.

Diaz, C. F. (2000). *Multicultural education in the twenty-first century.* Boston: Allyn & Bacon.

Duncan, W. R., Jancar-Webster, B., & Switky, B. (2005). *World politics in the twenty-first century* (3rd ed.). White Plains, NY: Longman.

Finn-Stevenson, M., & Zigler, E. (1999) *Schools of the twenty-first century: Linking child care and education.* Boulder, CO: Westview.

Friedman, T. L. (2005). *The world is flat: A brief history of the twenty-first century.* New York: Straus and Giroux.

Friedman, T. L. (2007). *The world is flat 3.0: A brief history of the twenty-first century.* New York: Picador.

Graves, M. F., Juel, C., & Graves, B. B. (2006). *Teaching reading in the twenty-first century* (4th ed.). Boston: Allyn and Bacon.

Hoyle, J. R. (1998). *Skills for successful twenty-first century school leaders.* Lanham, MD: Scarecrow.

Huetinck, L., & Munshin, S. (2008). *Teaching mathematics in the twenty-first century.* Upper Saddle River, NJ: Prentice Hall.

Kezar, A. (2001). *Understanding and facilitating change in higher education in the twenty-first century.* San Francisco: Jossey-Bass.

Martin, G. (2006). *The meaning of the twenty-first century.* New York: Riverhead Hardcover.

Mingst, K. A., & Karns, M. P. (2006). *United Nations in the twenty-first century: Dilemmas in world politics.* Boulder, CO: Westview.

Moriarty, L. J. (2006). *Criminal justice technology in the twenty-first century* (2nd ed.). Springfield, IL: Charles C. Thomas.

Obiakor, F. E., & Beachum, F. D. (2005). *Urban education for the twenty-first century: Research, issues, and perspectives.* Springfield, IL: Charles.C. Thomas.

Palmer, J. (1998). *Environmental education in the twenty-first century: Theory, practice, progress, and promise.* London: Routledge.

Quelch, A., & Laidler-Kylander, N. (2005). *The new global brands: Managing non-government organizations in the twenty-first century.* Boston: Thompson.

Sands, D., Kozleski, E., & French, N. (2000). *Inclusive education for the twenty-first century: A new introduction to special education.* Boston: Wadsworth.

Simplicio, J. S. C. (2007). *Educating the twenty-first century student.* Bloomington, IN: AuthorHouse.

Steffen, A. (2006). *Worldchanging: A user's guide for the twenty-first century.* New York: Harry N. Abrams.

Tompkins, G. E. (2005). *Literacy for the twenty-first century: A balanced approach* (4th ed.). Upper Saddle River, NJ: Prentice Hall.

Tonkin, H., & Edwards, J. (1981). *The world in the curriculum: Curricular strategies for the twenty-first Century* (Education and the world view). New Rochelle, NY: Transaction Publishers.

Acknowledgments

The editors would like to thank all contributing authors for generously sharing their passion for their work in education with us and for allowing their success stories to come alive on these pages. Our goal is to meet each of you in person!

We would like to recognize and extend a special note of appreciation to Kelley Cordeiro, Joshua L. Garfinkel, and Lucia Posillico for their ongoing assistance and exemplary support on this book project. We also wish to acknowledge individuals who have encouraged us to pursue this project, including Maureen Walsh, Ed. D. and Sister Bernadette Donovan, O.P., Ph.D., and all our friends and colleagues at Molloy College, Rockville Centre, New York.

On a personal note, we would like to thank the late Professor Rita Dunn, Ed.D. for her sustained role as mentor and inspiration.

Gratitude is extended to the staff at Rowman & Littlefield, who made this an enjoyable and exciting project: Dr. Thomas Koerner, vice-president and editorial director, Ashley Baird, production editor, and Maera Stratton, editorial acquisitions.

Part I

Classroom Innovations

Bickman (2000) argued that "genuine school reform can happen not through any change imposed from above but only through the consistent application of intelligence and steady thinking, by teachers and students, day by day, class by class" (p. 300). The chapters featured in this section certainly support his philosophy. As we visit with highly innovative educators from around the country, we can see their pioneering approaches are indicative of their deep thinking, passion for teaching, and courage to initiate change. These attributes will come alive on the following pages.

Sally Brown documents the story of Martín, a Latino English learner's journey evolving from an at-risk second grader to a student who excels socially, culturally, and academically as he is invited to share his expertise. Thomas DeVere Wolsey, Diane Lapp, and Douglas Fisher describe ways to create a culture of literacy in the classroom or the entire school community through meaningful interactions, high expectations, and challenging learning opportunities—across multiple themes, authors, texts, and text types. Karen Bostic Frederick invites us to take a look inside a classroom where Lani, a black Newfoundland, becomes an integral part of literacy instructional practices. Challenged by the lack of classroom space and concerns regarding adequate academic and literacy instruction for their English language learners, Maria G. Dove shows how she and her colleagues experimented with innovative, collaboratively taught classes to help both English language learners and their mainstream classmates. Lori Langer de Ramirez offers an extensive overview of new Internet tools for the language classroom along with her interactive, companion website designed to showcase the tools and allow readers to explore them for themselves.

1

REFERENCES

Bickman, M. (2000). Reforming all the time: Recuperating the tradition of the active mind for teacher education. *Phi Delta Kappan, 82*(4), 300–303.

Chapter 1

Being an Expert: Building Social, Cultural, and Academic Capital with an English Learner

Sally Brown

A PORTRAIT OF MARTÍN

Martín is a seven-year-old second grader from Mexico who speaks Spanish as his first language. His brown skin, black hair, dark eyes, and accent cause his peers to recognize him as Latino, maybe specifically Mexican. Now imagine Martín interacting in his English-only classroom with his English-speaking peers who have been bombarded with anti-immigrant sentiments in the media and their homes. Racism rises to the surface as Martín tries to find a reading partner. He is cut out of conversations at his table during writer's workshop. Science equipment is not shared and Martín is excluded from group play at recess. He spends his time outside walking along the fence waiting for an invitation to throw a football with the boys. Martín asks, *"Why don't they lets me play?"*

Ms. Davis, Martín's teacher, not only notices the social exclusion, she also found a wealth of information documenting Martín's academic deficiencies in his permanent record. The literacy results indicate that he is reading below grade level and is in need of intensive intervention. A language test from first grade shows lack of growth in English, which means Martín will spend another year working with the ESL teacher. A red dot next to Martín's name on the class list is a reminder that he is at risk of failure. She realizes the urgency to intervene so that Martín can engage in conversations and activities with his peers. She is determined to find a way to help Martín succeed as a reader, writer, scientist, Mexican, and a friend.

Ms. Davis began by discovering Martín's funds of knowledge (Moll & Greenberg, 1990) and getting to know him as a person. Giddy lunch conversations revealed stories of his family in Mexico while Martín sang "Happy Birthday" to himself in Spanish. He even admitted that his middle name was

3

chocolate. Of course, he was joking but he tried to convince Ms. Davis that his name was Martín Chocolate Gomez Mora because he loved chocolate so much. In the classroom, close observations and exchanges at center time revealed his interest in animals, drawing, and Legos.

Frequent, informal verbal exchanges between Martín and his teacher enhanced his oral language development in English and at the same time helped the teacher learn about his interests. As a result, Ms. Davis began to see all of Martín's strengths as a student and she looked for ways to connect his skills and interests to the academic world.

Apprenticeship for Academic and Cultural Learning

Ms. Davis embraced the notion of learning as an apprenticeship in which peers have the potential to support and broaden each other's understanding of the academic world (Rogoff, 1990). In her classroom, students' learning was extended by bridging different perspectives as groups engaged in discourse, created artifacts, and used cultural tools. Based on this framework, participation in academic events was required for Martín to transform his understanding of literacy and science concepts. Therefore, Ms. Davis developed a plan to capitalize on Martín's expertise.

This plan focused on building Martín's social and academic capital with his peers so that he was included in reading, writing, and science activities. In addition, Ms. Davis wanted Martín to view himself as worthy and smart. Throughout the entire school year, both Martín and Ms. Davis co-constructed expert identities that caused him to become an academically successful second grader who was excited about learning and coming to school.

THE EXPERT INQUIRER

The class was engaged in an interdisciplinary study of what it meant to inquire about the natural world. Students were busy asking questions about their world, which was followed by an investigation. Many children in the class struggled with this approach since they were accustomed to responding to teacher questions instead of creating their own. Ms. Davis intentionally decided to capitalize on this opportunity and used Martín as a model inquirer.

Martín was naturally curious about penguins. During independent reading, Martín spent a significant amount of time studying pictures in nonfiction penguin books. In many instances, he pointed to the pictures without using words. For the most part, Martín was not able to find a supportive partner during reading so he spent time alone with books. Eventually, he developed a type of self-talk as a strategy to comprehend the text. For example, Martín said the following as he looked through a penguin book. *"Where's their eggs? I don't see any eggs. I know penguins has eggs. But where are they?"* This began his journey as an expert inquirer. Martín yelled, *"Ms. Davis, penguins! I love 'em like gorillas, you know."*

In an ensuing reading conference, Ms. Davis prompted Martín to talk about penguins. Martín said, *"Seals and killer whales eat penguins. Look they jump [off cliffs] and climb back up."* The teacher continued the conversation by positioning herself as a learner. She initiated her own inquiries and read aloud until she found her answers. These actions served as a model for inquiry. Over the course of several days, Martín generated an authentic question about baby penguins. He wondered about the differences between the brown, black, and white penguins and the different types of feathers (adult versus chick). He shared this inquiry and his findings with the teacher as he encountered them. Ms. Davis specifically made time for Martín to offer his discoveries spontaneously and noted the development of his ideas.

After a shared reading session with a big book about Antarctica, the teacher asked Martín to reveal his inquiry and findings about penguins. Ms. Davis introduced Martín's inquiry by showing one of the books he read about penguins. Immediately Martín jumped to his feet, stood next to the teacher, and pointed to a picture of a baby penguin. He was rather nonverbal at first and appeared shy about speaking in front of his English-speaking peers. Ms. Davis persisted in drawing out Martín's discovery and positioned him as a model for everyone to follow.

The teacher introduced Martín's question to the class by encouraging him to show pictures of the two penguins. Ms. Davis scaffolded the event by providing the language to describe Martín's inquiry and intentionally began identifying Martín as the expert inquirer. She openly commented, "Martín made a discovery!"

This approach fully unfolded as Ms. Davis prompted Martín to continue sharing what he learned about the penguins. Once more, she used her knowledge of English to assist Martín in expressing his ideas. She repeated the words Martín said to her earlier. He responded, *"Umm. Gray, black, and white."* Finally, Martín revealed what he learned. The penguins with fluffy brown fur are baby chicks. They are not a kind of penguin. Through the process of molting the black and white feathers appear. It was as if Martín solved a problem and he smiled as he shared this information.

Martín's peers—his audience members—began to acknowledge his value as a contributing learner to the classroom community. The teacher's use of *we* indicated a collaborative effort between Martín and herself; thus, positioning them both as learners. The teacher altered her use of pronouns to direct the expert identity onto Martín, which was a subtle, yet important move. The teacher also skillfully scaffolded Martín's articulation of the inquiry process about penguins. In this context, Martín's understanding of penguins was valued as academic capital and a cognitive resource. As such, it was viewed as an asset by the class studying Antarctica. As the unit continued, Martín was sought out by his English-speaking classmates when questions about penguins arose. This was the first time that he was valued by his classmates. It was a turning point in Martín's status as a reader, writer, and scientist.

Martín's and his classmates' learning was enriched through the communal interactions that allowed a deep processing by the group of what it meant to be an inquirer. According to Vygotsky (1978), an internalization of the inquiry process can unfold during this type of interaction. Martín's literacy development evolved as he attempted to tell about the process in his own words. An inquiry into penguins permitted the teacher to co-construct an expert identity with Martín that encouraged him to pursue other inquiries throughout the school year. Thus, Martín worked with increasingly harder materials and concepts as the year progressed.

SHARING AS A CULTURAL EXPERT:
IT'S OKAY TO BE MEXICAN

During the school year, every child was given multiple opportunities to share their culture with the classroom community. The teacher perceived this as an open invitation embraced by a large number of the children. At different times, students brought in artifacts from home or shared personal stories. However, Martín never participated in these experiences. He remained a quiet listener in the background. In fact, he often tried to hide his identity as a Mexican. He refused to speak Spanish in the classroom and explained, "*I don't wants the kids to know I speaks Spanish. They won'ts like me.*"

After the inquiry event and other similar instances in which the teacher worked to elevate Martín's social and academic status, he finally brought in artifacts from home to share with his class. His collection consisted of a Mexican flag, a picture of Mexico City, and a postcard of a volcano in Mexico. Martín walked to the front of the rug and stood next to his teacher. With her prompting, he held up the flag of Mexico for his classmates to see. With an enormous sense of pride, Martín spoke about his country and places his family visited. He said, "*I'm from Mexico and this is my flag. We have ones at home, too.*" His classmates were so interested, they began asking questions about Mexico and Martín ended up talking about dancing. With the teacher's scaffolding of English, Martín explained that, "*every single Sunday there's a dance. People are dancing, Mexican dance like this. In the street.*"

Martín called up a Latino classmate, Evita, to assist him in demonstrating the dance. He was frustrated by his lack of English and the lack of understanding of his classmates about this type of boy-girl dance. Evita stood in front of the class and Martín showed her the girl part. Evita kicked her legs in the air with her hands on her hips, while Martín skipped around her in a circle. He smiled and said, "*Yeah, like that.*" The class clapped with joy and celebrated this Mexican tradition while Martín ended with a bow.

Martín's deep sense of Mexicanness was revealed to the class; he disclosed an important part of his personal life history. This sharing event also provided Martín access to a successful English literacy experience. The sharing activity illustrated the fluidity of Martín's cultural identity. He was proud of his Mexicanness and portrayed his culture as an asset to the class.

By the end of the school year, Martín's social, cultural, and academic capital improved (Bourdieu, 1986). His academic and cultural capital emerged through the development of the two expert identities, but the social capital surfaced naturally. Two boys began valuing Martín as a person after the Mexican dance episode. These boys initiated play in the classroom during center time, as well as at recess. Although some students still did not interact socially with Martín for a variety of reasons—including racist language from the media and home—Martín developed friendships with several of his classmates. He found friends who partner read with him, listened to his stories at lunch, and played basketball at recess.

Martín and his peers' attitudes were socially constructed and changed depending on space and time (Norton, 2000). Opportunities to gain academic competence or pride depended on contextual interactional conditions, which was why Ms. Davis intervened to assist Martín in creating opportunities for him to be an expert. Language was used as a personal resource and—with the teacher's planning and assistance—Martín claimed his voice and took part in co-constructing an expert identity for himself.

CONCLUSION

Martín's portrait is intended to serve as an inspiration for others working with students in need of building social, cultural, and/or academic capital. Ms. Davis continues to use the expert identity strategy successfully with non-English speakers, low socioeconomic students, and struggling readers. It is through intentional actions and use of scaffolded language that she is able to create a space at school where all students experience success.

Author's note: Both names are pseudonyms.

REFERENCES

Bourdieu, P. (1986). The forms of capital. In J. Richardson (ed.), *Handbook of theory and research for the sociology of education* (pp. 241–258). Westport, CT: Greenwood.

Norton, B. (2000). *Identity and language learning: Gender, ethnicity, and educational change.* Harlow, UK: Longman/Pearson.

Moll, L., & Greenberg, J. (1990). Creating zones of possibilities: Combining social contexts for instruction. In L. Moll (Ed.), *Vygotsky and education: Instructional implications and applications of sociohistorical psychology* (pp. 319–348). New York: Cambridge University Press.

Rogoff, B. (1990). *Apprenticeship in thinking: Cognitive development in social context.* New York: Oxford University Press.

Vygotsky, L. S. (1978). *Mind in society: The development of higher psychological processes.* Cambridge: Harvard University Press.

Chapter 2

Breaking the Mold in Secondary Schools: Creating a Culture of Literacy

Thomas DeVere Wolsey, Diane Lapp,
and Douglas Fisher

Throughout her school career, Dalila knew she was what her teachers called a "struggling reader." When teachers called on her in class, she mumbled her words to hide potentially inaccurate pronunciation, demurred from reading aloud when she could, and avoided reading on her own or in small groups as much as possible. In her experience, student work displayed in the hallways was always created by the same students; she could not remember a single instance of her work being put up in the classroom or in the hallway since she started middle school.

Most of the books she was asked to read made little sense to her; writing tasks seemed a mystical art for a chosen few. She wrote notes to her friends and sent text messages, but she did not think of these as reading or writing for the simple reason that the school banned both these practices during school hours. Her cell phone had been confiscated more than once as a result of these policies.

When Dalila's family moved, she enrolled in a new school. She expected the new environment would not be any different than the last one. But on her first day of school, she found that some things were not the same at all. This school seemed to invite her to be part of a community, and the disposition of that community demonstrated how each student was a worthwhile member. How is a community of this type developed? This chapter illustrates how literate communities might address students who struggle with literacy tasks or who may need to be challenged.

THE LITERATE SCHOOL CULTURE

School cultures that invite students to literacy are interactive across a wide range of conditions. No one condition is sufficient, yet all conditions require the attention of the school if every student is to believe that literacy is valued and valuable. This is especially true of secondary schools given the wide range of disciplinary literacies schools demand (Moje, 2008), as well as school experiences, home culture, talents, and skills of the students in the school. Some of the conditions that contribute to the literate school environment include attention to learning spaces, use of technology, access to a wide variety of texts and other materials, teacher expectations, and challenging learning opportunities.

Space for Learning and Literacy

Learning spaces contribute to student achievement and the school learning climate. Students need ample room to move around classrooms that are set up in a flexible manner and are responsive to the needs of both learning tasks and learners. Students form their identities as learners, in part, as a result of the interactions of school climate, academic press, and the physical school environment. These factors add up in significant ways.

At one rural middle school serving students in the lower half of socio-economic status indicators, students showed one author of this chapter where

Photo 2.1.   Wall of Inspiration, courtesy of Douglas Fisher.

their work appeared on school walls. Without exception, students could find examples of their work as literate members of the school community, usually in many locations throughout the school. As important, schools that invite students to literacy as a way of learning provide spaces that promote effective literacy practices. In the corners of classrooms, students can find books and comfortable spaces to read and to discuss what they learn (Henk, Moore, Marinak, & Tomasetti, 2000).

Hallways and common spaces provide gathering points as students read, compose, and discuss the important questions that arise as part of a challenging curriculum. At Dalila's new school, classrooms have shelves with books and other reading materials related to the subject matter. There are comfortable chairs and computers in every room and student work on every wall. Imagine her surprise when she saw her work posted in the hallway. She was very proud that the book cover she designed for her book was displayed for all to see.

Technology and Literacy Learning

The great strength of technology lies not in its ability to bring information to students; rather, the educational strength of technologies lies in the capacity of the tools to bring students together across time and space. In short, technology as a tool of instruction permits students to engage with others of like mind, but also connects them with others whose diverse views and experiences are unlike theirs. It is from diversity, as much as commonality, that communities are born.

In order to realize the potential new literacies offer, students need (a) access near the physical point of learning (Zandvliet, 2006) and (b) school policies that promote considerate use of technologies among learners (Frey & Fisher, 2008). While computer labs are useful for some tasks, students need access to computers and the Internet in or near all classrooms. In most cases, this means that students need an interface with the computer and the Internet where they may access information when they need it in the service of learning, not when the teacher is able to sign up for a whole-class lab on occasion. This may mean laptops are available for students to check out as Dalila's school does or small banks of five or six computers are placed in each room. In schools that promote literacy through technology use, students can find and use computers depending on the learning task, not the school computer lab schedule.

At Dalila's new school, technology is a teaching tool and students are taught to be courteous with their phones and MP3 players. The school adopted a courtesy policy, not a technology ban, in which students learn to be responsible and respectful with their technology. Imagine Dalila's surprise when her history teacher used his cell phone to text a colleague to find a word's meaning.

Expectations and School-wide Practice

Teachers who hold high but achievable expectations for their students make powerful and positive differences in student achievement (Hawley, Rosenholtz, Goodstein, & Hasselbring, 1984). Similarly, school-wide practices help foster climates for learning built on common values and trust. For schools that appreciate and promote literacy, the implications of expectations and school-wide practices are of particular import.

At Dalila's new school, there is significant consistency in the instructional routines that teachers apply. For example, all of the teachers use graphic organizers, Cornell note-taking, shared readings, vocabulary, and writing-to-learn prompts. As a result, school becomes predictable for students and they develop habits that they can take with them from class to class and year to year. When Dalila learns to take notes in one class, the habit transfers to other classes, because of this consistency.

MANY TEXTS AND MULTIPLE LEVELS

Effective programs to promote reading tend to make use of multiple sources of information rather than relying on a single textbook (Lapp & Fisher, 2009). Sources of information need not be uniform, requiring all students to read the same materials at the same time. Even as students work toward common standards, many sources upon which students might rely can result in a variety of benefits. Among these are critical thinking skills that ask students to determine the validity, reliability, and suitability of the source given specific tasks, purposes, and evaluative frameworks.

Opportunities to Read

A variety of easily accessible materials is a critical feature of a literate environment. Students should be able to find materials in their classrooms, in their bookbags (Fader, 1976), in their homes, and on the Internet. The library—while important—is not the only place where students should be able to find and access the tools of a literate environment.

Prime conditions found in schools that foster literacy are the opportunities to read (Fisher, 2004), familiarity with a wide range of discipline-specific materials, and choices for students. While choices fall within certain constraints, effective teachers know that some students cannot make sense of textbooks that are too difficult, whereas others need challenges beyond the textbook. To that end, appropriate materials that can account for variability in literacy proficiency are available. At the same time, the choices about which texts they wish to read from among designated choices are often left to students.

Students assigned to specific groups based on assessments of their literacy proficiency rarely escape the label of *struggling* or *below proficient* readers. Students with choices often challenge themselves to read increasingly difficult materials in order to participate in the community of readers with something to contribute. Choices add depth and complexity because everyone contributes something to the class discussions and learning tasks as a result of reading different materials.

Time for Literacy

Another feature of effective school-wide literacy practice is the time dedicated to reading, writing, and discussion during school hours. Dalila sensed the value her school places on learning, in part, as a result of the time allocated to the activity. In schools that promote lecture over time to read, write, and discuss topics and issues, students learn that active construction of knowledge is not valued. This is not to say that lectures do not have a place. However, lecture dominates in many schools at the expense of students learning through active construction of knowledge—the tasks of literacy. Schools that value literacy make time for literacy activities in class rather than relegating these to the status of homework.

At Dalila's new school, students read widely from books they have chosen. She reported to her English teacher that she "never really finished a whole book." When asked why, Dalila said that they were too hard or too boring. When she found out that she could pick her own book to read she was ecstatic. For her first book, she selected a recent Newbery award book, *The Higher Power of Lucky* (Patron, 2006). When asked why, Dalila said that she liked the idea that a kid was spying on an Alcoholics Anonymous meeting. She shyly added that she heard that the word *scrotum* was in the book and wanted to see if she could get away with reading that for school.

THE ESSENTIAL QUESTION AS COMPLEX THINKING

At Dalila's school, teachers work together to develop essential questions. Essential questions serve as "signposts to big ideas" (Wiggins & McTighe, 2005, p. 106) and guide student inquiry. The interplay of learning spaces, access to technology and print-texts, teacher expectations, and opportunities to engage in literate activities in school creates the case for the interdisciplinary essential question. The four questions for the first year Dalila attended this new school were:

- What sustains us?
- If we can, should we?
- Does age matter?
- How do people care for themselves?

Given that the questions are used by the entire school, they change every year and are not repeated. This provides teachers with opportunities to make new connections between big ideas and the content they teach. In responding to the question, students draw on multiple sources from many disciplines. The following review of some responses from students in Dalila's school to the question *What sustains us?* demonstrates the various ways in which students answer the question, integrating their ideas with course content.

- Nico, a 9th grader, focused his essay on water as a sustaining force. He drew on his earth science class, a trip that he made with his family to the natural history museum, and his reading of the book *Out of the Dust* (Hesse, 1997).
- Ahmed, a 10th grader, wrote on religion and faith. He reflected on his world history class, his personal belief system, a conversation he had with his Imam, and his reading of *Comparative Religion for Dummies* (Lazarus & Sullivan, 2008).
- Destini, an 11th grader, examined family as a sustaining force. She drew on her U.S. history class, specifically World War II, made a connection with the idea of bonds in chemistry, and referred to several books about family ties, including *Letter to My Daughter* (Angelou, 2008).
- Doumas, a 12th grader, focused his essay on his teachers who he believes taught him that reading widely and evaluatively sustains him. He gained his insights from the multiple sources he read as he thought critically about his inside and outside of school worlds.

CONCLUSION

At Dalila's school, students are encouraged through instruction and interactions with their teachers and peers to realize that they are valued and so too are their insights, questions, and unique qualities. Her teachers believe these interactions are the heart of literacy and disciplinary learning. Essential questions serve as a center on which to address issues across multiple themes, authors, texts, and text types. As teachers and students consider how best to make sense of the physical environment of the school, the tools available there, the potential to read from a variety of texts, coupled with high expectations and challenging learning opportunities, schools can truly break the mold of literacy learning.

REFERENCES

Fader, D. (1976). *The new hooked on books: How to learn and how to teach reading and writing with pleasure.* New York: Berkley Books.

Fisher, D. (2004). Setting the "opportunity to read" standard: Resuscitating the SSR program in an urban high school. *Journal of Adolescent & Adult Literacy, 48,* 138–150.

Frey, N., & Fisher, D. (2008). Doing the right thing with technology. *English Journal, 97*(6), 38–42.

Hawley, W. D., Rosenholtz, S., Goodstein, H. J., and Hasselbring, T. (1984). Good schools: What research says about improving student achievement. *Peabody Journal of Education, 61*(4), 1–178.

Henk, W. W., Moore, J. C., Marinak, B. A., & Tomasetti, B. W. (2000). A reading observation framework for elementary teachers, principals, and literacy supervisors. *The Reading Teacher, 53*(5), 358–369.

Lapp, D., & Fisher, D. (2009). It's all about the book: Motivating teens to read. *Journal of Adolescent and Adult Literacy, 52*(7), 556–561.

Moje, E. (2008). Foregrounding the disciplines in secondary literacy teaching and learning: A call for change. *Journal of Adolescent & Adult Literacy, 52,* 96–107.

Zandvliet, D. B. (2006). *Education is not rocket science: The case for deconstructing computer labs in schools.* Rotterdam, The Netherlands: Sense Publishers.

YOUNG ADULT LITERATURE CITED

Angelou, M. (2008). *Letter to my daughter.* New York: Random House.

Hesse, K. (1997). *Out of the dust.* New York: Scholastic.

Lazarus, W. P., and Sullivan, M. (2008). *Comparative religion for dummies.* Hoboken, NJ: Wiley.

Patron, S. (2006). *The higher power of Lucky.* New York: Atheneum.

Chapter 3

Canines in the Classroom

Karen Bostic Frederick

When Morgan, a classroom teacher, considered teaching her lesson on Lewis and Clark's travels, she decided that she wanted to engage her students better. For many of them, the task of memorizing names and dates along with the new vocabulary would prove to be unappealing, even daunting. In an attempt to bring new life to her classroom, Morgan chose to use the novel *The Captain's Dog,* by Roland Clark (2000). In this tale, the students learn of the travels, tribulations, joys, and experiences of Lewis and Clark through the eyes of Seaman, the Captain's Newfound land dog.

Why is this worthy of discussion? As teachers, we sometimes find it hard to keep our students attentive and motivated to learn. Morgan took her knowledge of Lewis and Clark, her love of dogs, and her desire to try an innovative approach to teaching to a new level. She brought a Newfoundland named Lagniappe to class with her!

MEET LANI

Lagniappe, or Lani for short, added a new dimension of learning for Morgan's students and to her teaching. Morgan's original reasoning for bringing Lani to class was to introduce her students to the breed of dog. In southern Louisiana, where Newfoundlands are scarce, students were unfamiliar with the breed. They were struggling to identify with the character in the story because they lacked the background knowledge to which they could connect their new information.

Photo 3.1. The author with Lani, courtesy of Karen Bostic Frederick.

How could a dog pull a pirogue full of supplies? That would be too heavy. Using students as supply weight, Morgan was able to demonstrate the ease with which Lani could accomplish this task—outside on the playground, of course. However, through the course of the unit, Morgan found Lani to be a valuable teaching tool in several ways.

A PET WITH PURPOSE

What are some legitimate purposes a dog can serve in the classroom? As with other instructional practices, we must justify the need to bring a dog into our classroom. It must serve a purpose, preferably one that cannot be met easily through another, more traditional instructional practice. Additionally, this must be a collaborative practice. While the dog will generally be in a specific teacher's classroom, it is unrealistic to believe we can simply walk into school one morning with a dog.

Once the dog gets to school, what will it do all day, for instance, when it is not in class? Of course, it can take a nap, but we do not allow our students to do that, nor do we do it ourselves. The challenge is to make the most of this unique resource when it is available to us. We will have a beautiful animal, waiting to please and serve, so we must consider how to make the best use of this learning tool. While there are numerous ways to incorporate dogs into instruction, here are just a few of the more prominent and easier ones.

As with any innovative instructional practice, bringing a dog to school is not without concern or controversy. There are precautions to take as well as safety issues to address. There are legitimate concerns involved in bringing a dog to school, and it would be irresponsible to ignore them. The students' and faculty's health, fear, and safety should be considered, as well as working cooperatively with the building/district administration.

Why do we choose any practice or methodology in our classroom? We do so because we believe it is the best instructional practice for teaching our students a given concept or content. So why bring a dog to school? Ideally, it is because we believe that dogs will bring a higher level of comprehension of the target content. Historically, we have not seen dogs in our classrooms; it is a relatively new practice, though one growing by leaps and bounds (Jalongo, Astorino, & Bomboy, 2004; Katcher, 1997; Katcher, Friedmann, Beck, & Lynch, 1983; Serpell, 2000). While many teachers do keep classroom pets, this is something more. We are talking about using dogs to aid instruction.

When Morgan brought Lani to school, she worked to develop a program to utilize her presence and skills. Lani's primary academic function involved assisting students in improving their reading skills. Morgan used Lani not only for one-on-one oral reading, but also as a means of promoting silent reading. Morgan decided on this idea after having read about a program that utilizes trained dogs as reading partners to motivate reluctant readers (Jalongo et al., 2004).

Teachers who bring dogs into their classrooms find that this approach changes their students' perception of them as teachers. It makes teachers more approachable and takes away some of the intimidation students may feel. Dogs can often generate an environment of warmth, intimacy, and protection. What better learning environment is there than one in which our students feel comfortable and safe? As with students, dogs comfort adults as well. Morgan found that Lani could sense apprehension; thus, in order to keep Lani calm, she had to remain calm herself. It is much easier to maintain control of our classroom when we maintain our own calm, which makes teaching anything more effective.

DOGS AS READING BUDDIES

Dogs often help students deal with their own fears and stress. Serpell (2000) estimated that over 70 percent of children of all ages talk to and confide in animals. Students who are introverted or shy will often choose to talk to a dog rather than a person. Reluctant readers will sit on the floor and read aloud to a canine partner. Have you ever heard a dog correct someone for overlooking a word or reading one incorrectly? Dogs do not worry about fluency or inflection, they just enjoy the attention. Lani did not mind that Morgan's students often read the same book over and over to her; she still listened.

Reading to dogs offers students a fun, nonjudgmental atmosphere in which they can improve their reading skills. Dogs do not embarrass their readers by pointing out mistakes. Children know this without being told, thus they may be more willing to practice their oral reading skills with a dog rather than with a peer or teacher. Student readers can find comfort in reading to a dog because the dog is patient and offers undivided attention. Dogs as accommodating reading buddies relieve much of their stress. For example, Lani also doubled as a warm beanbag to lean on while reading.

Morgan labeled each book in the class library with paw prints, depicting the reading level. Students were encouraged to read 10 books at their reading level with Lani during their designated reading time. A job chart showed whose turn it was to read to Lani. If students were not reading, they lost the privilege of having a canine reading partner. According to Morgan, this only happened once or twice before the students caught on.

After documenting the reading of ten books on their reading charts, students were permitted to choose a book from the book carousel to take home. Lani would "pawtograph" it for them by having her paw traced on the inside of the book. Talk about an incentive to get the kids to read! It was a win-win situation for everyone. Morgan had her students reading; their motivation to read skyrocketed, and both parents and the administration were thrilled.

This is not to say a dog can teach a child to read. However, if a dog is able to help a child relax and read aloud, it affords the teacher an opportunity for informal assessment. In listening to the child read, the teacher can identify the areas in which the child is struggling. This also offers the opportunity for casual, yet specific praise to the child for something he or she has done well. In so doing, we are helping lower that child's level of resistance to reading.

ADDITIONAL BENEFITS

Animal-assisted activities show great promise in motivating students to complete academic tasks across the curriculum. Additionally, the presence of dogs can support the inclusion of children with disabilities in general education classrooms. In one study, a child without disabilities was 10 times more likely to interact with a peer who had disabilities if the child was accompanied by a dog (Katcher, 1997).

One of the issues that arises when attempting to include students with disabilities into the general instructional setting is peer acceptance. If a dog can help a child's inclusion process go a bit more smoothly, shouldn't we at least explore the possibility?

Teachers have discovered additional benefits of having a dog in the classroom, including a decrease in classroom absenteeism, increased frequency of work completion, improved social skills and self-confidence. Furthermore, it gave students who may have had difficulties at home a friend who would listen and offer unconditional affection (Jalongo et al., 2004).

Most children respond well to animals. They can confide in a dog and know their secrets are safe. They can reach down and scratch furry ears if they need a moment to gather their thoughts during a test. They can look forward to their turn brushing Lani or taking her outside to "do her business." While these are tasks many children shy away from at home, they are like magnets students cannot resist at school. These tasks can help students in alleviating depression, improving self-esteem, and helping to establish mutual trust (Katcher et al., 1983).

PLANNING FOR THE POOCH

It seems when teachers try something outside the box they often encounter naysayers. Collaboration involves working with more than one person or group. When bringing a dog to school, this is an area of critical interest. First and foremost, if you are an educator, it is recommended that you meet with your building administrators. You need them on your side, because you must adhere to their policies. Arrange a meeting at a convenient time, without distractions, and prepare your list of talking points. Ideally, you should cover:

- Why you are bringing a dog to school.
- Why another method or practice will not work better.
- What the dog will be doing at school.
- How you will address health concerns. (Allergies are a genuine concern. Students cannot miss class because they are allergic to a dog. Morgan bathed Lani daily in addition to keeping a heavy-duty air filter going in her room.)
- Some people fear dogs; how this will be addressed.
- What precautionary measures you will implement to keep the students and the dog safe.

You need to have an action plan in place before you meet with your administrators. If you do not, you may have difficulty garnering their support from the beginning. Morgan went through a specific planning sequence before she brought Lani to school. Gaining an insight into what she did prior to introducing Lani to her class might make it easier for you to bring a dog into your classroom.

1. Decide why you want to bring a dog to school. How will your students benefit from having a dog at school? Would another instructional practice work better? Why is bringing the dog so important?
2. Predict the questions that will arise from administrators, parents, and students and determine your answers in advance.
3. Arrange a time to meet with your building administration to discuss your goals.
4. Find the right dog to bring to school. You need a mild-mannered, well-behaved, tolerant dog to work with children. Trained therapy dogs work best, but if you know of a well-trained, vaccinated dog that meets the previous requirements, you might consider her as well.
5. Once you have permission, set up a face-to-face meeting with parents to present your plans, address concerns, answer questions, and introduce them to the dog.
6. Install a webcam and arrange for parents to have the ability to view lessons from alternate locations via the Internet.
7. Discuss with your students what will be happening. Answer their questions and concerns. Introduce them to the dog. Likewise, introduce the dog to your co-workers.
8. Bring the dog to school on a day without children to familiarize her with the surroundings.
9. Integrate the dog into class instruction and activities gradually. Introduce her to small groups first, then the large group.

With proper planning, you will already be aware of fears and health concerns and can address them with your students prior to bringing the dog to school. The best thing you can do is be honest, upfront, and demonstrate understanding to their potential unease.

Finally, remember that not everyone will welcome this innovation. Many people favor more traditional approaches to learning—and while we do not have to agree with their views—we should respect them. The best chance of successfully bringing a dog like Lani to your classroom is to plan for every question, concern, and situation imaginable.

REFERENCES

Clark, R. (2000). *The captain's dog.* Orlando, FL: Harcourt.

Jalongo, M. R., Astorino, T., & Bomboy, N. (2004). Canine visitors: The influence of therapy dogs on young children's learning and well-being in classrooms and hospitals. *Early Childhood Education Journal, 32*(1), 9–16.

Katcher, A. H. (1997). New roles for companion animals means new roles for veterinarians. *The Newsmagazine of Veterinary Medicine, 29*(6), 12–16.

Katcher, A. H., Friedmann, E., Beck, A. M., & Lynch, J. J. (1983). Looking, talking, and blood pressure: The physiological consequences of interaction with the living environment. In A. H. Katcher & A. M. Beck (eds.), *New perspectives on our lives with companion animals* (pp. 351–359). Philadelphia: University of Pennsylvania Press.

Serpell, J. A. (2000). Creatures of the unconscious: Companion animals as mediators. In A. L. Podberscek, E. S. Paul, and J. A. Serpell (Eds.), *Companion animals and us: Exploring the relationship between people and pets* (pp. 108–124). New York: Cambridge University Press.

Chapter 4

Grassroots Approach to Co-teaching for English Language Learners

Maria G. Dove

Eileen Haydock was certainly tenacious. She had strong opinions about nearly anything you can imagine and had no problem expressing herself. Yet, one could not help but be drawn to her strong passion for teaching and unswerving devotion to her young students. As a trained reading specialist and experienced classroom teacher, Eileen knew much about developing her first graders' early literacy skills. She also had wonderful instincts when it came to teaching English language learners (ELLs).

If you were to step inside Eileen's class, you would observe a room filled with carefully categorized, hand-made posters, which helped her young students connect written words with their corresponding illustrations. She collected and displayed artifacts from her travels so that her first graders could better understand the world around them. Her classroom was filled with rocks, seashells, starfish, and other assorted ocean creatures. She never missed an opportunity to bring the natural world into the classroom.

As an avid progressive educator, Eileen provided many hands-on learning opportunities to the delight of her youngsters. Considering the responsive learning environment she created and provided for ELLs, there is little wonder why I chose to approach Eileen with ideas to teach English as a Second Language (ESL) lessons inside her classroom.

IN THE BEGINNING

Approximately ten years ago, ESL instruction in elementary schools was predominately provided via a pull-out model. ELLs were taken from their mainstream classrooms to a separate, usually abbreviated, classroom setting for one to two periods a day and given lessons in listening, speaking, reading, and writing. Coupled with the lack of collaboration between mainstream teachers and specialists, this practice often caused ELLs to miss the lesson material presented in their regular classrooms during their absence, and they frequently fell behind their classmates in regard to their academic achievement.

From time to time, ELLs in pull-out programs are viewed by others as different, less capable learners or lacking intelligence. They experience more difficulty becoming a part of their regular classroom community. Mainstream teachers often feel less able to develop their learning or adapt lessons for these students. They may even believe an ELL's education is best left in the hands of the ESL specialist. Sometimes these youngsters are treated as second-class citizens by their fellow students and even can become the targets of class bullies because of their weak classroom status.

FIRST STEPS

By the turn of the twenty-first century, class size steadily increased due to the continuing rise in our school's population. Classroom space was scarce, and many educational specialists had to vacate their teaching spaces to make way for new, grade-level classrooms. Music and art teachers started to teach from carts, which they rolled from classroom to classroom. ESL teachers were asked to *push-in* and *pull-aside* the ELLs in their regular classrooms as a space-saving measure.

This new push-in model of ESL instruction was even less desirable than its pull-out predecessor. More than ever before, ELLs felt like outsiders in their own classrooms. Groups of two to five youngsters sat apart from their other classmates and practiced language skills that were not connected to what the rest of the class was learning. In addition, the lack of space inside some of the classrooms made instruction difficult, and sound as well as movement from the mainstream teacher's lesson distracted those who were with the ESL teacher.

After completing a course on literacy strategies, I was anxious to try the newly learned ideas with my ELLs. Many of these reading strategies were more conducive to a whole-class setting in the mainstream. One strategy involved building a word wall to help young learners develop their literacy skills. Using this strategy, ELLs were exposed to reading-and-writing support the entire school day.

For the word-wall-word strategies to be effective, it simply was not enough just to display a word wall in the room. It was important to do a word wall as a part of daily instruction (Cunningham, 2000). Therefore, Eileen and I formed a team to create a word wall in her classroom. It eliminated the use of the push-in model, as we endeavored to create a new model of instruction for our ELLs.

Co-Teaching Off the Cuff

At the time, little was established in the literature concerning co-teaching as an ESL instructional delivery model at the elementary school level. Yet, after many years as an ESL teacher, I was interested in finding alternative ways for my ELLs, not only to acquire their new language skills but also to stay connected to learning in their classrooms. I went into Eileen's class and began to model word-wall lessons. After several weeks, Eileen and I developed a routine with our word-wall activities. At the beginning of each week, we introduced six new words. Eileen and I took turns directing students to write each word and to chant the spellings of new words. As the week progressed, we played word games to reinforce the words on the wall.

For the remainder of the school year, one of us led full-class word-wall activities, while the other circulated throughout the room and assisted ELLs and other students who needed support or clarification regarding what they had to do and learn. Soon enough, other first-grade teachers became curious about what we were doing. Eileen invited her peers into the classroom to view our word wall and observe some of our shared activities. In a few years' time, pairs of ESL and mainstream teachers had built word walls in every classroom in grades K-3.

DEVELOPING CO-TEACHING MODELS

Co-teaching patterns began to emerge through team-teaching practice and simple trial-and-error. Some paired teams of ESL and mainstream teachers preferred one or two classroom configurations to deliver instruction, while others experimented with a variety of ideas. Table 4.1 identifies various ESL co-teaching models.

Co-teaching Procedures and Strategies

Co-teaching literacy instruction using word walls provided the framework and established routines for learning that benefited all students in the classroom. Using the development of word walls and various reinforcement activities, both the ESL and mainstream teaching teams established certain instructional procedures that were followed on a weekly basis. These procedures made lesson planning more predictable and streamlined.

Students, particularly ELLs, benefitted from the routines because they could predict what was expected of them and readily participate in the mainstream setting. Table 4.2 illustrates how we instituted a lesson-plan pattern

Table 4.1.   Co-teaching Models

Model Type	Model Description
One Student Group: One Lead Teacher and One Teacher *Teaching on Purpose*	The mainstream and ESL teachers take turns assuming the lead role. One leads while the other provides mini-lessons to individuals or small groups to pre-teach or clarify a concept or skill.
One Student Group: Two Teachers Teach the Same Content	Both teachers direct a whole-class lesson and work cooperatively to teach the same lesson at the same time
Two Student Groups: Two Teachers Teach the Same Content	Students are divided into two learning groups; teachers engage in parallel teaching, presenting the same content while employing differentiated learning strategies.
Two Student Groups: One Re-teaches; One Teaches Alternative Information	Flexible grouping provides students at various proficiency levels with the support they need for specific content; student group composition changes as needed.
Multiple Student Groups: Two Teachers Monitor/Teach	Multiple groupings allow both teachers to monitor and facilitate student work while targeting selected students with assistance for their unique learning needs.

Adapted from Honigsfeld & Dove, 2008.

Table 4.2.   Lesson Plan/Co-teaching Strategy Map

ESL Co-Teaching General Plan: Grade 1				
Days	Monday	Tuesday	Wednesday	Thursday	Friday
Literacy Instruction	Introduce new word wall words	Reader's Workshop	Word Wall Activity	Writer's Workshop	Word Wall Activity
Co-Teaching Strategy	One Lead Teacher and One Teacher *Teaching on Purpose*	Two Teachers Monitor/ Teach	One Lead Teacher and One Teacher *Teaching on Purpose*	Two Teachers Monitor/ Teach	One Lead Teacher and One Teacher *Teaching on Purpose*

that specified what literacy activity and accompanying co-teaching model would be applied according to the days of the week.

Why Did Co-teaching Capture the Faculty's Attention?

Our practice affirmed that good partnerships fundamentally help educators support one another when they have a common goal. Today's classrooms have many different challenges, and working with a colleague to meet those challenges is far superior to working in isolation, as teachers frequently do (Blase & Kirby, 2009).

Classroom teachers must often put forth much effort to maintain high expectations for all students, especially for ELLs who may not be able to participate fully in general classroom activities. Co-teaching allowed our ESL and mainstream teachers to share responsibility and lighten the workload in order to differentiate instruction for their students. Our co-teachers modified and adapted classroom and homework materials. Together, they furnished the necessary literacy strategies ELLs need to meet with academic success.

According to Zwart, Wubbels, Bergen, and Bolhuis (2007), much has been written describing the advantages of reciprocal peer coaching for in-class professional development. Peer coaching is a strategy for educators that facilitates the discussion of shared teaching practices. It also promotes cooperative interaction among teachers to ensure quality instruction for all students. A peer-coaching opportunity is often created when co-teaching relationships are established. When teaching teams systematically attempt new lesson ideas, they are better able to provide insight to each other through shared observations and reflections.

Co-teaching lessons can form favorable conditions for ESL and mainstream teachers to learn new problem-solving strategies and classroom management techniques. Teachers frequently feel not only supported in their instructional efforts but also share an equal responsibility to help all students succeed. For our co-teaching teams, working cooperatively eliminated the *your versus my students* mentality. Both teachers on each team were able support each other to include all students in the learning process. In this way, there were common goals set and a sense of mutual accountability in achieving those goals.

HOW TO GET STARTED WITH GRASSROOTS CO-TEACHING

If you are interested in making an innovative change such as co-teaching, here are some basic ideas to help you get started:

- *Begin from where you are.* In this case, ESL teachers have already been working inside the general education classrooms. Both the mainstream and ESL teacher agreed to change *how* they delivered instruction. You may wish to start by reflecting on all existing and potential collaborative practices.
- *Spread the word.* Let colleagues know *how* you are working differently in the general education classroom. You may also want to informally share some of the strategies you have implemented with administrators.
- *Showcase the results.* When other teachers viewed the word-wall activities, they too wanted to participate in building a word wall for their classrooms. Showcasing helps others learn *how* it could be accomplished.
- *Build trust.* According to Fullan (2001), the most important factor common to every successful change is the development of strong relationships, which foster meaningful cooperation. Creating trusting relationships is *how* you can build a co-teaching partnership.

FINAL THOUGHTS

Much time and attention must be focused on the success of the co-teaching team's collaborative relationship. However, other professional affiliations are also necessary to sustain a co-teaching plan. Grassroots co-teaching requires a combination of direct teacher leadership as well as cooperation from key decision-makers.

After co-teachers have developed partnerships with one another, they then must establish partnerships with all administrators who can lend their support in terms of the scheduling of classes, the development of necessary resources, time for joint lesson planning, and the careful placement of ELLs in general education classrooms.

REFERENCES

Blasé, J., & Kirby, P. C. (2009). *Bringing out the best in teachers: What effective principals do* (3rd ed.). Thousand Oaks, CA: Corwin Press.

Cunningham, P. M. (2000). *Phonics they use: Words for reading and writing.* New York: Longman.

Fullan, M. (2001). *Leading in a culture of change.* San Francisco: Jossey-Bass.

Honigsfeld, A., & Dove, M. G. (2008). Co-teaching in the ESL classroom. *The Delta Kappa Gamma Bulletin, 74*(2), 8–14.

Chapter 5

Language Learning 2.0: New Internet Tools for the Language Classroom

Lori Langer de Ramirez

Teaching world languages in the computer age has taken on new meaning. Gone are the days of rote memorization of vocabulary lists and verb paradigms. With the advent of communicative methodologies and the natural approach (Krashen & Terrell, 1983), language classrooms are designed to simulate real-world language use in context. Gone are lessons that are disconnected from cultural topics and practices. Gone are grammar translation activities that involve learners in word for word translation between first and second languages. Language education in the twenty-first century involves the synthesis of language, culture, and content (Curtain & Pesola, 2004), and web-based technologies are ripe with opportunities to facilitate these connections.

WHAT IS WEB 2.0?

When the World Wide Web first came into widespread use—and up until a few years ago—it was known as the place to search for and find information on almost any topic. It still is an excellent place to begin research. The use of the word *google* as a verb (meaning "to look something up online") is indicative of just how pervasive the use of the Web for information gathering has become.

But times have changed, and alongside the use of the Web as a search and retrieve tool, new Web programs allow users not only to read or listen to information in a passive way, but also to create and share information in a more active and dynamic way. This new version of the World Wide Web is called *Web 2.0*. The reference to the number 2.0 comes from the way that software products are distinguished from older versions when they are updated (such as the move from Microsoft Word version 3.0 to version 4.0). The name implies that Web tools have progressed and been upgraded by allowing users to become collaborators and active participants in the creation of material for the Web.

Web 2.0 sites enable users to post opinions, beliefs, and ideas in visual and text form. Web 2.0 tools include blogs, wikis, and social networking sites like Facebook and MySpace. These Internet-based services allow users to collaborate, share, and co-construct information in real time, providing authentic contexts in which to communicate in any language.

What Can Web 2.0 Tools Do?

Web 2.0 tools allow students to become creators and not merely recipients of knowledge. Whereas in the past, students were sent to the World Wide Web to find out information or do research (as with WebQuests where students are guided through the search and retrieval process of finding sites on specific topics), now they can use the Web as an arena in which to share their writing and speaking skills with a worldwide audience.

What begins with the passive skills of reading a blog entry or listening to a podcast quickly evolves into an active task in which students post comments and reactions to what they read on a blog or what they hear in the podcast. They can interact indirectly with the creators of the blog or podcast and offer their input regarding the information. As they leave comments—in text, voice, or even video form—their posts can be accessed by native speakers from around the world. As World Language (WL) teachers, we spend a great deal of time simulating authentic contexts for our language students. Web 2.0 tools offer *real* communicative contexts for language learners—and, for the most part, they are free of charge and available 24 hours/day.

How Can Web 2.0 Tools Link to Standards?

Web 2.0 tools can help language educators connect to a variety of national professional standards and initiatives. For example, according to the Partnership for Twenty-first Century Skills (www.twenty-firstcenturyskills.org), students must not only be able to consume information, but also to be critical of that information and be able to create some information on their own. The Twenty-first Century Skills (2009)—which connect well with the general goals of world language education—include:

1. Core subjects and twenty-first century themes
2. Learning and innovation skills
   - Creativity and innovation skills
   - Critical thinking and problem solving skills
   - Communication and collaboration skills
3. Information, media, and technology skills
   - Information literacy
   - Media literacy
   - Information and communication technology (ICT) literacy
4. Life and career skills
   - Flexibility and adaptability
   - Initiative and self-direction
   - Social and cross-cultural skills
   - Productivity and accountability
   - Leadership and responsibility

Language learners in the twenty-first century connect to these skills via technology in many ways. Web-based tools offer students a variety of opportunities to share information (for example, a visual presentation could include a video on YouTube, a wiki page, a blog entry, or a VoiceThread conversation). They must take the initiative by deciding how to express information and in designing a site online. But one of the most impressive connections to the twenty-first Century Skills—and to the American Council on the Teaching of Foreign Languages (ACTFL) standards—is the direct link that Web 2.0 tools provide between language learners and native speakers of the target language around the world. When students know that they are potentially communicating with native speakers—and not just with their world language teacher—they feel a different level of motivation and attention to the precision of expression. Students also become keenly aware of cultural identity and cross-cultural themes, thus raising their level of discourse and enabling them to develop cross-cultural skills.

Internet tools also connect to specific language learning standards. For example, the American Council on the Teaching of Foreign Languages (1996) established the five Cs of language learning:

- Communication: communicate in languages other than English
- Cultures: gain knowledge and understanding of other cultures
- Connections: connect with other disciplines and acquire information
- Comparisons: develop insight into the nature of language and culture
- Communities: participate in multilingual communities at home and around the world

SUCCESSES WITH WEB 2.0

Students across Long Island, New York, schools meet these standards as they communicate, explore cultures, and connect to communities—at home and abroad—through wikis, podcasts, and interactive Web sites. They make science, math, history, music, and art connections by creating informative videos or podcasts in the target language. They make comparisons to their home languages via blog posts and in sharing materials with native speakers throughout the world.

With Web 2.0 tools, World Language teachers implement an additional set of "Cs":

- Creativity: students create videos, slideshows, poetry, and other products without the typical constraints of time and space that often come with classroom presentations.
- Collaboration: students work on projects with classmates via the Web.
- Co-construction of knowledge: Ideas emerge in virtual spaces while students contribute their thoughts synchronously or asynchronously.
- Connectivity: In facilitating communication among students from around the globe, students begin to see the interconnectedness of our world.
- Computer Literacy: students become proficient at problem-solving by incorporating Web tools into their collection of tools for creating and communicating in the computer age.

Which Web 2.0 Tools Work in the WL Classroom?

There are many Web 2.0 tools currently available online and more are developed every day. What follows is an overview of some of the most promising of these tools for teaching and learning languages, along with specific examples of language educator projects using these tools.

Web sites are often transient: some may function one day, but might have moved or been taken down the next. For this reason, rather than providing URLs here, all links referred to in the following section can be found on the companion Web site to this chapter available at www.miscositas.com/webtools.html.

Blogs

There are many Web sites designed to offer free blogs to all (Google's Blogger) or specifically for educators (ClassChatter). Blogs are an excellent place to build online portfolios or to house student journals. They allow users to post text, photos, and audio or video files in chronological order. Other students can be invited to post comments on blogs and, if made public, visitors from around the world can comment and create an international dialog on a given topic.

World Language teachers set up classroom blogs in which students respond to a variety of prompts. Prompts might include thought-provoking questions, images, lines from films, lyrics from songs, or short video clips in the target language. Students respond from home and include links and even video or audio clips to support their writing. Students comment on each other's posts and also receive comments from native and heritage speakers from around the world.

Wikis

A wiki is a Web site that allows invited users to post, delete, and change information and content on the Web. Since several invited users can work on the same Web page at once, a wiki is particularly useful for collaborative and group projects. Students can work on the same project together at school or from home simultaneously or at different times during the day. Wikis are also useful as easy-to-edit class Web pages.

Wikis are great for collecting information from a variety of different contributors. Teachers can set up wikis to help organize a class event or to help students work in small groups on a writing or video project. Video, images, and links can be embedded into wikis, which in turn can serve a simple web-based portfolio for student work.

Podcasts

Podcasts are collections of digital audio files that can be listened to via the Internet. Contrary to the name, podcasts can be accessed without having an iPod (the Apple product). Podcasts usually contain digital sound files that can be listened to online, or often downloaded to any MP3 player or even a computer's hard drive. Using an RSS (Really Simple Syndication) feed, users can also subscribe to podcasts by having new episodes downloaded automatically to their computer.

Podcasting is best when students are encouraged to produce episodes of interest in the target language. Language teachers use podcasting to help students practice pronunciation and presentational skills. Students can record themselves speaking about a particular topic and then ask them to listen to the file to determine areas in need of improvement. They can also be used for pair or group presentations in which students record conversations, stories, monologues or dialogs, and poetry or non-fiction reports.

Avatars

An avatar is a digital representation of oneself. Students can design their own
avatar to look just like them, or they can take on the persona of a famous celeb-
rity, an animal, or a historical figure. Avatar sites often allow users to record
their own voice and to send messages to others using the avatar persona.

World Language teachers use avatars to allow students to practice speaking
and listening skills through the image they have created for themselves. Often
students who are reticent in class will find that they feel more comfortable
speaking in the target language through their avatar.

VoiceThread

Users of VoiceThread create online albums of images, text, or videos that can
be commented on by others. The comments can be posted in text, voice, or
video format and they usually refer to the central image or serve as responses
to the other comments. In this way, conversations are initiated and fostered
around a central theme, image, or topic.

Students upload images (photos or illustrations) and leave comments about
them on the site. Teachers then ask other students in the class to post their
own comments about the images or about their classmates' posts. Students
can practice their writing or speaking skills when they post, and their listening
or reading skills as they interpret the comments posted by their peers.

Video Sharing Sites

YouTube and TeacherTube are two of the most common video sharing sites.
They allow users to create a channel (a Web page) in which they upload,
arrange, label, and share videos on a wide array of topics.

Though banned in many schools due to the potential access to inappropriate
videos, sites like YouTube and TeacherTube can be a rich source of cultural
and linguistic information for language educators. Language teachers can ask
students to create videos ranging from the informative (i.e., weather reports,
cultural themes, science topics) to the creative (i.e., original short stories,
screenplays, soap operas). The videos can be shared in class and students can
be asked to comment on each other's creations using the comments feature
on both YouTube and TeacherTube.

Social Networking Sites

Web sites like Facebook and MySpace allow users to post personal information, leave comments, take online quizzes, and participate in discussions with

invited friends. When users post something to their page, all other friends in that network receive the same information. In this way, social networking sites allow and encourage users to communicate with a large group of friends with one simple post.

In a school setting, teachers can use Facebook as a means of communicating with students about class requirements and club events. There are excellent, interactive sources of information about famous artists, singers, and political figures from the target culture that students can explore.

WHERE TO BEGIN?

Teachers might consider choosing one or two technologies from the list and start playing with them for their personal use. Upload videos of family to a YouTube channel or create VoiceThread slideshows with photos of a recent vacation. Once you feel more comfortable with the technology, it is easier to think of ways in which to use it in teaching languages. The world of Web 2.0 tools can transform the language learning experience for students by connecting them with the *real world* in a very direct and creative way. After all, it *is* called the *World Wide Web*. Web 2.0 tools allow learners to communicate with the world—in all its languages!

REFERENCES

American Council on the Teaching of Foreign Languages. (1996). *Standards in foreign language learning: Preparing for the twenty-first century*. Lincolnwood, IL: National Textbook Company.

Curtain, H., & Pesola, C. A. (1994). *Languages and children: Making the match*. New York: Longman.

Krashen, S. D., & Terrell, T. D. (1983). *The natural approach: Language acquisition in the classroom*. Hayward, CA: Alemany Press.

Part II

Positive (Unconventional) School Leadership

Many of the educational success stories we focus on in this book share descriptions of authentic leadership and examples of relationship-building. Although these are not new concepts, the leaders in these chapters embrace the active participation of their teachers and encourage discussion as well as feedback. The leaders depicted seem to understand intuitively that their vision needs to be shared to empower others. Duignan (2006) explained that this is not often the case as "achieving a dynamic balance between coping with current realities and keeping a strategic eye on the future is difficult for most educational leaders" (p. 23).

The heading for this section is Positive (Unconventional) School Leadership, which begins with a narrative by Marc Ferris describing how teachers and administrators in a middle school created the E^3 movement to improve the quality of an already thriving school. James H. Powell, Patricia Chesbro, and Nancy Boxler introduce the success of an electronic professional network which provides Alaskan language teachers space to support and honor their work, even though they are distanced by miles. In another account, Audrey Murphy describes how to create a school infrastructure based upon shared leadership and student performance in an area of high poverty with struggling students. Similarly, Alice E. Ginsberg explores the visionary leadership of a principal at a new urban high school who offers a model for diverse students to become future leaders and engage in meaningful social change. In a chapter by Alan J. Daly, we examine the positive relationships that celebrate the strength and spirit of one group of educators as they transform a school from a culture of despair to one of success. Joan R. Fretz offers an explanation of invitational theory as she describes both messages and mindsets as powerful tools for transforming schools. As a final theme, Judith R. Merz defines spiritual leadership through the example of one superintendent who models it on a daily basis.

REFERENCES

Duignan, P. (2006). *Educational leadership: Key challenges and ethical tensions.* New York: Cambridge.

Chapter 6

Everyone Matters, Everyone Cares, Everyone Learns: Supporting School Communities in the Twenty-First Century

Marc Ferris

Meeting Roland Barth at a conference in Philadelphia during the fall of 2007 changed his life forever. Roland was a charming professor from Harvard, a former school principal, and the author of several bestselling books about education. During lunch, Roland spoke as eloquently as he wrote, with a clear vision about the importance of supporting powerful school communities from within the walls of the school house. "Such a shame," the principal thought, "that I'm here alone. Wouldn't it be great if all of my teachers were here, too? We could ask so many questions, learn so much!"

The principal of North Shore Middle School settled for hearing Roland's lecture and reading his books by himself. But as he read, he realized that he would need to share these ideas with his staff and engage them in what Barth (2001) described as improving everyone's learning curves.

That year, the principal set his mission to developing a healthy school culture so that teachers and students alike would become highly motivated learners. He began, as he had hoped, by sharing Barth's work with the faculty. It was his responsibility not only to support teacher learning and collaboration, but also to empower and motivate *all* teachers to take on leadership and learning roles. If change was going to come, it would have to come from the leadership ranks of the faculty (Phelps, 2008).

In looking for ways to motivate teachers to take on leadership roles and to support teachers in motivating students to engage in learning, the principal began to explore Self- Determination Theory (SDT) with teachers (Ryan & Deci, 2000). SDT is a research-based and well-established theory that explains how meeting three basic emotional needs of a human being enhances motivation and improves engagement.

When people experience competence (feeling that they know what to do to succeed), autonomy (feeling they have a voice), and relatedness (feeling they are cared about), they become more motivated and are more likely to complete tasks, volunteer for opportunities, and engage in learning or leadership roles (Assor, Kaplan, & Roth, 2002; Klem & Connell, 2004; Miserandino, 1996; Furrer & Skinner, 2003). When students' emotional needs are met, they become more engaged in learning. "If teachers understand these basic concepts behind SDT," the principal thought, "they would take on leadership and also begin to apply these principles in their classrooms." The end result: teacher leadership and engaged students.

During a spring superintendant's conference day, the faculty explored the concepts of SDT and tried to build these ideas into an emerging vision statement. As the school year began to wind down, it became clear that the faculty was generally interested in SDT, but no one was certain about where this was heading or how they would use these ideas on a daily basis. To make a difference, they needed some way to make these concepts practical and more meaningful for all members of the learning community.

How could the principal and his staff take these well-known theories to a level where people believed in them and put them into action on a daily basis? Nobody was really sure, but a few of the teachers became committed to figuring it out. Though it would take the next four seasons to build what would become the E^3 movement, the adventure began by energizing teachers as they journeyed to a state far from home.

SUMMER: A PLAN HATCHES

Nine teachers from North Shore Middle School landed in a small commuter plane on the tarmac at Charleston International Airport in South Carolina. They arrived to attend a middle-level leadership conference, hoping to refine the school mission statement and encourage all staff members to become invested in building a powerful school community that inspired teachers and students alike.

The walk from the plane to the small, two-gate terminal was short but productive. The hot Carolina sun and the fresh southern air ignited the kind of conversation that is rarely sustained during a busy school year in a fast-paced Long Island school district. "Do you think this conference will really help us?" a teacher asked. Nobody was sure, but everyone was curious to find out.

At the end of the first day, the teachers gathered around an outdoor table at a well-known Charleston eatery. The cobblestone street was dimly lit; and, from the blank stares on the teachers' faces, it was apparent to everyone that the answer to the young teacher's original question, was "no." This conference, focused on a theme that the North Shore teachers were already deeply familiar with, was not going to help them.

So, armed with more readings by Barth (2001) and an article about Self-Determination Theory (Ryan & Deci, 2000), the teachers and their principal made the decision to escape from the main conference and hold their own meetings at the hotel.

In a small workgroup, sitting with marked up copies of the school mission statement, a teacher finally cried out "This is not working!" The entire group fell silent and stared, waiting for her to continue, "We need something simple. We need something real, something that kids, teachers, parents—everyone—can connect to."

After more discussion, the teachers came up with a simple statement that reflected SDT, the thoughts of Roland Barth, and what everyone wanted for the school community. Scribbled in blue marker on a wrinkled hotel cocktail napkin, E^3 would become the keystone of the school's mission statement: "North Shore Middle School must be a place where *everyone matters, everyone cares,* and *everyone learns . . . E^3*"

FALL: TEACHER LEADERS INTRODUCE E^3 TO THE FACULTY

Upon returning from Charleston, the nine teachers joined with other team leaders who had not been able attend the conference, to create a plan for introducing E^3 to the faculty. When the whole faculty assembled in the middle-school cafeteria during the first Superintendent's Conference Day in September, each teacher received a colored puzzle piece. The principal's opening remarks began, "All of us play a role in shaping what this school is and how we move forward. We are all leaders and innovators, teachers and learners, and we are all responsible for being an important piece of a much larger puzzle."

With that, teachers divided into small groups of eight, based upon the color of the puzzle piece they were holding. The small-group members put their puzzle pieces together and then, with teacher leaders facilitating, they discussed the meaning of the E^3 concepts and implications for their work with students. They listed teacher actions that could show students that they mattered (Everyone matters!) and that the teachers cared about them (Everyone cares!). They also recorded teacher practices that would engage students in learning (Everyone learns!).

Once the small groups finished, the whole faculty came together again to report back. Each of the ten groups joined their completed puzzle to create one larger, more richly textured puzzle that revealed the image E^3. "For E^3 to work," the principal explained, "for people to really feel a difference, everyone in this building has to feel like an important piece of this larger puzzle."

At this first full day workshop, reactions differed. A few teachers were hesitant that this was just one more of the many initiatives that come and go. Some felt overwhelmed thinking about the big idea and were hoping that specific tasks would help clarify how E^3 would work. Others were enthusiastic, hoping that E^3 would make a difference in the school culture. Regardless, the faculty made a commitment to move forward with the E^3 concept. The teacher leaders suggested that the first after-school meeting of every month be dedicated towards further developing the faculty's understanding of E^3 and how it could be applied.

The first faculty meeting focused on what it means to feel cared about and how important that is for children. Teacher leaders showed a video clip from *The Wonder Years* where a student, Kevin Arnold, forged a powerful relationship with his math teacher that changed the way he saw himself as a student. Because the teacher believed in him and showed him that he would be there for him, Kevin went from Ds to Bs. While watching the clip, teachers were able to identify moments when the math teacher provided Kevin with a sense of relatedness—and strengthened his sense of competence.

A few days later, a teacher was talking about how he was about to let Kyle, one of his students, "have it" for forgetting the homework again. He thought about the discussion at the faculty meeting and wondered if another approach would make a difference. Instead of reprimanding him, he asked Kyle how he could support him in getting his homework done. Slowly, a new relationship developed and the student started doing his homework and engaging more in class. Would other teachers begin to think about E^3 and respond to students differently? Only time would tell.

WINTER: MOMENTUM BUILDS

Upon returning from the winter break, the principal invited all teachers to participate in the E^3 Leadership Collegial Circle. Sixteen teachers joined, dedicating their time after school to discussing teacher-leadership roles and how they could promote and support the E^3 movement. These teachers began planning faculty meetings, considering how school policies could be designed to support E^3 and how teachers could be inspired to use E^3 language on a daily basis.

The E^3 Leadership Circle was not the only group that began asking to take on leadership roles and share their knowledge with teachers. Three teachers created a Web site on Ning.com called NSMSE^3 (North Shore Middle School E^3). They developed a group page where teachers would post articles to share, start threaded conversations about specific issues, swap ideas for planning future faculty meetings, and even chat live late into the night.

This site served as an online community for teachers and made it possible for teachers to communicate outside the confines of the busy school day. As time went by, the NSMSE^3 site soon took on a life of its own as teachers began collaborating in entirely new and inspiring ways.

Because interest in the site increased so significantly, the technology teacher asked if she and a few of her colleagues could run a faculty meeting to train all staff in how to use it. These teachers also volunteered to run *lunch & learn tutorials* for teachers as additional support. It was clear that by the end of the winter, teachers were seeing the benefit of sharing their ideas and expertise with each other. They were beginning to feel that what they had to offer mattered to others around them, and, as a result, they began to show that they cared by helping others to learn.

As time went by, more and more teachers stepped into leadership roles. The guidance department asked if they could run a faculty meeting about student support services, how the guidance department mattered, and how all faculty and staff need to care about students from a social and emotional perspective. Momentum was building and teachers were taking additional responsibility for the leading and learning of others.

SPRING: CONCEPTS BEGIN TO BLOSSOM

By mid-March, examples of E^3 began to crop up in a variety of places. A home-and-careers teacher e-mailed the entire staff with the subject line reading, "An E^3 moment." In the e-mail, the teacher thanked the science teacher for showing her that she mattered by going out of his way to support her in a project she was doing with her students.

An English teacher wrote to her 7th-grade English colleagues, "I'm feeling so E^3 today as I spent the night making this PowerPoint on the grammar units we discussed yesterday. Let me know what you think."

Whether working to improve upon the grammar program, supporting professional development to help teachers to incorporate differentiated instructional techniques, or even in the midst of discussions about the school policy for gum chewing, all conversations about school improvement revolved around the E^3 question: How do teacher and school actions influence people's feelings that they matter, that they are cared about, and insure that learning occurs?

As the year moved to a close, the School Site Based Team, the E^3 Leadership Collegial Circle, Team Leaders, and other teachers from various parts of the building began to think about how E^3 could be introduced to the students at the middle school. They decided on a day in October to halt all regular instruction so they could have an E^3 Day for the students. The goal would be to develop hands-on, small group activities for students to create meaning for everyone matters, everyone cares, and everyone learns.

Close to 60 of the 79 teachers volunteered to participate in a local overnight retreat to prepare for launching E^3 with the students during the fall semester. If nine teachers could spend a day creating the E^3 concept, imagine what 58 teachers will bring back for students after the summer vacation! By the end of the spring semester, several teachers were seeing a difference in how people were interacting with each other and they were excited to see if E^3 would have a similar impact on the students.

E^3 COMING TO FULL CIRCLE

Powerful things can happen when teachers take on leadership roles in a school building. Over the course of four seasons, teachers from North Shore Middle school began rising from their classrooms to participate in the E^3 movement.

When teachers felt that they were cared about (relatedness), that their voices could lead to real change (autonomy), and that what they had to offer mattered to others, they began to engage in learning and leading each other. As more teachers successfully took on leadership roles, a forum for leadership (competence) evolved, inspiring others to join in.

Twenty-first-century schools are sure to be places that are full of unimaginable technology. However, the real future of successful twenty-first-century schools lies in their ability to create positive school communities where everyone feels that they matter, where everyone cares about the success of others around them, and where everyone feels safe in teaching, leading, and learning from one another.

While the E^3 movement has made a difference at North Shore Middle School, there is still a long way to go. There will always be skeptics. However, if the core of the learning community strives to make a difference, then E³ has unlimited potential. At North Shore Middle School, the core is growing and the E^3 journey is continuing.

REFERENCES

Assor, A., Kaplan, H., & Roth, G. (2002). Choice is good, but relevance is excellent: Autonomy-enhancing and suppressing teacher behaviours predicting students' engagement in schoolwork. *British Journal of Educational Psychology, 72*(2), 261–278.

Barth, R. (1990). *Improving schools from within.* San Francisco: Jossey-Bass.

Barth, R. (2001). *Learning by heart.* San Francisco: Jossey-Bass.

Ellis, J., & Silver, J. (Producers), & Tennant, A. (Director). (1989). *The wonder years: Math class,* Season 3, Episode 2 [Television program]. United States: New World Television

Furrer, C., & Skinner, E. (2003). Sense of relatedness as a factor in children's academic engagement and performance. *Journal of Educational Psychology, 95*(1), 148–162.

Klem, A. M., & Connell, J. P. (2004). Relationships matter: Linking teacher support to student engagement and achievement. *Journal of School Health, 74*(7), 262–273.

Miserandino, M. (1996). Children who do well in school: Individual differences in perceived competence and autonomy in. *Journal of Educational Psychology, 88*(2), 203–214.

Phelps, H. P. (2008). Helping teachers become leaders. *A Journal of Educational Strategies, Issues and Ideas, 81*(3), 119–122.

Ryan, R. M., & Deci, E. L. (2000). Self-determination theory and the facilitation of intrinsic motivation, social development, and well-being. *American Psychologist, 55*(1), 68–78.

Chapter 7

Creating Space to Tell Our Stories: Collaborative Networks as Professional Development for Language Educators

James H. Powell, Patricia Chesbro, and Nancy Boxler

What does professional development look like in a state where schools are often small and off the road system? How do you stay connected with your colleagues to share successes and to examine practice when meetings within the district require air travel? If, as Jackson and Temperly (2007) contend, the typical school has become too small and isolated to provide the depth of professional development educators need in a knowledge-rich, networked-world, what catalysts move educators from being geographically isolated, individual practitioners to engaged members of state-wide professional learning communities?

How do you establish learning communities with the permeability to allow knowledge to flow freely between colleagues, schools, and public sectors, but defined enough that members feel like they still belong to a group? These are critical questions in a state where bilingual educators are working with Native Alaskans to maintain, and in many cases resurrect, their languages and recent immigrants seeking to retain their home language while acquiring English.

ESTABLISHING A FRAMEWORK FOR PROFESSIONAL DEVELOPMENT NETWORKS

The Alaska Educational Innovations Network (AEIN) was conceived as one way to respond to issues of distance and permeability. Funded by a U.S. Department of Education, Title II, Teacher Quality Enhancement grant, AEIN was involved in developing partnerships to enhance professional development and student learning. AEIN was conceptualized as a way to connect educators in sustainable, professional learning communities. Each community was focused on a single educational issue and recruited members interested in reading and discussing that issue.

Though the *network* idea seemed a reasonable extension of an earlier partnership, the proposal designers had little idea of the powerful potential that networked learning offered its participants. These communities would not be isolated, but would be permeable, allowing knowledge to flow freely between colleagues, schools, and public sectors.

One such community grew from a group of bilingual and Alaska Native educators. Some were working to maintain, and in many cases resurrect, heritage languages, while others sought to support recent immigrants in retaining their home languages while acquiring English.

THE LANGUAGE ACQUISITION NETWORK

All stories have a beginning and every beginning creates its own story. The language acquisition network story is still unfolding, but it began with a group of four teachers in Chevak, Alaska, who were planning an observation at Ayaprun Elitnaurvik in nearby Bethel. Ayaprun is a K-6 Yup'ik immersion school. The visit would support development of a similar Cup'ik immersion program. Since both schools were partners in the U.S. Department of Education Teacher Quality Enhancement grant, AEIN's assistant network director and a College of Education faculty member attended to listen to the conversation and to provide additional support as specific needs were identified.

Much of the discussion centered on the philosophy, values, and cultural goals behind native-language immersion programs. While methods and materials also received attention, the primary purpose of both groups was building a school capable of regenerating interest in the language, including the cultural values embedded in each language. It became apparent that the short visit could not provide the time needed to explore these questions of practice and belief. Some way had to be found to overcome the distance between these two schools to continue the conversation.

Initial Key Supports for the Network

The initial response to the distance issue was technology, but what kind of technology? For members of the AEIN language-acquisition group, the solution to respond to the challenge of vast distance became Elluminate© Live, an electronic meeting format. Yet, the group soon learned that the technology would not provide the catalyst for participation, only the means to do so.

Since each school was a part of AEIN, the Assistant Network Director was given the task of turning the excitement of the initial visitation into a true collaborative network. This led her back to the two schools for further exploration. In conversations with teachers and administrators, several key elements began to emerge:

Identifying a Purpose

First of all, what was the purpose for the network? Strengthening and supporting immersion programs was an obvious purpose. After years of boarding schools and other educational systems that allowed only English, there was a generation that had lost fluency with its language. Chevak educators agreed with the principal of Ayaprun Elitnaurvik that academic achievement is enhanced through bilingual education. For her, the hard work and dedication meant the students who came to the school would be fluent in the Yup'ik language and connected to their culture.

However, there were very vocal community members opposed to native-language programs. They believed that the students needed English to survive in modern Alaska. They argued that the immersion program hindered the students' acquisition of vital English skills. The network became a vehicle through which these passionate educators could support each other when faced with similar challenges and celebrate their shared wisdom.

Who Am I as an Educator

The second issue was identity. Network facilitators asked, "How do you see yourself as a teacher in an immersion program?" Like the question of purpose, all the participants' responses tended to be similar and built around their vision of who they were in the context of their culture. One of the Cup'ik immersion teachers reflected, "If I had to teach who I am, I would be out on the tundra, not in this building. I would teach them about hunting and gathering. I would be like my dad, and I would show them how to do things, not tell them how to do things." From these discussions it became clear that the participants were delicately balancing their cultural ideas about teaching with the more colonizing concept of teacher.

Purpose and identity became the framework for the following questions: *What drew you to your work? Do you teach who you are?* In examining these questions, participants explored their moral purpose as language teachers. They began grappling with their roles within the school and community. They kept coming back to the question: Who am I as an educator?

PROVIDING THE STRUCTURE FOR
NETWORKED LEARNING

Facilitation was essential in keeping the network going, including setting up the meeting times and attending to logistical tasks. Facilitators also provided frames to hold the stories, listened for emerging topics, and kept the balance between theoretical and practical knowledge. As a result, the group created its own new knowledge.

Each meeting focused on the two core questions. *What drew you to your work? Do you teach who you are?* As they each listened to and reflected on responses to these questions, they began to construct new roles as colleagues. They recognized that everyone's experience had meaning and that as colleagues they were bound by shared professional ideals. Their stories transcended "the particularities and idiosyncrasies of specific schools in specific circumstances . . . those compelling qualities find their educational significance and enduring validity within the context of a wider collegium whose nature is dialogic and whose intentions are inclusive" (Fielding, 1999, p. 17).

With each new story and the dialogue it generated, the network began to emerge as a powerful place for educators to meet and engage in honest critical discussions about practice. From that start, a network emerged: rural and urban Alaskan P-20 educators engaged in substantive conversation around language acquisition.

Shifting Perceptions of Roles and Responsibilities

There was a substantial shift from the participants' initial expectations. Although the expectation for the network organizers was that the network would provide a non-hierarchical and collaborative context for the development of collective *intelligence* (Lacey, 1988), network participants initially tended to treat the university faculty and staff as leaders. Comments about teaching second-language methods and questions about being able to obtain course credits for participation were a part of the network's initial discussions.

Facilitators were forced to examine their practice to discover ways to create a more collegial environment needed for a true learning network to emerge. The key was found in the power of story that each member carried with them. The stories of *who I am as a teacher* that emerged from the two core questions had the power to transform the discussions and the language acquisition network.

The Power in Stories

After the first two stories that members told, everyone realized how powerful they were to deepen discussions about language and culture. It was unanimously decided that time and space at every meeting would be allocated for the participants to tell their stories. In this way the network was recognizing that "Oral cultures depend on respect, on allowing full space for people's words" (Brody, 2001, p. 207). Here, the technology helped to create the conditions. When only one member holds the microphone, no one can interrupt. As one participant stated, "this space is created so that we cannot interrupt. We tell stories rather than trade them. We actually listen to stories instead of just waiting for them to end. Stories take space and a place. This format demands that it be given."

GROWING THE NETWORK

At the start of the second year, the facilitators reached out to more language educators. The facilitators sent out an invitation to P-20 educators that included the stated purpose, the identified themes, and a definition of the group. This had some unforeseen consequences as invitees forwarded the e-mail to others they thought might be interested in participating. The participants who responded to these forwarded invitations enriched the discussions through the different perspectives they brought to the discussions.

A filmmaker from New York joined the group. Having grown up in Southeast Alaska, he was involved in a film about Haida culture and received the invitation from one of the faculty in the University of Alaska–Anchorage College of Arts and Sciences. A teacher new to the state and teaching in rural Alaska joined the group to try to better understand what was happening in her classroom. An experienced kindergarten teacher in Anchorage joined to find better ways to reach out to his native students and their families.

In addition, one of the facilitators connected with the Alaskans for Language Acquisition (AFLA) group. AFLA extended an invitation to the language-acquisition network to present and participate in their upcoming conference. At this point, connections were made because of commonalities in acquiring all world languages, including the heritage languages of Alaska natives. Language educators from around Alaska became aware of each other's work.

The positive growth in participants throughout the second year provided evidence that the network was becoming self-sustaining. Every member of the network had to miss meetings occasionally. However, with the growth in numbers there were always enough people to ensure great discussions about practice.

THE LANGUAGE ACQUISITION NETWORK TODAY

As the number of participants continued to grow during the second year, the group adopted an appreciative inquiry protocol that allowed examination of successful practice. Identifying the strengths of the group framed further inquiry. Synchronously, the Alaska Commissioner of Education fostered statewide dialogue about how place-based education impacts language acquisition for students. Place-based education resonated with the two primary questions and became the focus of every meeting.

A set of questions continues to provide a loose framework for the stories:

- What do you do?
- Where do you work?
- Who are your students?
- What drew you to your work?
- As a professional how do you see yourself living out the definition of place-based education?

The stories, deeply rooted in teacher identity, lead to further questions from the network:

- How does place based education include language acquisition?
- What do you see and hear at your school that values the stories of staff, student and faculty?
- What will it look like and feel like for you and your school/community if we have space for these stories?

CONCLUSION

The Language Acquisition Network evolved from a group of individuals with common concerns to an entity that co-constructs its learning and crosses cultural, linguistic, and hierarchical boundaries. Members are colleagues engaged in examining practice. Collectively, the AEIN Language Acquisition Network has created a safe space for P-20 educators to share as well as pose difficult questions.

The growth in membership and the richness of the dialogue during this past year confirms Little and Horn's (2007) finding that "talk within teacher communities is likely to be generative of professional learning and instructional improvement to the extent that it invites disclosure of and reflection on problems of practice" (p. 91).

Although the AEIN project began in predictable fashion with highly organized and tightly controlled professional learning seminars that reflected a
trainer-student approach, throughout the multi-year process *trainers* became
presenters, then *facilitators.* These titles chronicle a shift in role and in
behavior. Now, project directors consider themselves *colleagues.* This view
is accompanied by intentional practices designed to capture and honor the
wisdom of participants. The scripts have become collegially written, based
on the needs of the group rather than the needs as perceived by a hierarchical
instructor.

The results only hint at the potential of networked learning. Participants are
describing the interaction as rich and rewarding. They note that their thinking has been changed in ways that affect their professional practice. Project
directors, as colleagues and co-learners, report similar reactions. This is deep
professional learning that combines the wisdom of many for the benefit of all.
As Shaull (2000) pointed out, education is never neutral. It is either an instrument used to bring us into conformity or it "becomes 'the practice of freedom,'
the means by which men and women deal critically and creatively with reality
and discover how to participate in the transformation of their work" (p. 34).

Authors' Note

The authors want to recognize and thank Panigkaq Agatha John-Shields—
Ayaprun Elitnaurvik administrator and Naqucin Flora Ayuluk—Kashuna-
miut School District Cup'ik Immersion teacher for their tireless work on
making the Language Acquisition Network successful and their invaluable
insight and feedback on the writing of this chapter.

REFERENCES

Brody, H. (2001). *The other side of Eden: Hunters, farmers, and the shaping of the
world.* New York: Macmillan.
Fielding, M. (1999). Radical collegiality: Affirming teaching as an inclusive profes-
sional practice. *Australian Educational Researcher, 26*(2), 1–33.
Jackson, D., & Temperley, J. (2007). From professional learning community to
networked learning community. In L. Stoll & K. S. Louis (Eds.), *Professional
learning communities: Divergence, depth, & dilemmas* (pp. 45–62). Berkshire,
England: Open University Press.
Lacey, C. (1988). The idea of a socialist education. In H. Lauder & P. Brown (Eds.),
Education: In search of a future (pp. 91–98). London: Falmer Press.
Little, J. W., & Horn, I. S. (2007). "Normalizing" problems of practice: Converting
routine conversations into a resource for learning in professional communities.

In L. Stoll & K. S. Louis (Eds.), *Professional learning communities: Divergence, depth, & dilemmas* (pp. 79–92). Berkshire, England: Open University Press.

Shaull, R. (2000). Foreword. In P. Freire, *Pedagogy of the oppressed: 30th anniversary edition* (pp. 29–34). New York: Continuum.

Chapter 8

The Link Between Accountability and Collaboration: Creating an Infrastructure Based upon Shared Leadership and Student Performance

Audrey F. Murphy

Is there a connection between accountability and collaboration? Can a school hold itself accountable and, at the same time become a center of collaborative learning? This chapter will highlight the progress of one school from a School in Need of Improvement (SINI) status to the status of Good Standing, while developing a culture of collaboration. This progress was accomplished by making bold strategic moves in the areas of school infrastructure, instruction, and professional training.

THE STATUS OF THE SCHOOL

Our school is located in an urban setting in a high poverty area. This elementary school had recently opened to relieve the overcrowding in three neighborhood schools, all of which are in walking distance. The population consisted mainly of Latino youngsters, many of whom spoke Spanish as their first language. In fact, 92 percent of the students came from a home where English was not the first language. Our first year's performance scores were disappointing: 28 percent were at proficiency in English Language Arts and 19 percent in mathematics. As principal of the school, I met with my assistant principals and together we decided on a course of action.

SCHOOL INFRASTRUCTURE CHANGES

Our first challenge was one of organization. How can we structure the school so that all of our resources were focused upon improving student performance and at the same time building a collaborative community? We knew that a professional learning community is based upon a shared vision and commit-ment among all people within a school (DuFour & Eaker, 1998). As a result, the first change we made was in the school's framework: we offered all of our classroom teachers a common preparation period which enabled them to meet weekly. The common time allowed teachers to plan together and provide instructional uniformity throughout the grades. It also facilitated goal setting by the teachers for their classes, individual students, and themselves.

Our second infrastructure change empowered our teachers by giving them a voice in the decision-making process and established structures to communicate those decisions throughout the school. We created a *Strategic Planning Committee,* consisting of representatives from each grade and all faculty constituencies (academic intervention providers and cluster teachers). The agenda was set at the beginning of the meeting and would consist of any matter from instructional to organizational to custodial issues.

A very important challenge for any principal is to assure that the ideas and initiatives decided upon by the school community are accurately conveyed to students, teachers, and parents. Effective communication is necessary so that the exchange of ideas is occurring on a regular basis (Marzano, Waters, & McNulty, 2005). With this in mind, we established multiple means of con-veying our messages to all stakeholders within our school community. Daily announcements advised students of upcoming events and school initiatives. Assistant principals prepared weekly newsletters highlighting daily events and upcoming priorities, as well as organizational and safety issues. The inclusion of personal events—such as birthdays and graduations—was an addition that contributed to creating a positive school community in our building.

Bi-monthly walk-through letters were prepared for the staff, detailing what was noted throughout the school during classroom visits, the new informa-tion gathered by the school leadership, and the appropriate next steps for improvement. We instituted an open door policy, encouraging staff members to come in to discuss their ideas, while keeping our conversation focused primarily upon instruction. We provided structures to regularly involve both students and staff in the contribution of ideas to revise current school plans, and develop new programs.

INSTRUCTIONAL DECISIONS

We decided on instructional initiatives within a collaborative framework so that all stakeholders were involved, creating buy-in among the staff members. At our school, we wanted to be clear and explicit about our instructional steps for the year, communicating these to the teachers at faculty and grade conferences as well as through walk-through letters. Believing that one of our goals as supervisors was to make the observational visits real and meaningful for teachers, we eliminated the planned, pre-dated observational visit. This type of observation often caused teachers to feel obliged to put on a performance for the observer in order to receive a good evaluation and did little to support them with instructional practices. We proposed unannounced observational visits based upon agreed-upon expectations that should be in place in each classroom.

Our instructional walk-throughs with resulting feedback to teachers were happening frequently throughout the year, so all faculty were aware of how well initiatives were implemented and the next steps needed. As a result, it was very unlikely that a lesson would suddenly result in an unsatisfactory rating, since the supervisors were consistently visiting classrooms and addressed any concerns before the official observational visit.

Teachers were advised by a dated notice that they would be observed in the upcoming weeks, but no specific date or time was given. The *give back* was one of compassion: if the teacher was not feeling well or if an emergency arose, the administrator would return at a future date to conduct the observation. Unannounced observational visits became the protocol, enabling us to view meaningful instruction and assist our teachers in their areas of need. Our support became formative in nature, used to guide teachers onto their next steps in order to inform their instruction.

We decided on our instructional priorities in collaborative teams and shared them with the entire faculty. For example, a new schoolwide design, such as a *Reading Level Assessment Sheet* to record data on literacy growth, would be introduced over a six-week period, giving teachers time to become familiar with the parameters of the initiative. Through the use of a snapshot assessment form, we were able to concisely specify the main points of each initiative and use these points as a lens during our focus walks. As part of a successful peer review process, teachers walked in groups with this form in their hands as they visited each other's classrooms and fortified their own practice. After the six-week period had ended, the items in this initiative became a staple in our classrooms, and the next instructional priority was decided upon by our teams.

Clear goal-setting became important to our school community. We needed to identify best practices within our building in order to improve academic performance results (Reeves, 2006). Our school had a comprehensive plan in place; now we needed to create goals for grades, classes and individual students, as well as have the teachers set goals for themselves. We accomplished this by modeling our own learning and goal-setting for both teachers and students. Through team collaboration, we created goals for each grade and class. Teachers met in groups during their common preparation time to align their class goals with each other and establish individual goals for each of their students.

An innovative instructional approach was the establishment of literacy benchmarks for each grade. We developed goals based upon the established ending levels for each grade and refused to promote students not meeting the criteria. At first, we experienced resistance from some parents. But after parent education workshops detailing what reading should look like at the end of each grade, our parents became our best allies.

No Child Left Behind regulations focus on accountability for various subgroups within each school. One of the largest populations at our school was second-language learners. We developed a model to service these children, while celebrating our school's diversity, providing strong instructional support, and meeting accountability targets. After meaningful research and discussion, we decided upon the formation of a Gifted Dual Language program. This model serviced English language learners and native English speakers by providing first and second language support as it alternated the language of instruction (Spanish and English) each day so that learning took place in both languages (Soltero, 2004).

Our enrichment program was attractive to all students since learning activities were supplemented by weekly trips, after school activities, interactive technology in the classroom, and language support in both Spanish and English during after school sessions. By the time the Dual Language students were in the second grade, they were fluent in two languages. This created a classroom in which both language groups developed native-like fluency in the other language. By the third grade, an additional language, Chinese, was added to the curriculum, so that our Dual Language students would become tri-lingual and tri-literate.

PROFESSIONAL TRAINING

To strengthen our newly formed professional learning community, it was important that all faculty view themselves and the administration as continual learners. To build upon this philosophy, we took advantage of every opportunity to share our learning, to discuss every discovery, and to invite staff members and students be proactive in their own learning. To build this learning community, we initiated the following comprehensive training program:

- A Professional Book Club was established. We met before school to discuss cutting-edge publications and their ramifications for classroom practice. Teachers were not paid for their attendance, but received the books. Our group consisted of self-motivated members who wanted to read and participate in the ensuing discussions.

- *Lunch and Learn* trainings were carried out by our literacy and math coaches. Sessions were held weekly during lunchtime for those who wanted to deepen their understanding of a current initiative.
- Weekly meetings with the administrative and professional development team were held throughout the year. The administrative team met to discuss implementation of district instructional priorities and ways to support teachers. The professional development team—consisting of both literacy and math coaches—met to focus upon the actual training of teachers and decide upon the next professional development focus.
- Professional development was differentiated. We created a menu of training opportunities which allowed staff members to choose an area in which they wanted assistance or wished to further develop their interest. The self-selection of training not only empowered teachers, but resulted in more responsibility taken for their own learning (Senge, 2000).
- Accountability for the professional development was essential. To ensure that all of us continued to enhance our own learning on a regular basis, we needed to implement new training in our classrooms and share what we had learned with others who had not attended. Upon returning to the building after an off-site training session, each workshop participant completed a form detailing what was learned and how this training could be implemented in classrooms. These forms were then used by our teams to decide upon the professional development which would be useful for each faculty group, as well as the best venue in which to deliver the training.

ACCOUNTABILITY MEASURES

Under NCLB, all schools are held to the same high performance standards and are evaluated using the same rubric. Our initial student performance scores demonstrated that a strong focus was needed to address the improvement of student performance. To formulate immediate measures, we formed teams of teachers and administrators to decide on priorities for three domains that most impact student performance: instructional delivery systems, parental support options, and the measurement of student progress.

- The instructional team decided to reduce the student-teacher ratio for those students who were struggling in literacy and mathematics. Academic Intervention Specialists (AIS) pushed into classrooms and provided small group instruction to students at risk. The team also determined that additional instruction was necessary before the high-stakes exams were administered in January (for literacy), and in March (for mathematics). Starting in September, extended day programs and Saturday institutes were offered to struggling students. Additionally, vacation academies were added during week-long breaks throughout the year. This supplementary instruction afforded students additional time to absorb and review crucial skills necessary for success on the upcoming state assessments.

- The team working on parent support options realized that family partnerships were an integral part of student academic success. Building upon this vision, the team set up weekly workshops to share strategies with parents on topics such as helping children with homework, understanding the school's new literacy initiatives, and improving parents' own literacy skills. To strengthen parental support and increase their familiarity with high stakes assessments, ELA and math nights were held at strategic points during the year. During these events, parents were instructed in their own children's classroom on the different components of the actual exam. At the same time in another location, their children were coached in test-taking strategies as an additional preparation before the exam administration.

- The third team focused on tracking student progress. Team members developed rubrics for reading, writing, mathematics, and end-of-year benchmarks for student achievement in math and literacy consulting Fountas and Pinell (2006). Working backwards, we established interval goals at strategic points in the school year. Student performance was assessed four times a year and aligned to the benchmarks set by the team so that teachers were able to track student progress throughout the year. If students experienced difficulty, they were immediately identified and offered AIS interventions to address their area of need directly. Teachers were able to meet with AIS providers to discuss students at risk. During common planning periods, intervention strategies were shared with colleagues, so that teachers were able to provide immediate support to struggling learners early enough in the year to make a difference in their year-end performance.

WHAT HAVE WE ACCOMPLISHED?

A unique learning community was built on a shared goal: to improve learning for all students. Each succeeding year brought an increase in our student performance scores. By working collaboratively and keeping our team focus, our professional conversations and our action steps on accountability targets, we witnessed student scores rise from 28 to 66 percent at proficiency levels in ELA and from 19 to 87 percent in mathematics.

Building trust became a core component for initiating change. Transparency about our intentions, present thinking, and future plans resulted in clear communication and a high level of trust. Together we learned that collaboration and accountability can go hand in hand by working together with a shared purpose, committing ourselves to a common vision and making high performance standards part of the fabric of our daily instruction.

REFERENCES

Dufour, R., & Eaker, R. (1998). *Professional learning communities at work.* Alexandria, VA: Association for Supervision and Curriculum Development.

Fountas, I. C., & Pinnell, G. S. (2006). *Teaching for comprehension and fluency: Thinking, talking and, writing about reading, K-8.* Portsmouth, NH: Heinemann.

Marzano, R., Waters, T., & McNulty, B. (2005). *School leadership that works.* Alexandria, VA: Association for Supervision and Curriculum Development.

Reeves, D. (2006). *The learning leader: How to focus school improvement for better results.* Alexandria, VA: Association for Supervision and Curriculum Development.

Senge, P., Cambron McCabe, N. H., Lucas, T., Kleiner, A., Dutton, J., & Smith, B. (2000). *Schools that learn: A fifth discipline fieldbook for educators, parents, and everyone who cares about education.* New York: Doubleday.

Soltero, S. (2004). *Dual language: Teaching and learning in two languages.* Boston: Pearson Education.

Chapter 9

Becoming Leaders: A Visionary Educator Leads the Way

Alice E. Ginsberg

"How do we learn?" "What can we create?" "What does it mean to lead?"

These three questions are at the heart of the mission of the Science and Leadership Academy (SLA), which is a three-year-old public high school located in downtown Philadelphia (www.scienceleadership.org). Christopher Lehmann, the school's founding and current principal, helped to craft these questions, which permeate every aspect of learning at the school.

On the surface, one would think these are reasonable questions to guide an educational institution, yet, curiously, they are rarely asked.

- Why? *Perhaps*, because asking "how do we learn?" suggests that learning is more complicated than the traditional method of lecture, memorization, and testing. Learning is a collaborative and on-going process. Often there are many different right answers and approaches.
- Why? Because asking "what can we create?" suggests that knowledge is not simply internalizing a fixed list of data (Hirsch, 1987), but needs to somehow be put into use to become meaningful and sustained.
- Why? Because asking "what does it mean to lead?" suggests that students might become empowered and thus voice opinions or take actions that are controversial or disorderly.

This is not to say that principals and teachers at most urban public schools do not care deeply about their students and make a profound difference in their lives. On the contrary, many urban public schools provide opportunities for students to achieve far greater than their parents or grandparents ever did.

Yet these schools often exist on a shoestring budget. Classrooms typically have over thirty students. They are often housed in buildings that look much like factories or prisons—even to the point of having bars on the windows and metal detectors at the door. In many such schools, the yearly dropout rate is over 60 percent. The long-standing crisis in public urban education has been well documented (Delpit, 1995; Kozol, 1991; Meier, 1995; National Commission on Excellence in Education, 1983; Tyack & Cuban, 1995).

At SLA, Principal Lehmann provides a role model for students interested in becoming leaders by his very own way of leadership. After working at an innovative school in New York City, he returned to his home town, Philadelphia, and wrote the original proposal for SLA. He soon connected with the nationally renowned science museum The Franklin Institute (www.fi.edu) to create a community partnership and make SLA become a reality. Lehmann has been widely recognized for his educational leadership, including being a finalist for the Association of Supervision and Curriculum Development's 2008 Outstanding Young Educator Award.

Of course, a school is far more than the vision of one person, yet without that person providing leadership and support from the top, and without a clearly defined mission that is embraced by all of the school's stakeholders, schools may be very limited in what they can accomplish. Even the most innovative teachers cannot make lasting change in an environment where they are being evaluated and rewarded for a way of teaching and learning they do not embrace.

Lehmann gives his staff a lot of leeway (no pun intended); however, everyone working at the school is expected to buy into the school's core values. They include using inquiry, research, collaboration, reflection, and presentation. In all learning students are at the center. Teachers do not so much impart knowledge to students as they foster student engagement in creating it. Teachers meet together with Lehmann on a weekly basis to discuss how they are using these values in the classroom, and to reflect, as a community, on current issues in the school.

Principal Lehmann readily admits that the adults in the school do not know everything, and that they have a great deal to learn from the students themselves. This translates into a larger aspect of the leadership he models: everybody has voice which should be listened to and respected.

LOOKING THROUGH THE LENS OF LEADERSHIP

When you walk into SLA, Lehmann's forward-thinking mission is immediately obvious. There is a continual buzz of conversation on each floor of the building. The school's core values are posted in every classroom and on every wall of the school, along with current examples of students' work. Students wear white lab coats (which they are free to personalize), and carry laptop computers, loaned to them for the duration of their stay at SLA.

Principal Lehmann's vision for the school is still a rare one. Students at SLA learn in a project-based environment where they must create something concrete and meaningful, something which has value and may indeed change the world for the better.

Lehmann has a background in using technology for teaching and learning. Most of the projects students engage in require understanding and using the most up-to-date technologies in new and creative ways. Assignments range from making commercials on subjects of social change, to creating on-line magazines about their unique cultural backgrounds, to designing Web pages and blogs, to conversing with other students around the globe. During class, all students have their laptops open and rarely use paper for anything.

Indeed, Lehmann feels very strongly that technology has a central place in all kinds of learning and in creating a new generation of leaders. Regarding a recent bill to ban certain kinds of technology in schools, Lehman notes on his blog:

> If we want to teach students to be twenty-first century citizens, we shouldn't ban—by state law—the tools of the twenty-first century. . . . This law creates more distance between our schools and the lives our kids lead. That makes it harder for us to teach, not easier. The short-term gain of keeping distractions out of our classrooms is, in my belief, far outweighed by the long-term loss of making our schools less and less relevant to kids.

CULTIVATING AN ETHIC OF CARE

Speaking of distractions, Lehmann's office has two open doors at either end and he is constantly being sought out. He is obviously more than a figurehead, he is a problem solver. He knows the students well, cultivating personal relationships with each, and demonstrating another core value of the school, the ethic of care. According to Lehmann:

> we have to create classrooms where students are taught to value their own work, to understand the relationship between freedom and responsibility, to understand how to dedicate themselves to an idea, a passion, to their work, not just for a grade, but . . . for themselves and their community as well.

Lehmann has designed the school in a way that collaboration among students is more common than competition. Students need to figure out who brings what skills to the table, and how the group can most effectively achieve its mission.

This collaborative approach does not mean that students do not get letter grades. They do. It also does not mean that they are not assessed. They are. SLA teachers remain authority figures in the school, as does the principal. Yet as Lehmann explains, it is possible to successfully create a mix of high expectations and authority, while still cultivating an ethic of care:

> We must expect our students to work hard, we must expect our students to learn to make deadlines—we must set the bar as high for our students as we set it for ourselves, but we must also remember to set up structures that help students when, inevitably, they sometimes miss the bar. We should do so if for no other reason than we hope someone does that for us when we fail.

ASKING *WHERE DOES IT LIVE?*

In his daily blog, Lehmann emphasizes that "every system, every policy, every structure in schools represents a pedagogical choice." On his blog, Lehmann urges:

> whenever we hear or read schools or districts or teachers or administrators make a claim that their school/district/PD session/whatever is about "twenty-first Century Learning" or "Life-Long Learning" or "Project-Based Learning" or whatever claim we may see or read, our first question should be—"Where Does it Live?" Educational ideas only have lasting power if *they exist within the systems and structures of institutions that claim them.* (Emphasis added.)

Lehmann affirms that every aspect of the design and administration of a school states something about its mission and values. To persuade students to work cooperatively, for example, he designed longer class periods that allow for the building of new relationships and trust.

To encourage students to care about the community around them, Lehman created the partnership with The Franklin Institute, giving students regular opportunities to go into and interact with their community in a genuine and meaningful way. During all four years of high school, students intern at the museum and help design exhibits, use technology, thus bridging theory with action while embracing twenty-first-century tools.

CREATING A CURRICULUM THAT PUTS STUDENTS IN THE CENTER

How, exactly, is learning different at SLA as compared to more traditional schools? Several recent assignments stand out:

In an African American history class, students are asked to make a 30-second commercial about an African American person who made a difference. Students do not shy away from controversy or hard-to-look at images. One commercial shows Emmett Till, only fourteen years old, being taken away in a body bag after his brutal assassination, with the voice over stating that Till was killed because he whistled at a white woman.

Another example takes place in a 10th-grade English class in which students are asked to explore the relationship between language, power, and culture. After reading a variety of novels and personal narratives, they are asked to explore questions such as: is language an area of conflict in your home? in school? in other aspects of your life? How do you consciously change your ways of speaking? Do you code-switch?

A Spanish teacher overhears students discussing the latest fad diet. Writing in Spanish, students are asked to blog for five days about what they have eaten and how much exercise and sleep they get. Then each student reads another student's blog and acts as his or her personal trainer.

Students are asked to write an essay titled "This I Believe" and submit it to National Public Radio (NPR). Students write on topics such as: I believe that intelligence is not measurable by mankind; I believe your voice is your strongest weapon; I believe that everyone should love and be loved by someone, no matter what their sex; and I believe mistakes make you stronger. Several students' essays were published on the NPR website.

LEADERS CULTIVATING LEADERSHIP

Although SLA is particularly strong in science because of its relationship with The Franklin Institute, Lehmann makes sure that whether science or math, English, history, or art, the goal is the same: to help students use their new knowledge to make a positive difference in their lives, in their communities, and in the larger world. Indeed, this is where the Leadership in the school's title comes in. Lehmann explains his vision for learning:

> Why do we study history? Because we must be able to understand what has come before us if we are to understand what may follow . . . and what our role is in what comes next.

Why do we study foreign languages? To remind us of the incredible diversity of our world. So that we never allow ourselves to fall victim to the simplistic idea that our culture, our ideas, our language is the only one that matters.

Why do we read books? Because every book we read gives us the ability to view the world through the eyes of someone else.

Under Lehmann's direction, the school thus cultivates a sense of agency in place of widespread apathy.

CONCLUSION: A NEW KIND OF LEADERSHIP, PASSIONATE BUT NEVER BLIND

"As we all rush to change the world, and as we hear more and more about a sense of urgency to change our schools. . . . Let us be passionate, but never blind" (from Lehmann's Blog, *Practical Theory*).

Lehmann's greatest hope for the school is that graduates are thoughtful, wise, passionate, and kind. He also hopes that they are highly prepared to succeed in college and make positive life choices. In such an economic downturn and politically turbulent times for our country, and indeed around the globe, we need to nurture wise and compassionate future leaders. At SLA, every student is taken seriously as a learner and as a potential leader.

It has been said that nothing is more beautiful than potential. At SLA, there are countless opportunities for students to express their opinions, provide leadership, and engage in real community problem solving. We cannot take this kind of learning for granted, but we can support its growth.

REFERENCES

Delpit, L. (1995). *Other people's children: Cultural conflict in the classroom.* New York: The Beacon Press.

Hirsch, E. D. (1987). *Cultural literacy: What every American needs to know.* New York: Vintage Books.

Kozol, J. (1991). *Savage inequalities: Children in America's schools.* New York: Crown.

Meier, D. (1995). *The power of their ideas: Lessons for America from a small school in Harlem.* Boston: Beacon Press.

National Commission on Excellence in Education. (1983). *A nation at risk: The imperative for educational reform.* Washington, DC: U.S. Department on Educational Reform.

Tyack, D., & Cuban, L. (1997). *Tinkering toward utopia: A century of public school reform.* Cambridge, MA: Harvard University Press.

Chapter 10

The Power and Potential of Strengths-Based Connectedness: New Directions in Leadership and Organizations

Alan J. Daly

In organizations, real power and energy are generated through relationships, and the capacity to form those relationships is more important than tasks, functions, roles, and positions.

—Margaret Wheatley

EMBRACING YOUR TIME

They sat around the oval table as they had so many times in the past. Conference Room 5 had a small Seth Thomas clock that hung on the faded walls. The clock was a gift from the most recently retired superintendent who, at his celebratory dinner, said to his former colleagues, "Now is your time, your time to lead, your time to grow, your time to take Crisálida to the next stage." Despite the festive atmosphere, the words hung in the air that Friday evening as a reminder of the work at hand. The press of accountability, the media, and strained relationships within the district added to the urgency of the retiring superintendent's words.

The Crisálida School District in the city of Monarch was facing a significant shift in demographics as well as potential sanctions under No Child Left Behind for continued underperformance. Monarch had grown from a small, rural bedroom community of Los Angeles to an urban fringe city in what seemed like the blink of an eye to the life-long residents. It may have been the building of the prison or the arrival of vast tracks of affordable homes or just simply city-dwellers wanting to escape the urban sprawl of Los Angeles that spurred the transformation.

Whatever the reason for the growth, the district had now expanded substantially and was attempting to serve a linguistically, culturally, and socio-economically

71

diverse student population. Perhaps similar to many communities across the country, while the demographics changed, teaching practices and attitudes did not follow. In fact, if anything, the new student faces seemed to bring forth a desire for the good old days.

THE JOURNEY HOME

Despite being the son of a long line of educators, school never came easy to Jose. In fact, he struggled through most of his education. He majored in outright defiance, suffered from desperate bouts of apathy, all of which were underscored by a pervasive sense of boredom. He would have left school if it was not for Mrs. Hausmann, his tenth-grade English teacher. She saw the strengths in him that he had worked so hard to bury. She believed in him, treated him as an equal, and most importantly, never gave up despite his highly developed lack of caring.

When he graduated with his Masters in education, it was Mrs. Hausmann who received one of the four coveted tickets to his graduation. His brother, also a teacher, could not attend. She died the year he was hired as an assistant superintendent in Crisálida, and it was her spirit that brought Jose back home. He often reflected on the irony, the boy who never wanted anything to do with education now found himself a career educator.

Leaders in Crisálida, under the direction of the assistant superintendent, began the intentional and purposeful process of building relationships grounded in mutual respect, trust, interdependence, and individual strengths. District leaders focused on the *co-construction* of change efforts that included both a learning orientation toward reform and a focus on mutually supportive and respectful relationships (Datnow, Hubbard, & Mehan, 2002).

The idea of reform as a co-constructed learning process between partners was a radical departure for Crisálida, which traditionally had relied strictly on external expertise and programming. All too often the district's previous efforts were implemented in a top-down hierarchical manner concerned primarily with the fidelity of implementation rather than on a focus of learning and mutual engagement. Approaching change as a learning-oriented partnership suggested that reforms are not based solely in fidelity to implementation, but rather represent the intersection of the knowledge, skills, and expertise of members as they act within a specific context. In this sense, reform is truly a partnership building not only on the human capital of participants, but also on the social capital/relations between members.

WITH A LITTLE HELP FROM FRIENDS

The quality of relationships an individual has to others may support or constrain opportunities for resources such as information, knowledge, and expertise to be accessed and diffused throughout the organization (Daly & Finnigan, 2009). The idea of a social network suggests a change in the emphasis of the old maxim: it is not what you know, but who you know, to who you know *defines* what you know. The balance of network research confirms what Mrs. Hausmann instinctively knew: the relational linkages between people based in strengths are as important to success as the technical aspects of schooling.

The leaders in Crisálida realized that change could no longer be mandated from a central office, but needed to be co-constructed through a process of learning and support enacted in a network of relationships. This significant shift embraced the idea that change is socially constructed, and individuals are more likely to take up a new practice from a trusted colleague than from an outside expert with whom they had no social connection.

Therefore, if leaders were to create reforms that provided for greater collaboration, distribution of leadership, and change in practice they would have to attend more closely to the existing structure of social relationships. Changes in practice are ultimately modified and adapted based on individual attributes, context, skills, and social interaction, much of which occurs outside the realm of formal dictates (Mohrman, Tenkasi, & Mohrman, 2003).

District leaders recognized that the social ties between teachers were important in the uptake and enactment of change, but also that the existing social structure may well moderate, influence, and even determine the direction, speed, and depth of a planned change. Leaders, therefore, needed to intentionally create the conditions for strong relationships to develop in order to support the transfer of tacit professional knowledge important in enacting complex change. They knew that in order to really build district capacity they would have to return to their roots.

THE MIGHTY OAK

The new superintendent—if you can call someone who has been in Crisálida for almost twenty-five years new—looked out the window at the California Oaks as they bent in a gentle breeze. He remembered when the trees were first planted. As a young teacher in the district, he could not imagine how these saplings would grow into the sturdy trees that intermittently lined the street near the district office, creating an inconsistent patchwork of cover against the California sun. The thought of those days both comforted him and served as a reminder of how quickly time passes.

The trees were originally spaced evenly along the street to create a natural network of dense, interwoven branches, but in the late 1990s some of the trees suddenly began to weaken, whither, and die. It seemed these mighty oaks were being destroyed from the inside out, their strength being slowly drained away by a disease deep in the core of the tree. The slow death of the oaks became the focus of the community, and through quick and concerted effort many of the trees were spared.

As the superintendent related this story to his cabinet, many of whom, like the oaks, had also grown up in the district, realized that they too were being weakened from the inside out. Although external factors such as changes in demographics and demands from accountability had certainly affected them, it was the slow decay of hope, a diminished sense of efficacy, and a sparsely connected social network that sapped their strength.

The administrators knew that in order to move forward they had to recommit to improving the district climate. For change to occur, teachers and administrators in the district had to once again believe in their own ability to affect change. Crisálida had been identified as a failing district, and that label took its toll on morale. Worse yet, some educators began to assign blame for the dismal state of affairs to the students and their families. Even many of the very best in the district began to doubt their ability to meet the educational needs of the community.

Across the district there was a sense of loss among the teachers and administrators—a loss in their own sense of individual and collective efficacy. In Crisálida, teacher efficacy had been stripped away and replaced with a personal sense of doubt. The responsibility for the current state of the district also shifted from the educators to the students and community. Excellence did still exist in Crisálida. However, in order to move the district forward it would take reconnecting these caring educators to their own success and to one another.

At the core of this effort was a purposeful and intentional strategy on examining the existing strengths in the organization. A focus on strengths suggests a different and perhaps counterintuitive course of action. Instead of merely documenting those areas in which the organization has broken down, the focus shifts to rigorously examining the elements of excellence in the system and determining how to diffuse that excellence.

A strengths-based approach has been used in a number of other disciplines apart from education, but is now slowly taking hold in educational circles (Daly & Chrispeels, 2005). This work suggests that a focus on strengths results in improvement in organizational outcomes as well as numerous positive individual level effects including: increased job satisfaction, morale, and professional commitment (Cameron, Dutton, & Quinn, 2003).

District administrators in consultation with the teacher's union and school board decided to undertake a strengths audit in which each principal and school leadership team would seek out the excellence that resided in every corner of the district. An interview protocol that included questions around high point experiences in the district, conditions that supported success, and resulting outcomes was developed. This process provided educators with the opportunity to interview one another and share powerful stories about successful experiences in Crisálida.

Teachers were also asked what they imagined, hoped, and dreamed for both the district and school. The act of searching out excellence, focusing on what works, and carefully considering how that knowledge would be shared became the centerpiece of the change effort.

What was most important in this approach was not the actual strategies that the teachers generated or the ways in which practices would be diffused, but the fact the educators engaged in an inquiry process of their own successes, hopes, and dreams. It was in the process of sharing and memorializing stories of success, and the approaches contained within them, that ultimately provided the collection of Crisálida-specific strategies for improvement. Experiencing the process prompted many teachers to also start strengths-based audits in their classrooms in which students interviewed one another about the best aspects of themselves and how that quality added to the fabric of the classroom.

Starting from a point of excellence raised the level of conversation and oriented staff to a focus on what they did well. For far too long the district had enumerated failures, used valuable resources to document what was not working, and relied on external experts and district mandates for improvement. Now with a renewed spirit and focus on the existing excellence in the system, one could sense the increased efficacy throughout the district.

It is not to suggest that focusing on strengths eliminated the need for addressing concerns, but rather when educators started from a point of success and imagined what was possible it made addressing those challenging areas appear more possible. It is the robust combination of powerful external strategies coupled with a systematic examination of the successful strategies *within* a system that holds the greatest promise for empowerment, improvement, and excellence.

For one of the schools, stories of successful collaboration between the principal and teachers was a theme. Drawing on that idea, the principal began actively participating in grade-level meetings, encouraging collaborative lesson studies, and supporting reflective practice through book clubs and teacher-designed professional development. These efforts supported the identification and diffusion of knowledge and expertise through the school and, most importantly, were derived from the lived, successful experiences of teachers, not from a top-down mandate.

RENEWING A COMMUNITY

A focus on strengths also spread to Monarch's neighborhoods. Educators held focus groups with community members in which parents shared stories of a time when the district/school exceeded their expectations. In the beginning, the principals and central office leaders were concerned about engaging in such conversations for fear of a backlash of complaints or unhappiness. However, to their surprise, most of the parents and community members responded well to the questions, and as they related their stories, faces lit up and a wellspring of positivity flowed.

The themes shared by the community were charted and published for all of Crisálida to celebrate. A sense of pride began to appear slowly in the spirits of teachers and leaders that ultimately had the effect of renewing the connection between the district and community. It was the intentional change in the narrative of the district from one of failure and blame to one of success and connectedness that made the difference. These conversations provided an opportunity for both the district and community to heal from years of mutual distrust and animosity and move toward imagining what *could be* in both Crisálida and the city of Monarch.

(All names are pseudonyms.)

REFERENCES

Cameron, K. S., Dutton, J. E., & Quinn, R. E. (eds.). (2003). *Positive organizational scholarship: Foundations of a new discipline.* San Francisco: Berrett-Koehler.

Daly, A. J., & Finnigan, K. S. (2009). A bridge between worlds: Understanding network structure to understand change strategy. *Journal of Educational Change.* Retrieved April 2, 2009, from http://www.springerlink.com/content/1040n7231740m232/fulltext.pdf

Daly, A. J., & Chrispeels, J. (2005). From problem to possibility: Leadership for implementing and deepening the processes of effective schools. *Journal for Effective Schools, 4*(1), 7–25.

Datnow, A., Hubbard, L., & Mehan, H. (2002). *Extending educational reform: From one school to many.* London: Routledge/Falmer.

Mohrman, S., Tenkasi, R., & Mohrman, A. (2003). The role of networks in fundamental organizational change. *The Journal of Applied Behavioral Science, 39,* 301–323.

Chapter 11

Messages and Mindsets: Powerful Tools for Transforming Schools

Joan R. Fretz

School leaders spend many hours conferencing with teachers about instructional strategies to increase student achievement. We expect teachers to be masters of curriculum and to implement the very latest instructional practice. Yet, two significant influences on student achievement and behavior are seldom discussed. These are the *Messages* that teachers convey to students in their words and actions and the *Mindsets* that guide our teachers' and students' behavior.

Messages and mindsets are powerful teaching tools that positively or negatively influence a student's self-concept and behavior. School leaders will discover that staff members are eager to try new strategies for inviting, rather than demanding effort and cooperation. The benefits of increased academic achievement and decreased behavioral issues are far greater than what is gained through punitive approaches. Just like any successful business or organization, schools need a service mission and shared agreements to frame how all members of the learning community will contribute to the mission. The moment that we begin the discussion of shared goals and practices, the vision of the school becomes clearer and the contributions of school adults more intentional.

AN INVITATIONAL FRAMEWORK

Invitational theory and practice provides a simple and effective framework for creating a service mission and shared agreements for schools (Purkey & Novak, 2008). The mission of an inviting school is "to cordially summon people to realize their potential in all areas of worthwhile human endeavor" (p. vii). Staff

Table 11.1.   Shared Agreements for Positive Mindsets and Messages to Students

The Mindset:	The Message:
I am optimistic.	I see you as able, valuable, and responsible. I see your talents, strengths, and potential. I believe you can make responsible choices.
I am respectful.	I respect your unique individuality. I will not embarrass, insult, or humiliate you. My respect for you is unconditional.
I am trustworthy.	I am consistent in my behavior. I am truthful and genuine. The intent of my actions is for your benefit. You can depend on me.
I am caring.	I care about you as a person, not just as a student. I wish to be a beneficial presence in your life. I strive to help you to realize your potential.
I am intentional.	I strive to communicate all of the above to you by intentionally choosing words and actions that are optimistic, respectful, trustworthy, and caring.

members assert that "all students are valuable, able, and responsible and are capable of behaving accordingly" (Purkey & Strahan, 2002, p. 74). They maintain an intentionally inviting stance of optimism, respect, trust, and care and choose actions that reflect their understanding of perception and self-concept theories. When efforts to create a supportive learning environment are driven by identifiable theories and practices like these, skills will develop and meaningful reflective conversations will take place. Table 11.1 provides an example of shared agreements that school adults might use to communicate supportive messages to students.

FROM THEORY TO SKILLED PRACTICE

We often introduce a new concept during a faculty meeting and then expect educators to implement it successfully the next week. Teaching is a performing art, and like playing an instrument, it takes time and coaching to develop strong skills. The administrator who explores messages and mindsets with teachers in a nonjudgmental manner will positively influence their actions and consequently, the actions of students and the climate of the school.

With this skill-based practice in mind, let us explore how knowledge about behavior and self-concept might shape a teacher's mindset and her approach to helping Dan, a student in her class, replace a disruptive behavior with a more beneficial one. Thinking about ways to illustrate *Messages and Mindsets* led me to create an analogy with a favorite candy that I am sure you will recognize. Represented by two M's these round chocolate treats come in many colors and are fragile on the inside, just like the precious children in our care.

Think of the hard candy shell as representing our behaviors and the soft chocolate center as our self-concept. The hard and colorful shell has several functions: It serves to protect, maintain, and enhance the chocolate center. In a similar fashion, all behaviors serve a function: to help us gain or avoid something. We select a behavior based on how we perceive our world at that particular moment. The behavior is chosen to protect, maintain, or enhance our self-concept.

THE CONSERVATIVE SELF CONCEPT

Self-concept is what a person thinks to be true about him or herself. Additionally, self-concept is a very complex organization of the many characteristics and attributes that make up who you think you are. As such, it is also very conservative. The more you identify with a trait, the harder it is to let go of it. Many invitations may be needed to help someone change a behavior.

What method do you use to eat these chocolate candies? Do you forcefully crush the shells or patiently let them melt in your mouth? When you are eating candy, personal preference is quite acceptable. However, when you are an educator who understands how conservative the self-concept is, you'll strive to be more patient and *let the shell melt.*

Sometimes when teachers disapprove of a student's choice of behavior, they use forceful words or punishments to dissuade the child from repeating the behavior. Basically, they bite the candy shell to crush or extinguish the behavior. While this controlling approach may be the most expedient way to eat the candy or stop a student from interrupting your instructional plan, it is not the most beneficial in the long run.

In their frustration to maintain control in the classroom, some educators use this *bite and crush* approach quite often. For repeat offenders, they immediately assign a consequence for a disruptive action, which might include sending the child to the principal or dean's office. As Purkey (1992) pointed out, our colleagues may not be aware that

> people who have learned over a long period of time to view themselves in essentially negative ways are not likely to change readily. Whether a self-concept

is psychologically healthy or unhealthy, productive or unproductive, the person clings to his or her self-concept and behaves accordingly. (p. 18)

It takes time and multiple opportunities to be willing to change our behavior!

As an illustration, sometimes after that reflective chat with the principal, Dan returns to the classroom only to repeat the behavior. The teacher then exclaims, "Didn't you learn anything down there in the office?" She thinks, "What's the use of sending him to the principal?" Without knowledge about the nature of self-concept, she may not realize why the behavior is not yet changing. Teachers who assume that the student will never change the behavior may give up and resort to assigning a more severe punishment.

READING BEHAVIOR BACKWARDS

When educators understand that all behaviors serve a purpose, they will try to "read behavior backwards" in order to "understand what is occurring within the student's perceptual world" (Purkey, 1996, p. 71). Perhaps our disruptive student, Dan is trying to avoid being called on because he has difficulty with reading comprehension and is afraid of looking inadequate. The teacher considers what the function of the behavior might be and then invites him to choose a replacement behavior.

Remembering the conservative nature of the self-concept, the teacher is prepared to provide Dan with multiple invitations to choose a less disruptive behavior. She might put a caring hand on his shoulder and ask him his opinion about information the class has already discussed and then acknowledge and build upon his contribution. After class, she will arrange a two-minute private conference in order to engage him in a genuine dialogue: a conversation in which "neither party knows at the outset what the outcome or decision will be" (Noddings, 2005, p. 23). When Dan senses that the teacher already has a consequence in mind, he will be reluctant to participate in what he considers to be a pointless dialogue. If he trusts that the teacher truly wants to know what he has to say, he will participate in a discussion.

Dan and his teacher might then agree to use a silent signal to alert the teacher that he is feeling anxious about the task at hand and needs to pass. Simply acknowledging that the student is uncomfortable and providing a solution will communicate a message of trust: "This agreement is for your benefit, not mine. It's important to me that you feel safe in my class." Less public ways to develop the child's reading comprehension would then be utilized.

MESSAGES THAT NURTURE SELF-CONCEPT

This educator demonstrated respect, care, and democratic practice by engaging the student in a genuine dialogue and reaching an agreement to work differently together. She did not ignore or excuse the inappropriate behavior. She chose to discuss it privately and gather more information; instead of confronting Dan in the middle of the lesson and assuming he wanted to be disruptive. In striving to contribute to the school's service mission, the teacher used intentionally inviting messages to convey optimism, respect, trust, and care. Here are some examples of messages that help a child develop a more positive self-concept:

> *"Tell me how things are going with you."* instead of *"What's your problem?"*
>
> *"Help me understand what happened."* instead of *"Why am I not surprised that you don't have your homework again?"*
>
> *"When you work hard, you always do well."* instead of *"If you paid attention you'd get it."*

An inviting educator provides opportunities for students to demonstrate personal and social responsibility, while still holding students accountable for their actions. To permit students to behave irresponsibly does not help them to realize their potential, for there are always consequences in life for our choice of actions. As Dr. Purkey explained during a recent conversation, "You will be tomorrow where your actions of today take you." (W. W. Purkey, personal communication, March 13, 2009).

It is important for school administrators to also model messages and mindsets that support the school's mission. A positive school climate depends on everyone following the shared agreements; otherwise, there are mixed messages. School adults will be quick to note when a principal fails to be respectful or caring of staff. An intentionally inviting school leader invites the staff to realize their potential as well.

Every school leader has at least one member of their staff that advocates for a control-oriented, zero-tolerance school climate. When introducing a more optimistic approach to the staff, the leader anticipates a negative and reluctant response. While moving forward with those who are interested, the leader continues to invite this person to experiment with the ideas, maintaining the optimistic belief that even the most resistant teacher wants to connect positively with students.

"When opportunities to change are seen by the experiencing person as an invitation, rather than a threat, then changes are most likely to occur" (Purkey, 1992, p. 20). Extending positive invitations to teachers is just as important when trying to change the school climate. Sometimes we forget that they are protecting their self-concepts, too!

FOSTERING A GROWTH MINDSET

An exploration of messages and mindsets would be incomplete without the work of Dweck (2000) on fixed and growth mindsets. People with a fixed mindset have an entity theory of intelligence. They are concerned with looking smart and continually need to validate their intelligence by getting the best grade. They think that effort is for people who are not able, so they avoid challenging work. When they experience failure they may blame others, respond helplessly, and lose confidence in their abilities.

On the other hand, growth mindset people have an incremental theory of intelligence. They believe that their aptitude can increase through effort and experience. They are mastery-oriented and thrive on challenge. A growth mindset person is more interested in learning, than proving they are smart. They are not defined by failure. Instead, they view failure as a cue to try a new strategy and work harder. The growth mindset person remains confident in the face of obstacles (Dweck, 2000). This compelling research illustrates the importance of teaching children about brain plasticity: the ability of the brain to change with learning. We can thank our neuroscientists for providing this message: the more you learn new things, the more your brain grows. Simply sharing this information with children encourages effort and helps to foster a growth mindset.

Fixed mindset children are particularly at risk in middle school, when they make the transition to multiple teachers and increased expectations. During these years, many students who were high achievers in elementary school develop a helpless response to challenging work. As young students, they seldom had to work hard to succeed. So now, when more effort is required they begin to doubt their ability.

A fixed mindset child may have heard their parents and teachers say, "You've aced every exam without studying. You're brilliant!" A more helpful message might have been "These terrific scores tell me you are ready for more challenging work." The second message avoids praising intelligence and encourages children to challenge themselves.

This knowledge is of critical importance in education. A fixed mindset can contribute to a negative self-concept and avoidance of effort. Does that describe some students you know? Teachers who possess this knowledge strive to acknowledge effort and incremental progress. They encourage children to use positive self-talk, such as "If I keep trying, I'll get it." And,

"I just need to try a different strategy and I'll find the answer." Positive self-talk and teacher messages are key components in a supportive learning environment.

Educators with a growth mindset will contribute greatly to their students' success and the climate of their school. While fixed mindset educators continue to judge and label students as less able or less responsible, the growth mindset educator sees each student's strengths and special gifts and invites them to realize their potential. Through their messages, they intentionally convey their belief that all students are capable of changing their intelligence and behavior. These are the Messages and Mindsets that will transform our schools and invite all students to succeed.

REFERENCES

Dweck, C. S. (2000). *Self-theories: Their role in motivation, personality, and development.* New York: Psychology Press.

Noddings, N. (2005). *The challenge to care* (2nd Ed.). New York: Teachers College Press.

Purkey, W. W. (1992). *Avoiding erosion in the foundations of invitational education: The seven deadly sins of self concept theory.* In J. M. Novak (Ed.), *Advancing invitational thinking* (pp. 15–23). San Francisco: Caddo Gap Press.

Purkey, W. W., & Novak, J. M. (1996). *Inviting school success* (3rd ed.). Belmont, CA: Wadsworth.

Purkey, W. W., & Novak, J. M. (2008). *Fundamentals of invitational education.* Kennesaw, GA: The International Alliance for Invitational Education.

Purkey, W. W., & Strahan, D. B. (2002). *Inviting positive classroom discipline.* Westerville, OH: National Middle School Association.

Chapter 12

The Superintendent as Spiritual Leader

Judith R. Merz

On a frigid January morning at 6 a.m., Tom and his fellow custodians worked to clear the overnight snowfall from paths for a delayed opening of the school. Hard into their labor, they were not surprised to see Dr. Julia Moore, the superintendent, stopping to inquire how the work was coming along, encouraging them to keep warm, and thanking them for their extra effort.

After contract discussions stalled for months, Dr. Moore asked the teachers to come to the bargaining table in a collaborative mode. Both sides—union and board—gave up the lawyers who had been representing them and worked face-to-face with open discussion of the issues involved. The contract was settled within thirty days and was easily ratified by the full teaching staff.

Retiring superintendent Dr. Moore was escorting newly-appointed Dr. Paul on a tour of district schools. As they paused to acknowledge a 1st-grade class, the teacher introduced the new CEO of the district to her students. Six-year-old Anthony popped from the class line to embrace the retiring leader at the knees, and then turned to Dr. Paul to ask, "Will you take care of us the way Dr. Moore does?"

In the current demanding educational environment of accountability and reform, a spiritual leader such as Dr. Moore is both an unusual and a necessary model for school superintendents and indeed for leaders at every level in school systems. This chapter seeks to define spiritual leadership, both theoretically and operationally, through the example of Dr. Moore.

THE SPIRITUAL LEADER: A FOCUS ON DEFINITION

The goal of a spiritual leader is a definition of self, of others, and of the synergy between self and others. Such a leader is, at core, a sense-maker. First and foremost, she is dedicated to exploring and understanding her own inner

85

life and purpose. The heart of her leadership resides in such understanding, which provides a touchstone for her actions and interactions. But this quest for personal definition necessarily occurs within the larger context of others.

The spiritual leader seeks to define and understand the hearts and minds of those around her. Even more significantly, she embraces the key challenge of leading others to find their own personal meaning. Finally, the spiritual leader seeks to define the *bigger picture* within which she and others interact. Intuiting that the whole is more than the sum of these parts, she works to grasp the nature of that whole—to achieve a holistic understanding of how the synergy of self and others creates a larger meaning—and to convey that meaning to others.

This view of a spiritual leader is readily elaborated in the familiar context of religious vocation. A minister, for example, is one who has a calling—whose definition of self invariably returns to the context of the religious life. His long preparation involves considerable academic work, but even more significantly, this formation period includes ample time for reflection and development of exceptional certainty in his beliefs. Such reflection is an essential part of the minister's life, as his beliefs anchor his actions. As he works with others, he defines the larger context in which they interact—in this case, God's plan for the world and for each individual. No matter the specific belief system, the spiritual leader is focused on defining himself or herself, others, and their place in that which is larger than themselves.

Some might argue that schools (other than those based in religious settings) are not places for spirituality or spiritual leadership. They point to separation of church and state and emphasize the secular nature of most school systems. However, if one understands spiritual leadership as defined above, schools are clearly an ideal setting for such leadership. At their best, educators have the very spiritual purpose of helping young people define themselves, their thinking, and their role in the larger community. The best teachers enter classrooms to inspire and motivate students to discover and refine their unique talents and interests. They teach subjects not as ends to themselves but as portals to deeper understanding of self and others. Furthermore, they define their own success in terms of the success of their students, recognizing the transcendent nature of their profession that literally touches the future.

RECOGNIZING SPIRITUAL LEADERSHIP IN SCHOOLS

Can such spiritual leadership transcend the intimate setting of the classroom? Can such innovative leadership be seen in district administrative offices? What marks a spiritual leader at the district level?

Defining Self

The superintendent as spiritual leader must develop a strong definition of herself as an individual, an educator, and a leader. Accordingly, she reads widely and interacts with others as a way to gather insight and information and to refine her own thinking. Perhaps most importantly, the spiritual leader includes time for *reflection* in her day. She writes a personal vision and mission statement and revisits it regularly, not only for revision but also as a touchstone for her actions. She develops a core certainty of who she is, what she stands for, and what is important.

The spiritual leader is *political* in the best sense: she understands that many viewpoints frame an issue and is accordingly attentive to many voices in making decisions. However, she recognizes that she cannot lose herself in an attempt to please diverse personalities and constituents. In this sense, she firmly rejects playing politics. From the moment a potential superintendent interviews for the position to the moment she closes her office door for the last time, the spiritual leader is true to her personal definition. This is not an easy task, given the political nature of many boards of education, but being true to oneself is critical if one is to lead spiritually.

Recognizing the pervasive influence of her words and actions on the culture of the district, the superintendent who is a spiritual leader walks the talk. She clearly expresses her vision and mission to others as a framework for her behavior, and she models the behaviors she wants to see in others. Most importantly, she has the courage to stand up to those who violate her professional ethics, and she consistently reminds herself and others to do the right thing—not just do things right. In short, by maintaining fidelity to her clearly articulated self, the spiritual leader displays the unity of purpose and action that is called *integrity*.

Interacting with Others

The superintendent who is a spiritual leader interacts with all members of the school community—students, teachers, administrators, parents, community members—with unconditional positive regard. This concept, from the work of humanist psychologist Carl Rogers (1961), suggests that one approaches others with openness, trust, and nonjudgmental acceptance. At its core, the theory is based on a belief that all individuals have the inner resources for personal growth. The spiritual leader's job is to facilitate that growth.

Such facilitation begins with understanding of, and respect for, the roles that individuals play within the district. Although her role carries positional power, the superintendent understands that leadership is about power with rather than power over others; it is about bringing out the best in others. The spiritual leader strives to understand the full dimension of the work that others do and thanks others for their work. She helps individuals recognize their part in the mission of the school system.

Reflecting this respect, the spiritual leader communicates directly with others rather than using intermediaries, particularly in situations of conflict, where she strives to settle differences in a win-win manner. Recognizing the strength and power of human emotion, a superintendent who is a spiritual leader avoids locking into adversarial positions, preferring to bring all parties to the table for direct discussion. There, she:

> works to build a solid foundation of shared goals by (1) listening deeply to understand the needs and concerns of others; (2) working thoughtfully to help build a creative consensus; and (3) honoring the paradox of polarized parties and working to create "third right answers" that rise above the compromise of "we/they" negotiations. (McGee-Cooper & Trammel, 2001, p. 144)

The spiritual leader also provides opportunities for growth for all members of the school community, not just for the students. She budgets for and ensures quality professional development for teachers and administrators, but she also provides learning opportunities for custodians, secretaries, bus drivers, classroom aides, lunch personnel, and security guards. In this way she helps them better understand their roles but also reinforces their importance as support person-nel. The superintendent ensures that parents are informed about their rights and responsibilities and about the activities and curricula of the schools. She also engages board members in growth by including lessons in board meetings or facilitating their attendance at training sessions. Whenever possible, wherever possible, the superintendent teaches, both formally and informally.

The Big Picture

Perhaps the most significant activity for the spiritual leader is defining and communicating the big picture to all stakeholders—in essence, providing meaning for the work of all. Of course, it is virtually impossible to separate the leader's self-definition and interactions with others from the effort to define the larger purpose. The special gift of the spiritual leader is the ability to create the links between individuals as they pursue meaningful collective goals.

Just as she maintains a personal vision and mission, the spiritual leader ensures that personal and collective visions and missions are articulated for the district, the schools, and the stakeholders, whom she brings to the table for direct input and consensus on goals. She keeps the district vision and mission in constant view as she communicates, referencing it in meetings, speeches, and publications, and she works to help others see how their individual goals fit within and support the larger mission. Rather than divide and conquer, she emphasizes the interdependence of members of the school community.

The spiritual leader welcomes questions and challenges as opportunities to refine the vision and mission. Recognizing change as opportunity for growth, she is not afraid of the messiness of brainstorming or the unsettled feeling that accompanies putting current assumptions and paradigms to the test. The spiritual leader takes learning risks publicly in order to encourage similar risk-taking and creativity among those she leads. She readily admits to and learns from her own errors and, in dealing with the errors of others, seeks steadily to fix problems, not blame.

One should not conclude, however, that a superintendent who is a spiritual leader is a laissez faire pushover who shelters everyone from consequences. Rather, such a leader requires all stakeholders to test their actions against the touchstones of personal and district vision and mission. She empowers others, not by letting loose of the reins but by communicating clear expectations, collaborating with those who will carry out the work, and defining the ultimate parameters within which they may make decisions. Because of the strength of the relationship that evolves during this process, those who are empowered more readily embrace the ideal of self-management with a view to the common good.

In short, the spiritual leader's high expectations motivate and guide those who follow her, for whom meeting those expectations becomes a more personal endeavor—and indeed a way to define themselves more clearly as part of a larger purpose. By leading at a higher level, the superintendent inspires others to perform at a higher level. By empowering others—increasing their capacity to make choices leading to desired action and outcome—the spiritual leader more efficiently and effectively moves the organization toward its larger goals.

WHY SPIRITUAL LEADERSHIP?

The path of spiritual leadership is important for modern school executives both for their own sakes and for the sake of the educational system as a whole. As a superintendent faces enormous external challenges and pressures, including dealing with massive *administrivia*, she runs the risk of succumbing to stress, cynicism, and disillusionment. As a spiritual leader, however, with a clear sense of who she is as an educator and of her role in the most important task of educating young people, the superintendent can more readily weather the challenges and accomplish the myriad tasks because they are imbued with meaning.

Accordingly, as educational reforms increasingly define young people by their scores, a spiritual leader can reform education to protect their spirits. Where a mechanistic leader (Gallegos Nava, 2001) emphasizes competitive values, a spiritual leader emphasizes human values. A mechanistic leader sees learning as acquisition of knowledge, readily assessed through multiple choice formats, and views test scores as meaningful and useful for categorizing and directing students.

A spiritual leader, however, sees learning as a process of integrating information for understanding, not easily captured in quick-scoring formats, and is more concerned with providing a context for understanding and addressing the meaning of test scores. In the broader sense of society, a mechanistic leader would see success in terms of financial success; a spiritual leader would see success in terms of personal satisfaction.

Again, some may mistakenly label such spiritual leadership as a touchy-feely attempt to avoid accountability. In truth, the superintendent who leads spiritually sets a higher level of accountability than the most complex regulations regarding test scores. The spiritual leader does not need to wait for annual test scores to judge her behavior; she is accountable to her own mission and vision on a daily basis. She does not need to enforce rigid external demands for accountability on others; by valuing and empowering them, she makes them accountable first to themselves and secondly to those around them. Such internal accountability, grounded in a clear sense of purpose, is far more powerful than external accountability measures.

CONCLUSION

Who am I? What is my purpose? What is the larger meaning of life? These questions are at the heart of human experience. Through reflective definition, the superintendent who is a spiritual leader answers these questions for herself and facilitates others' search for answers. In a world accelerated by technology, struggling with the disintegration of traditional support units such as family and church, and focused on one-dimensional models of reform and accountability such as NCLB, school systems need leaders who have a firm sense of themselves, of the intrinsic value of others, and of the larger purpose of education in our society. Superintendents who are spiritual leaders nurture the unique human soul of education daily and by their actions answer young Anthony's concern: "Yes, I will take care of you, too."

(All names are pseudonyms.)

REFERENCES

Gallegos Nava, R. (2001). *Holistic education: Pedagogy of universal love.* Brandon, VT: Foundation for Educational Renewal.

McGee-Cooper, A., & Trammell, D. (2001). From hero-as-leader to servant-as-leader. In L.C. Spears & M. Lawrence (eds.). *Focus on leadership: Servant-leadership for the twenty-first century* (pp. 141–152). New York: Wiley.

Rogers, C. (1961). *On becoming a person: A therapist's view of psychotherapy.* London: Constable.

Part III

School and District-wide Initiatives

If you were to ask experienced educators to *name* five words that describe the current state of educational practices, you would certainly get a varied response. Most likely, phrases noted would include standardization, accountability, responsibility, strategies, differentiation, objectives or assessment. These words all depict the educational focus at the beginning of the twenty-first century. What is rarely noted, however, are the words of excitement, engagement, or compassion related to teaching and learning. The range of school and district-wide programs that are seeking change and moving away from the status quo is exhilarating. This section of the book offers examples of such successes which create schools that students and teachers are eager to attend. Each of these selections offers illustrations of development and innovation that are school or districtwide and reflect a compelling vision for change.

Madeleine F. Holzer, Stephen M. Noonan, and Scott Noppe-Brandon introduce us to the High School for Arts, Imagination and Inquiry. Connected to the mission of the world renowned Lincoln Center, New York, this high school is an urban learning community which builds upon the imaginative capacities of its students. Anastasia Legakes and Suzanne D. Morgan invite us to take a look inside the portal of a marine and oceanography academy in Fort Pierce, Florida with a nontraditional focus and hands-on science at its best. Nadine Binkley takes us to a magnet school in Leominster, Massachusetts that has undergone a process of transformation and become one of the most sought-after schools in her district. In another chapter, Lois Favre and Susan Rundle offer a behind the scenes look at the development of a Learning-Styles District of Excellence in Lakeland, New York. In yet another initiative, Diane W. Gómez, Diane E. Lang, and Suzanne M. Lasser portray a home-school literacy intervention program in White Plains, New York that offers hope for struggling families and has yielded significant academic gains for incoming kindergarten children. Lastly, Mary Ellen Freeley and Richard Hanzelka describe a successful high school redesign plan from New Hampshire that pioneered personalized learning in a flexible environment entitled *Follow the Child.*

Chapter 13

Imagination is Our Middle Name: The High School for Arts, Imagination and Inquiry, and Lincoln Center Institute

Madeleine F. Holzer, Stephen M. Noonan, and Scott Noppe-Brandon

In September 2005, the High School for Arts Imagination and Inquiry (HSAII) opened its doors on the Martin Luther King Educational Campus, across Amsterdam Avenue from Lincoln Center for the Performing Arts. It could be said that, in many ways, Amsterdam between 65th and 66th Streets is one of the widest streets in America: on one side is Lincoln Center, the premier performing arts center in the world, and on the other side is the old Martin Luther King, Jr. High School, once among the most troubled schools in New York City.

Lincoln Center Institute (LCI) is the educational cornerstone of Lincoln Center. For nearly 35 years, LCI has brought experiences with works of art in performing and visual arts to students in and around New York City, nationally and internationally. Its practice of imaginative learning through aesthetic education is based on the work of its philosopher-in-residence, Maxine Greene, who defines aesthetic education as:

> an intentional undertaking designed to nurture appreciative, reflective, cultural, participatory engagements with the arts by enabling learners to notice what there is to be noticed, and to lend works of art their lives in such a way that they can achieve them as variously meaningful. When this happens, new connections are made in experience: new patterns are formed, new vistas are opened. (Greene, 2001, p. 6)

For years, the Institute had thought of founding a school that would be based on this premise, which, Greene (2001) implied, was applicable across the curriculum and would cultivate students' imagination and affect their lives. Being there from the beginning would enable the Institute to chart the progress of students engaged in imaginative learning and aesthetic education over time.

A 1991–1996 study supported by the Lila Wallace Readers Digest Fund found that most students engaged with the study of artworks through aesthetic education over short periods of time showed improved personal skills and general education strategies, such as working cooperatively, taking risks, finding new means of personal expression, and gaining a sense of accomplishment. Students involved with aesthetic education over several years broadened their notions of art and became increasingly comfortable expressing their views about it, expressed themselves more freely through art, and found connections between their art experiences and their everyday lives (Lincoln Center Institute, 1995). But this study did not address aesthetic education's broader philosophical promise.

In the focus schools, started by LCI in 1996, the study of works of art was integrated throughout the school in every grade. But even then, since the Institute had not been involved in setting the tone or the school's culture from the beginning, the philosophical promise could not totally be explored.

In part to further pursue this question, in part to serve New York City's most challenging students, in the fall of 2004 the Institute started planning a new small high school in collaboration with New Visions for Public Schools and the New York City Department of Education (DOE), as part of a DOE strategy to break troubled large high schools into small ones. LCI's drafts of the planning process show the difficulties in making a practice in the arts, grounded in an existential, progressive philosophy relevant to the lives of New York City eighth-grade students.

As represented in the initial mission statement, planners wanted the school to focus not totally on skills, but rather on developing capacities; integrate arts throughout the curriculum; respect dialogue, empathy, and cultural diversity; be faithful to the philosophies of John Dewey and Maxine Greene; and create constructive citizens; all the while cultivating students' imaginations (Lincoln Center Institute, 2004). They also knew that many students would have reading and mathematics scores far below grade level, be English Language Learners or Students with Special Needs, and have to pass five high-stakes examinations before graduation.

The grant application required the applicant to state—in language incoming ninth-grade students would understand—what they might learn at this high school that made it different from any other school. In response, the Capacities for Imaginative Learning were created. In their initial form, they were:

Noticing Deeply: To identify and articulate layers of detail in a work of art through continuous interaction with it over time.

Embodying: To experience a work of art through your senses, as well as emotionally, and also to physically represent that experience.

Questioning: To ask questions throughout your explorations that further your own learning; to ask the question, *What if?*

Making Connections: To connect what you notice and the patterns you see to your prior knowledge and experiences, as well as to others' knowledge and experiences including text and multimedia resources.

Identifying Patterns: To find relationships among the details you notice, group them, and recognize patterns.

Exhibiting Empathy: To respect the diverse perspectives of others in our community; to understand the experiences of others emotionally, as well as intellectually.

Creating Meaning: To create your own interpretations based on the previous capacities, see these in the light of others in the community, create a synthesis, and express it in your own voice.

Taking Action: To act on the synthesis of what you have learned in your explorations through a specific project. These include projects in the arts, as well as in other realms. For example: you might write and produce your own play; you might create a dance, you might plant a community garden as a combined service-learning/science project; you might organize a clothing drive for homeless neighbors as a combined service-learning/humanities project.

Reflecting/Assessing: To look back on your learning, continually assess what you have learned, assess/identify what challenges remain, and assess/identify what further learning needs to happen. This occurs not only at the end of a learning experience, but is part of what happens throughout that experience. It is also not the end of your learning; it is part of beginning to learn something else. (Holzer, 2007, pp. 4–6)

The Capacities were presented as a series of core competencies amid the components for school design that included:

- interdisciplinary study of subject matter that includes primary sources and the study of works of art in performing and visual arts
- a constructivist approach to learning
- team teaching
- integral use of library resources
- small classes
- advisory sessions
- inclusion classes and differentiated instruction
- rigorous ongoing assessment
- scheduling that permits in-depth exploration of content and process
- internships and/or service learning
- family workshops

A team of five teachers, one guidance counselor, and one principal, opened the school with seventy-five ninth-grade students. As the school's principal is fond of saying, we had a great philosophy, a great plan . . . and then we had students. He is not pointing to the students when he says this; he is pointing to the school's planners. What the students immediately (and not surprisingly) taught them was that the value of a theoretically-sound philosophy is measured by how successfully it interacts with real students. Like most urban students struggling in school, many in HSAII's first class had no reason to trust the place that was supposed to educate them. Teachers had to gain that trust, not only in them personally, but also in what the school could offer students. And yet, even as that trust grew, the students continued to challenge their teachers.

The unique elements of the original mission statement and vision that remain in practice are the integration of artworks across the curriculum, the effort to use the Capacities for Imaginative Learning as the common language at the school, and philosophic questions around the theme of "Who Am I?" that shape the work each year. Nonetheless, their implementation has been modified each year, as teachers learned from their students.

In the first year, teachers met almost weekly with the principal and Lincoln Center Institute's educational development director to discuss curricular issues. Four works of art were used as anchors for the curriculum, and teaching artists collaborated with teachers in math, science, social studies, and English to create curricular units. Teachers experienced professional development with LCI both before and during their first year at the school. They learned how to experience an artwork in depth through first-hand workshops, worked on questioning techniques, and tried out different ways to guide the students' noticing.

Students learned to notice, for the first time, the details on the Martin Luther King, Jr. memorial sculpture on the campus plaza; created their own sculptures to symbolize how they would want to be remembered after high school; and studied a flamenco dance performance, sculptures at the Metropolitan Museum of Art, and a play about refugees directed by Ping Chong. They made spontaneous connections between artworks and discipline-based subject matter. For instance, in social studies, they connected a Donatello sculpture and positions of power they had noticed in the flamenco dance. At the same time, they followed Regents curricula in math, science, social studies, and English, even though in this first year students did not take Regents Examinations.

In its second year, the school moved to a different floor. The number of staff and students doubled, causing some concern about discipline and communication in the less-intimate environment. A newly hired math teacher left after two days and could not be permanently replaced until the second semester. Students were scheduled to take two Regents exams, in living environment and in mathematics. It was decided that the 9th and 10th grade would study only three works of art. To improve students' test skills, a test preparation consultant was hired as both school administration and teachers struggled to integrate the original philosophy and practice with the realities of high-stakes tests. At the same time, Lincoln Center Institute brought in a consultant to work with a committee of teachers to create rubrics for the Capacities for Imaginative Learning.

A telling moment came during a class trip to El Museo del Barrio, taken by a group of 10th-grade students with the Spanish, science, and visual arts teachers toward the end of the year. At the first work of art, the docent *explained what the painting was* and prepared to move on, but the students rebelled. They wanted to spend more time with the painting, ask questions, and talk in small groups about what they had noticed, as they had learned to do with LCI's teaching artists. The docent agreed to let them have their way. At the end of the visit, she marveled out loud at their sophistication, while the teachers wondered why the students who exhibited such sophistication when studying art still struggled with other subjects.

Around the same time, teachers worked on defining rubrics for the Capacities that emphasized students' ownership of their learning. By the end of this year, both the principal and the teachers thought—from their own experiences—that if the Capacities were more fully integrated across subject matter areas that did not involve teaching artists or works of art, their students might thrive in them, including the areas with Regents Exams. The school's mission statement was revised to reflect what had been learned. It now reads.

> The High School for Arts, Imagination and Inquiry is a learning community in which deep engagement with works of art enhances the intellectual rigor expected of all students across the academic disciplines. Based on the work of Lincoln Center Institute, the community reinforces the imaginative capacities and sense of self-worth necessary for citizens who can constructively participate in a more just, humane, and vibrant world (Lincoln Center Institute, 2007).

During the first two years, a qualitative study was conducted regarding the students' reaction to the Capacities for Imaginative Learning. The data from a very small sample of students suggested that they were beginning to understand that the Capacities can be abstracted from a specific course content and applied across all subject areas, that they equip students with a framework for approaching and making sense of new situations, and that there is an emergent sense of ownership as students use the Capacities to generate their own ideas and questions. They are also beginning to see the value of the Capacities as a way to understand their own emotions and inform their choices and actions and to appreciate the predictive power of seeing patterns (Schwartz, 2007).

During the third year, many classes included a Capacity with the lesson aim of the day. Rubrics were completed that posited four types of achievement, each one with increasing student ownership of a particular Capacity. (For instance, the rubric on the *noticing deeply* Capacity asks whether students notice deeply only because they are told to or because they are curious and want to learn more.) Students, for the first time, helped choose the works of art they would study in the coming year. A number of them participated in internships at Lincoln Center Institute and witnessed the development of *Fly,* a play about the Tuskegee Airmen, developed and produced by LCI.

As the fourth year draws to a close, integrating imaginative learning with all school efforts is an even more prominent focus at HSAII. The inquiry team, which focuses on improving 10th-grade literacy skills, is looking at the *questioning* Capacity as a tool for improving reading comprehension. Students are learning to solve document-based questions by noticing details, asking questions, and making connections to their previous knowledge. Science teachers emphasize more connections between the Capacities and the scientific method; math teachers ask students to notice elements of an equation before they ask them to solve it. HSAII students consistently score well on social studies and the living environment Regents Examinations. All the while, works of art continue to be integrated across the curriculum, and studied in all grades.

In 2009 HSAII graduates its first class. As of April of that year, it is anticipated that as much as 65 percent of the class will graduate within four years, and a high percentage of those students will have Regents diplomas. It is expected that all will graduate in five or six years. Given that only 18 percent of the school's initial ninth-grade students were at grade level in mathematics and reading, this is progress. Those associated with the school know they can do better.

REFERENCES

Greene, M. (2001). *Variations on a blue guitar: The Lincoln Center Institute lectures on aesthetic education.* New York: Teachers College Press.

Holzer, M. F. (2007). *Aesthetic education, inquiry and imagination.* Retrieved March 12, 2009, from http://www.lcinstitute.org

Lincoln Center Institute. (1995). *Longitudinal study research findings.* New York: Author.

Lincoln Center Institute. (2004). *High School for Arts, Imagination and Inquiry: Concept paper.* New York: Author.

Lincoln Center Institute. (2007). *Culture and community at the High School for Arts, Imagination and Inquiry.* New York: Author.

Schwartz, F. (2007). *And then you make an idea: A report on target student interviews at the High School for Arts, Imagination and Inquiry, 2006–2007.* New York: Author.

Chapter 14

Opening the Portal to Innovative Learning: A Model for Science Education

Anastasia Legakes and Suzanne D. Morgan

Our Southeastern Florida school district recognized that the secondary school curricula had been regimented, watered down, and diffused. Learning expectations had been reduced to the degree to which students no longer had to demonstrate their mastery of the subject matter. The district decided to take the initiative . . . and we did.

Our students now claim, "You are so knee-deep in muck that you forget you are in school!" Working with scientists in a professional research setting, high school students attending the district's new marine and oceanographic program experience hands-on, real world, innovative learning. Our global economy and demographic trends are forcing educators to make drastic changes in the educational system to include meeting the necessities of the whole child. Effective school leaders are initiating community partnerships, involving parents, universities, and local businesses in the "business" of their school. Our district rose up to meet the needs of the whole child by commencing with a science-based program in a small learning community environment in the middle of a professional and higher-learning academic setting.

Armstrong (2006), author of *The Best Schools,* argued in support of Jean Piaget's claim that the primary goal in education should be to (1) train young people to think for themselves, and (2) that students should not accept the first idea that comes to them, but to ask questions, challenging themselves as well as the masses. Our program accomplishes this goal by offering a rigorous curriculum. The foundation for the curriculum is all honors and advanced placement level, not just in science and math, but in English and history as well. Students will graduate with eight credits of science, four credits of math, four years of history, four years of English, and two years of a foreign language, along with electives. These learners have an opportunity to choose an area of concentration in one of the following four categories of science: environmental science, marine biotechnology, ocean engineering, and aquaculture. Students come prepared to meet the business of the day.

Although this is a public school, the program partnerships with a research institution, a university, and is a school within a school. Twenty percent of students' learning time is with research scientists and professors. This uniquely designed program consists of a committee made up of these entities working collaboratively for the betterment of secondary education.

ENRICHING ENVIRONMENT

Located on the Indian River Lagoon, a unique ecosystem and estuary surrounds students attending our program. Exposure to wildlife, mangroves, plankton, sea grass, coral, dolphins, alligators, and a myriad variety of birds allocates more hands-on experiences. Warm days invite students to sit along the channel and study outdoors as manatee calves hug their mothers. In the distance, the sounds of a cormorant and osprey call out as students open their field books surveying nature.

This enriched-learning environment profoundly *nurtures* students by removing threats of a four-wall classroom with bell schedules, while creating a positive work atmosphere and eliminating the embarrassment and humiliation at-risk students often experience. Students learn to become one with nature in this transcendental atmosphere, as well as productive members of society in learning how to get along as an individual and a group.

Jensen (1998) proclaimed, "The brain can literally grow new connections with environmental stimulation" (p. 30). With this in mind, scientists immerse students' waist-deep in brackish waters, in order to seine. Plankton observation offers a deeper understanding and value of the ecosystem. Our future scholars realize the value of their place within the ecosystem in order to establish more positive changes for a longer lasting planet.

Changing instructional strategies creates a mental challenge. Computers, guest speakers, games, peer teaching, journaling, and multi-projects are incorporated into daily lessons. For instance, a professional lecture series given by university professors enrich our students by offering thought-provoking and novel experiences. Working with ships' crews, engineers, and lab techs offer scope for imagination and variety. A trip in a submersible helps a learner move from imagination to real life. The experience of one can influence many; this is part of the environment.

WORLD READINESS

"This school is about teaching us to think beyond the job description . . . job . . . meaning our studies," stated one student who would not trade the rigors of this learning community for anything. World readiness means preparing students for a variety of life's events, as well as meeting the needs of the individual. Students are exposed to different genres of literature (textbooks, college-level literature, field books, and lab texts), music, cultural diversity, and everyday occurrences. The program teaches students the need to be adaptable and flexible. Although each day has an outline of what it could look like, opportunities arise at a moment's notice. Students and staff use these teachable experiences as irreplaceable examples of real world learning. Another student remarked, "Flexibility and adaptability is preparing me for the real world better than any chapter in a textbook can."

Pride of ownership is an underlying theme within this community's culture. Students question daily what can the individual do to prepare themselves to cope with any situation. Working together *makes things work.* Participation in the daily functions of this learning community is an integral part of being a student in this program. These learners are negotiating, articulating, arguing, manufacturing, experimenting, planning, reflecting, designing, building, teaching, relating, and anticipating. Students work independently and collaboratively to problem solve as teachers facilitate learning.

Students participating in a field trip to Universal Studios conversed with professional engineers on site, while discussing the limitations, parameters, and safety features of the design of theme parks, rides, and, specifically, roller coasters. As scholars in a student-directed venue, they took on the role of engineers, wrote proposals to lenders asking for funding for the design and building of the theme parks. Included in these proposals were a research-based purpose, dependent and independent variables, and *the attack plan.* In addition, they generated a hypothesis, the scientific process, data diagrams, and interpretation. Some learners included in their process a three, five, and even ten-year projection plan. Model roller coasters were constructed following physics and biological constraints. As a culminating activity, students dressed in business attire and presented a professional proposal to a panel of stakeholders (staff members).

ENGAGING STUDENTS WITH TECHNOLOGY

Pearson and Young (2002) declared, "The purpose of technology education is to teach students about technology, while the purpose of educational technology is to use technology to help students learn more about the subject they are studying" (p. 59). We believe effective use of educational technology means integrating technology into the curriculum so subject areas become unified. For instance, learners in our program use calculators with probe ware to test the water quality and salinity and then create graphs based on data collection.

Simulated learning is a highly effective method of teaching problem solving through a series of manipulatives. A new age of global exploration has allowed simulated and Web-based exploration to engage learners in asking questions, changing variables, and evaluating outcomes at the touch of a button or mouse. This interactive method—an example of twenty-first-century literacy—helps to develop problem-solvers for the future and equip them with global knowledge. As one sophomore noted, "Technology enhances our learning by creating a more global connection to resources, which not only aids in teaching the lessons, but can also prepare us for the business world." A digital weather station located on campus provides yet another example of how students use technology. Current weather information feeds directly into the classroom where students can monitor and predict changes and patterns.

In addition to the technology provided at the campus facility, as freshman, students start a four-year project with a day-long expedition aboard a 137-foot sailing vessel. This floating classroom is used as a platform for inquiry-based science learning. Students rotate through four fundamental science stations exploring basic collection techniques before being introduced to the technologically advanced methods. Students are not just researchers but become crewmembers as well. Interrupting data collection for a shift in winds, students must move quickly to set and strike sails, as per captain's orders. Students use the basic nautical skills they have learned (knot tying, navigation, and nautical communication) as they sing out in unison to the sounds of "2-6, heave." It is anticipated that these expeditions will grow each year leading into a senior research project of a ten-day voyage.

Moving learners away from linear thinking and enhancing their knowledge base with situational learning has proven to be more stimulating and individualized. This form of student-centered learning allows educators to facilitate unique discussions with diverse students. As scientific learners, they have discovered new knowledge through technology and hands-on experiences. Davis (2007) stated:

More than ever, teachers of mathematics and science say, when digital tools are incorporated into the curriculum, the change motivates students to get through the drudgery and uncertainty of data collection to the payoff of results that simulate and showcase the theories they're studying. (p. 13)

Learners in our marine science program are engaged daily with interactive activities that are math and science based. Our students participate in hands-on, real world discoveries using equipment and technology only available to professionals. Field work and laboratory experience with data collection equipment offers instantaneous results; the immediate feedback needed to help increase students' coping abilities, while "lowering the pituitary-adrenal stress responses" (Jensen, 1998, p. 33). The digital tools used in this curriculum elevate math and science classes to new levels.

MOVING FROM ISOLATION TO INTEGRATION

Arthur Wise, former President of the National Council for Accreditation of Teacher Education (NCATE) made clear:

Professionals do not work alone; they work in teams. Professionals begin their preparation in the university but do not arrive in the workplace ready to practice. They continue their preparation on the job. In medical, legal, and architectural settings, services are provided by experienced and novice professionals working together to accomplish the goal-to heal the patient, win the lawsuit, plane the building. The team delivers the services . . . the novices learn by doing, with feedback and correction. (Schmoker, 2006, p. 25)

As part of the culture of this program, integration is vital for teachers as much as it is for students. The educators who have committed themselves to teach in this unique environment must break the mold of the *traditional* classroom setting where teacher autonomy and isolation are prevalent. As quoted from one educator in the program "working together to teach the whole child is more challenging than just teaching our individual curriculum; however, the end results for the student outweigh the obstacles for the teachers." Incorporating *innovative* integration is about teaching students the transference and entwining of knowledge from one subject to another.

Supporters of our program share the vision in helping each student grow in a globally connected society. Rigor and relevance play an integral part in contemporary education, preparing students academically and socially for twenty-first-century living. Our district has implemented an innovative program because of our understanding that this is not just about educating our future, but that this is the future of education.

REFERENCES

Armstrong, T. (2006). *The best schools: How human development research should inform educational practice.* Alexandria, VA: ASCD.

Davis, M. R. (Summer 2007). Digital tools push math, science to new levels. *Digital Directions, 1*(1), 12–14.

Jensen, E. (1998). *Teaching with the brain in mind.* Alexandria, VA: ASCD.

Pearson, G., & Young, A. T. (2002). *Technically speaking: Why all Americans need to know more about technology.* Washington DC: National Academy Press.

Schmoker, M. (2006). *Results now: How we can achieve unprecedented improvements in teaching and learning.* Alexandria, VA: ASCD.

Chapter 15

The Re-Invention of a City School: A Magnet (School) for Students and Parents

Nadine Binkley

This is the story of how new life was breathed into a school to which few parents wanted to send their children. It is also about how a middle school in a low social-economic area became one of the most sought after schools in the city. This chapter will explore the background, inception, planning, introduction to the community, resistance, and the implementation of a transformation.

BACKGROUND

Southeast Middle School was a neighborhood school that served the majority of the lowest income children in Leominster, Massachusetts, with 46 percent of students living below the poverty line and low-income housing existing directly across the street from the school. Many children came from single-parent households, were newly arrived immigrants, and sometimes were undocumented.

The parents of students who attended often called it a hidden gem because the teachers and administration were caring, cheerful, and helpful, who wanted more than anything for their students to succeed. But the school was seen differently from the outside. Few parents chose to school choice their children to Southeast, and many parents requested school choice to other middle schools in Leominster without giving Southeast a chance. Some of the reasons were justified—a lack of involvement from a significant number of parents, language barriers that often prevented communication with parents, and clashing cultures as early adolescents worked their way through a developmental stage of change and uncertainty.

There were other important questions that the school district was working through. Space and money were necessary to move from half-day to full-day kindergarten so students could get much needed early academic support. We found that often it is more efficient to solve two or more problems in a complex system than it is to respond to one issue at a time. The full-day kindergarten challenge gave us the excuse to reconfigure grade levels and the opportunity to redefine what Southeast School could be.

Collins (2001) discussed the need to continually refine the path to a great organization. We put together a broad-based reconfiguration committee to explore several options. They liked the plan that moved Southeast from a middle to an elementary school, kindergarten through grade 5. This may not have been possible without the full-day kindergarten issue on the table to use as a reason and an excuse.

INCEPTION

We had a chance to move Southeast beyond being just a small neighborhood school in a poor area of the city. We explored how we could service neighborhood students, but make the school attractive to the greater community, so that students of higher income parents with more time and resources to devote to their children's education would begin attending the school.

An overarching concern in this small urban district is student achievement, particularly in math and science. Students in our state are tested in both subjects from grade 3 on, with passage of the grade 10 exams a graduation requirement. We also were concerned with the small number of students going into math or science after graduation, particularly from our Hispanic population. According to a report published by the National Action Council for Minorities in Engineering (Frehill, Di Fabio, & Hill, 2008), the Hispanic population across the United States is underrepresented in study or work in the fields of mathematics and science.

Blankstein (2004), in his book *Failure is Not an Option,* stated that schools have the potential to be the great equalizer. The reinvention of Southeast was an opportunity to address the learning needs of this important part of the school population and to help students grow up with a love and sound knowledge of math and science. The new school would offer an opportunity to introduce inquiry-based pedagogy. Science and math education would be project-based with the emphasis on experiments and hands-on learning. This would be a school that pilots best practices in science and math education. Literacy would continue to be a focus as math and science were integrated through all curriculum areas. Writing about math and science explorations would strengthen students' writing skills as well as their understanding of the math and science content.

Next, we set out to determine how to open the school with a mix of students—the neighborhood students and an influx of students from higher socio-economic areas who had parents who understood how to be active partners in their children's education. We believed modeling for both neighborhood students and parents would be important to the success of this school.

The transformation of Southeast provided the opportunity to solve another issue with which the district was grappling. Leominster students have a wide range of academic achievement. We were more and more concerned that we were not meeting the needs of our most capable students and providing them with the challenging educational experience they needed.

We decided to use this opportunity to create a districtwide gifted and talented program and house it at Southeast. The program would be voluntary and students would test into it. We would target the top 10 percent of our students. Many talented and gifted programs admit only the top 2 to 3 percent of students; however, in an urban area where many students do not have the support at home to develop their gifts and talents, expanding to the top 10 percent would give more students a chance to discover their innate abilities. Because gifted and talented programs are often the first programs to be cut when financial times are tough, we decided to run the program like any other class with one teacher and a full class of carefully selected students. Project LEAP (Leominster Educational Accelerated Program) would be comprised of two classes each at grades 3, 4, and 5 and would bring students from all parts of the city to Southeast Elementary.

PLANNING

A new committee of academic partners was going to be necessary to develop the math/science concept. A planning committee was formed with representatives from local colleges—Fitchburg State College and Mount Wachusett Community College—the school principal, the superintendent, curriculum directors, teachers, and interested parents. Each college sent three to four faculty members to serve on the planning committee. We shared ideas about how to organize instruction, what kind of professional development was needed for teachers, and how students at both post-secondary institutions could be engaged in volunteering at the school. A separate committee of administrators and parents met to design the gifted and talented program, while yet another committee worked on the transition from half to full-day kindergarten.

Interested parents were brought together by the principal to envision what needed to be done to the building. One parent arranged to donate thirty gallons of paint to begin sprucing it up. Two other parents took charge of the outside of the school. Through their businesses, they were able to mobilize other businesses to do landscaping and prepare for a playground. One parent volunteered to lead a playground committee in an effort to build a math/science playground. In these difficult economic times, this part of the project is being done in stages.

The school needed some cosmetic and grade-appropriate work to transform it from a middle school to an elementary school. The superintendent wrote a proposal for funds to the mayor, who shared it with the city council. The superintendent toured the city council through the building. At first reluctant, the city council appropriated money for this project. In a second visit after the renovation, city councilors were pleased that for a relatively small amount of money, new life was breathed into this building.

The school board was instrumental in supporting and implementing this program. They were clear that they wanted to see changes in district schools that would bring students back to the public schools and keep future students in our schools. They were involved in planning and were kept informed of all developments. Presentations were given to the school board about the curriculum and pedagogy that would be used. The school board voted positively to open a math/science elementary school that housed a magnet gifted and talented program. They agreed to provide city-wide busing for the program and siblings of the students involved, so that families could be kept together. They actively supported the proposal to the city council to request money for renovations. Most importantly, individual members of the school board strongly supported the program both publicly and privately. They became active ambassadors for this new concept.

The principal took on multiple roles: planner, teacher, recruiter, salesperson, and tour guide. As a critical part of the planning process, she met with teachers to share the concept and the vision for the new school. Finding the right people to staff the building was of primary concern. Collins (2001) in *Good to Great* suggested that you put your best people on your biggest opportunities, which is exactly what we tried to do!

INTRODUCING THE IDEA TO THE COMMUNITY

We needed to share information in multiple ways with multiple audiences. We discussed the changes at school board meetings, which were broadcast on the local cable station. The superintendent devoted one of her monthly cable shows to the math/science school. Research on full-day kindergarten, early math and science learning, and gifted and talented programs were posted on the district Web site. The local newspaper was willing to publish information and to cover informational events. Sometimes this was helpful and sometimes not. The planning committee sponsored community forums with a panel of parents, teachers, and administrators to explain the plan and to listen to concerns. Every forum was followed by questions and answers posted on our Web site. A survey was distributed to all parents, in both English and Spanish, the results of which were brought to the school board.

In addition, the school board invited the community to comment on the reconfiguration during the public forum part of their meetings. At first, parents were skeptical and needed to talk directly with the principal. They wanted to see the building and know it was a safe and pleasant environment. In short, every conceivable way of getting word out to the public was used: television, the district Web site, a survey, school committee meetings, flyers, newsletters, e-mail correspondence, newspapers, an open house, guided tours, and many hours of conversations with individuals about the strength of such a program.

RESISTANCE

Change is never easy, even when the result is positive and is designed to benefit many. There were concerns from parents that their children would have to change schools. Parents and students were concerned that children may be separated from friends. Most discouragingly, some vocalized that students in higher economic areas would never want to go to school in *that* area. There were questions about the need for a full-day kindergarten, and a handful of parents argued that a full day would be too long for their child. There were questions about busing. But no one questioned the need for a strong math and science education at the elementary level.

IMPLEMENTATION

As this is written, Southeast Elementary is finishing its second year of implementation as a math/science elementary school with a magnet gifted and talented program. We promoted a definition of gifted education by Renzulli (2005) to help form the framework for this program. This is a program where students were identified because of above-average abilities, high levels of task commitment, and high levels of creativity.

Students come from all parts of the city to be part of the Leominster Educational Accelerated Program (LEAP) and part of the math/science initiative.

The students are exposed to the same curriculum as all other students in their grade level across the city. However, real-life applications to math and science abound. For example, every second grade class does a weather project which requires that two students go outside every morning and record the temperature, cloud formation, sun position, and tree life cycle. They take a digital picture of the clouds and a particular tree. They download the pictures and record their data and pictures in a daily log as well as graph the data monthly. Next year they will use this year's data to make comparisons as they discuss issues such as global climate change. The fifth graders participated in a biome project and shared their results with the rest of the school through a large display in the lobby.

First-grade students went to "Garden in the Woods" with their TufCams to take pictures of the large insect sculptures. They downloaded the pictures, then, using Photo Story, they made a presentation. This was a culminating event where the students had read a story about ants in reading class, learned about ants in science class, made three dimensional ants in art class, sang a song about ants in music class, and pretended to be ants at a picnic in physical education.

CONCLUSION

Each year more and more parents ask for their children to be tested into Project LEAP. The community shares our belief that the school has transformed. Each classroom is now named after a college or university, so the discussion of higher education starts at the very early grades. The school conducts a science night in conjunction with Fitchburg State College that attracts parents and students from all over the city. An inquiry-based approach in math and science is firmly grounded in the school. Not only is the education offered at Southeast of a high quality, but Southeast is now a sought after placement for students in the district. This is a school that has been reborn. Here, socio-economic lines are crossed and a high-quality education is offered to all students.

REFERENCES

Blankstein, A. M. (2004). *Failure is not an option: Six principles that guide student achievement in high-performing schools.* Thousand Oaks, CA: Corwin Press.

Collins, J. (2001). *Good to great: Why some companies make the leap . . . and others don't.* New York: HarperCollins.

Litow, S. (July 21, 2008). *A silent crisis: The underrepresentation of Latinos in STEM careers.* Retrieved March 17, 2009, from http://www.edweek.org/ew/articles/2008/07/18/44litow-com_web.h27.html

Frehill, L. M., Di Fabio, N. M., & Hill, S. T. (2008). *Confronting the 'New' American dilemma: Underrepresented minorities in engineering: A data-based look at diversity.* White Plains, NY: National Action Council for Minorities in Engineering.

Renzulli, J. S. (2005). The three-ring conception of giftedness: A developmental model for promoting creative productivity. In R. J. Sternberg & J. E. Davidson (Eds.), *Conceptions of giftedness* (2nd ed.). (pp. 246–279). New York: Cambridge University Press.

Thernstrom, A., & Thernstrom, S. (2003). *No excuses: Closing the racial gap in learning.* New York: Simon & Schuster.

Chapter 16

Creating a Demonstration Learning-Style District of Excellence

Lois Favre and Susan Rundle

Lakeland Central School District in northern Westchester County, New York, was already a district of excellence in many respects. With its renowned staff, it had earned the distinction of a *twenty-first Century School District* for its course offerings, innovations in technology, test scores, cutting-edge curriculum, and programs such as Science Research, the arts and music programs, not to mention its amazing food services (www.lakelandschools.org). So what could a new assistant superintendent bring to the district that would challenge the staff to remain cutting-edge participants as life-long learners and continually improve their teaching craft? How does one continue to ask teachers who give their all to give more? How does one do this in a district where test scores are outstanding?

THE CONTEXT FOR CHANGE

Lakeland teachers had studied differentiated instruction and had been incorporating the approach as a key component of their lesson design and delivery. A district-wide professional development survey indicated that they wanted to know more, and were interested in training on how to address students' learning-style strengths. Since 2005–2006, over one hundred teachers and administrators have attended extensive staff development on the Dunn and Dunn Model of Learning Styles (www.learningstyles.net).

In the Beginning

Educators often ponder the best way to determine how to meet the needs of learners in their classes throughout the day. While this question is often debated in professional journals, sometimes the most simplistic answer turns out to be the best and most efficient one: ask your students what they need! At Lakeland Central School District that is just what we did—we asked them! We wanted to find out what our students' learning-style preferences were since we intended to plan a new instructional framework around how they best learn new and difficult information. We asked all of our more than 6,000 students how they learn best—and more importantly than that, we listened to what our students told us.

During the 2005–2007 school years, we involved teachers and students in the test-retest research on two new web-based learning-style surveys: one for elementary students, *Elementary Learning Style and Assessment* (ELSA), and one for high school students, *Learning In Vogue: Elements of Style* (LIVES) (www.learningstyles.net). These assessments provided us with a personalized learning-style profile for each of our students and the ability to create group profiles for all of our classes. With student learning-style assessment in place, the next steps came naturally.

Next Steps

As researchers and staff developers trained in differentiated instruction, change theory, and learning styles, it didn't take long to determine what the next step would be. We agreed to target the already successful initiatives within the district and to continue to strengthen them through attention to student learning-style preferences. The process was additive: we never stopped doing anything that was already working, but we were committed to make improvements continuously on that which had been successful. We planted the seeds necessary to effect change in classrooms—one class-room at a time, one teacher at a time, one student at a time, and one parent at a time.

As a recently approved member of the International Learning Styles Network (ILSN), the Lakeland School community also realized that we needed to strive to become a Demonstration Learning-Style District of Excellence. Pre-kindergarten through grade 12 schools and institutions of higher education, as well as adult-training programs around the world, had implemented learning-styles with outstanding results. There has never been a District of Excellence as outlined by the ILSN. Now, there was a goal!

BECOMING A DISTRICT OF EXCELLENCE

Begin with the end in mind, which is the concept behind much twenty-first-century planning in schools, was fitting for this project. What is a Demonstration Learning-Styles District of Excellence? Could Lakeland attain this status? A Demonstration Learning Style School/District of Excellence is defined by the ILSN (Dunn & Rundle, 2008) as one in which:

1. At least 70 percent of the teachers in the school/district are engaged in using students' identified individual-learning styles as the teachers' primary instructional strategy.
2. Students' individual learning styles are identified with a reliable and valid instrument.
3. Teachers implement a learning-styles model directly related to the instrument used for identification.
4. Both students and parents demonstrate an understanding of the concept and selected practices related to learning styles.
5. Either a designated Learning-Styles Coordinator and/or Support Team are part of the continuing implementation process.
6. The school is open to visitors wanting to observe learning-style practices.
7. The school documents significantly increased achievement, attitudes, and behaviors, and/or attendance through accepted research practices.
8. Teachers are willing to: share learning-styles knowledge and practices with other educational professionals; conduct demonstration lessons; and provide staff development for other educational professionals. (p. 140)

With 50 trained teachers in learning-style strategies, we were on our way. At the ILSN board meeting in 2007, the District applied for and was granted provisional status as an International Learning-Styles Center based on the work that we had initiated around learning styles. Reviewing the above list, we were confident that we would be successful. We already had two certified learning-styles trainers on staff (#5) and the commitment of Dr. Rita Dunn of St. John's University (developer of the learning style model) to assist in any way. With items #2, #3, and #4 fulfilled, we were on our way to documenting our success (#7).

Information about our district's accomplishments was spreading locally and internationally. We started hosting visitors who wanted to hear more about our innovations from Denmark, Turkey, and across the United States. With six out of eight steps already underway, the two most difficult ones remained. Could we convince 70 percent of the staff to become engaged in utilizing the student profiles for both planning and lesson delivery? In addition, would teachers then be willing to share their learning-style expertise with local area teachers?

MORE PROFESSIONAL DEVELOPMENT

During the summer of 2008, the ILSN offered its annual Learning-Style Certification Institute in Denmark. It would not be cost effective to send fifty teachers to Denmark for training, so Lakeland decided to run a certification conference on a smaller scale. This would assure continuity of the training for our own teachers, as well as training teachers from the surrounding areas as part of our commitment as an International Learning Styles Center. We trained fifty more of our own teachers, alongside fifty teachers from the area and beyond (New York, New Jersey, South Carolina, and Colorado).

In the summer of 2008, we were awarded permanent status as the Lakeland International Center for Teaching and Learning Styles based on our continued work. With the entire administrative team ready for learning-style certification, and eighty teachers trained in differentiating instruction through learning styles, more than 20 percent of the Lakeland teaching and administrative team was on board. By November 2008, eight of the eighty individuals became fully certified as learning-styles trainers, with many others working towards the same. The excitement of those who had received the training was contagious. The wave of excitement continued as teachers incrementally added learning-style strategies and procedures to their planning and teaching repertoires.

OUR MANTRA

Trainers at the ILSN Annual Learning-Style Certification Institute have a mantra—begin small, and begin with what you are comfortable changing. This was the same mantra we used when bringing the information back to the district. When we first started in 2007, we began by inviting teachers to consider changes to the learning environment to accommodate for student learning-style strengths. Reluctant teachers were encouraged to try something small. From our experience with learning-style implementation, we knew that one small change would lead to another. We provided individual and group learning-style profiles for teachers and encouraged them to begin with what they were comfortable in modifying in their classrooms. All agreed that learning environments matter! There hasn't been even one teacher unwilling to begin in some small way.

REDESIGNING CLASSROOMS:
SCHOOL ENVIRONMENTS MATTER

Call it the feng shui of education—matching learning environments to the preferences of learners! Research indicates that changes in learning environments that match the preferences of learners result in increased achievement and improved attitude about and behavior in school (Dunn & DeBello, 1999; Favre, 2007). In addition to beginning small, most of our teachers also began by matching the environment to their learners' preferences, which permitted experimentation with the concept of learning styles without having to change their lesson delivery. The results have led to teachers wanting more.

Environmental Learning-Style Elements

Regarding the learning environment of a school, the Dunn and Dunn Learning Style model considers sound, light, temperature, and design (Dunn & Dunn, 1992) (see Fig. 16.1). Teachers must consider students who need sound,

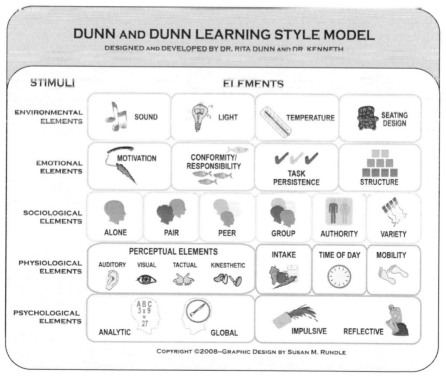

Figure 16.1. The Dunn and Dunn Model of Learning Styles, courtesy of Professor Rita Dunn.

quiet, bright lights, dim lights, formal design, informal-comfortable seating, warmer or cooler temperatures. When designing the classroom, teachers must also understand students' sociological learning-style preferences, whether they prefer to learn alone, with a peer, in a group, or with an adult nearby.

Additionally, it is beneficial to plan for the perceptual strengths of students such as addressing their visual (seeing), tactual (learning by manipulating with the hands), auditory (listening), and kinesthetic (requiring movement to process) strengths and assuring that appropriate space is available through the classroom design. Finally, when designing classrooms teachers should include space for students who require mobility (needing to move every so often) when processing information. With countless numbers of preferences on which to focus, it is abundantly evident that environments are crucial.

DOCUMENTED OUTCOMES

Elevated scores on standardized tests have been celebrated in our schools and classrooms where teachers began with room redesign as we embarked on our learning-style journey. Attitudes about school on the part of both teachers and students have been improving. Teachers began thinking differently about their classroom design. Librarians and principals worked to redesign our secondary libraries, which has once again made our school libraries the hub and heart of the secondary buildings. It is here where students and teachers come to work in a fashion that suits his or her learning-style preferences— each as unique and respected as the individual. It has been abundantly clear to the entire school community involved in this research-based initiative that *learning environments matter!*

BACK TO THE DEMONSTRATION DISTRICT OF EXCELLENCE

Learning-style instructional strategies have become a major focus for our administrative team, our teachers, and our families. In the fall of 2008, as the administrative team and the district curriculum council determined next steps to becoming a Demonstration Learning-Style District of Excellence, it was essential to strategize as to how to ensure that at least 70 percent of the teachers in the school and district were engaged in using students' identified individual learning styles as their primary instructional strategy.

After careful review of our handbook for teacher evaluation, the administrative team realized that one part of the evaluation process—the pre-observation conference—could be greatly strengthened. During the pre-observation, teachers indicate what they will be doing for their lesson, also requiring teachers to describe the students with whom they will be working.

A commitment by the administrative team to refer to the group profiles when conferencing with teachers guaranteed 100 percent engagement of the teaching staff in the use of learning-style profiles for lesson planning to meet the needs of learners. Individual and group learning-style profiles have become a required part of the Instructional Support Team (IST) process that identifies strategies for use by teachers for students having difficulty. Profiles are also required for Committee on Special Education (CSE) meetings to develop individualized educational plans for students with handicapping conditions, and make recommendations at Section 504 meetings. In addition, individual profiles are available for parents and teachers at conferences.

OUR GOAL: BE THE FIRST DEMONSTRATION DISTRICT OF EXCELLENCE IN 2009

We are in the process of examining our assessment of students and our report cards. The elementary report card was redesigned as a standards-based document. In response to parental requests, student learning-style strengths are now also noted on the report card. Similar adjustments will be made as we move forward with the middle school and high school assessment process. Our goal is to ensure that teachers are using the tools that provide them with information on their students' learning-style strengths and that their planning and lesson delivery reflect a strong knowledge of their learners' needs. Thus, we can assure 70 percent participation and aim for being recognized as a Demonstration Learning-Style District of Excellence as early as 2009.

CONCLUSION

Carefully documented data reveal that Lakeland has increased standardized achievement scores, attendance, and improved behavior in all classes that have embraced a learning-styles approach. With solid evidence to support success, there is little argument whether or not the learning-style approach makes a difference for our students. The administrative team is ready to work with teachers to assure that all of our students meet or exceed standards *in style* and their commitment is unyielding. The team has developed their leadership skills by focusing on teaching and learning through the application of learning styles.

In Lakeland, teachers' teaching styles and students' learning styles are respected, and every effort is made to assure that best practices of lesson delivery prevail in the classrooms. Many teachers have also emerged as leaders through this initiative and each is committed to giving students what they need. Good leadership becomes contagious—as do good results, great collaboration, and the willingness of the all too simple notion—*just give it a try*. Our story continues, as do all great success stories! Test scores continue to increase, morale is positive, and the willingness to *stick to it* is astounding.

REFERENCES

Dunn, R., & Dunn, K. (1992). *Teaching elementary students through their individual learning styles: Practical approaches for grades 3–6.* Boston: Allyn & Bacon.

Dunn & T. C., & DeBello, T. (eds.). (1999). *Improved test scores, attitudes, and behaviors in America's schools: Supervisors' success stories* (pp. 166–169). Westport, CT: Greenwood.

Dunn, R., & Rundle, S. (2008). *Bound for success.* Rochester, NY: Performance Concepts International.

Favre, L. R. (2007). Analysis of the transformation of a low socioeconomic status African American, New Orleans elementary facility into a Demonstration Learning-Style School of Excellence. *Journal of Urban Education: Focus on Enrichment, 4*(1), 79–90.

Chapter 17

Avenidas Nuevas: New Pathways for Modeling and Supporting Home-Based Literacy Strategies with Hispanic Parents

Diane W. Gómez, Diane E. Lang,
and Suzanne M. Lasser

A group of eager 5-year-olds sit "crisscross applesauce" in a circle on the carpet while Ms. Suarez demonstrates a "picture walk" through a book about a bus ride that is related to a thematic literacy unit on the local community. In an outer circle sitting on chairs, their parents, whispering acknowledgement in Spanish, smile as their children participate in the picture walk. Ms. Suarez reads the book and the children easily converse in English and Spanish about the story.

The teacher poses a question, "Why do you think the little boy did that?" Juan answers the question but does not supply an accurate answer. Modeling reaction and response to an incorrect answer, the teacher lifts her head above the book and directing her remarks to the parents says in Spanish, "See, it doesn't matter that he doesn't know the answer. Just follow up with a question allowing him to explain his answer to get the correct answer." Ms. Suarez then says to Juan, "Let's go back to the words and pictures and see if we can figure this out." Juan steps up to the book, and with the support of Ms. Suarez and the other children, he figures out the answer.

This vignette shares a few minutes of a parent workshop on early literacy designed to help the incoming kindergarteners avoid the achievement gap. Now in its third year, the Kindergarten–Providing Academic Skills and Strategies program (K-PASS) has shown remarkable results.

Our focus is to share the foundations and successes of an educator-developed program. It started with a problem that the district encountered: Hispanic immigrant students registering for kindergarten were far behind their non-Hispanic peers in the area of literacy readiness skills. Hispanic students needed to catch up before they even entered kindergarten. The steps that educators, with limited resources, took to solve the problem and create a district-wide model are discussed. Narratives from parents, teachers, and school administrators illuminate and document the components and successes of how K-PASS addressed the achievement gap.

School districts, whether urban, suburban, or rural, endeavor to respond to the needs of English language learners (ELLs). However, most school districts only begin to address these learners' unique needs once they become officially registered students. Unfortunately, the delay in reaching out to these students and their families may inadvertently reinforce a cycle of underachievement in school. For some ELLs, socio-economic factors—such as poverty or family literacy—may work against school achievement and the acquisition of the English language. These factors may also make the achievement gap between ELLs and their English-speaking counterparts difficult to bridge.

DESIGNING THE K-PASS PROGRAM

Three ESOL teachers and their director set out to tackle a problem they repeatedly saw when ELLs entered kindergarten: they scored lower on the district's kindergarten academic screening instrument, the DIAL-3 (even when screened in their native language), than their monolingual peers.

The teachers designed the K-PASS program on what they knew about the critical importance of early literacy foundations such as letter recognition, phonological awareness, story grammar, and background knowledge (Adams, 1995; National Literacy Panel, 2009). More critically, the idea that parents with limited literacy skills themselves were seen as having the power to forge a new pathway for their children to avoid academic deficits prior to kindergarten sets this program apart from others that have tried to address the achievement gap for Hispanic children. This vision for parents as literacy coaches was innovative as it did not define illiterate and semiliterate Spanish-speaking parents as the cause of the problem. Rather, they were seen as collaborators who with the right tools, in-hand and in-mind, could create *avenidas nuevas*—new avenues for literacy for their own children and families.

The components of the K-PASS are a series of three parent workshops taught in Spanish, three workshops for children, and bilingual academic materials/supplies that are given to the families. Three ninety-minute workshop sessions were conducted in Spanish during the month of June prior to the children's September entrance to kindergarten. The curriculum included three thematic units of study with an overarching focus on family literacy activities that could be woven into the fabric of everyday life (Gutierrez, Larson, Enciso, & Ryan, 2007). The themes were: "What's in a Name?" "All Around Town," and "Shapes and Colors."

Drawing from the state and local kindergarten curriculum standards and research on early literacy development, academic content and skills were selected and embedded in the thematic curricula. Teachers worked with parents to ensure that the children could identify their first and last name, names of family members, letter names, colors, and shapes. Additionally, certain readiness skills were taught such as book handling, holding a pencil, and cutting paper. Finally, beginning reading foundations such as being able to listen to a picture book and recall details, using the pictures to understand the story, and knowing the direction of the text were targeted.

Specific outcomes were discussed with parents and then strategies for mastering these outcomes with children at home and in the community were modeled. By the end of the three parent training sessions each family received:

- a bilingual alphabet chart
- letter cards, sight word list with instructions on how to teach children to make words
- pencils
- a blank book
- sentence stems in English and Spanish for each of the three themes
- scissors
- crayons
- a glue stick
- shape sorting cards
- two bilingual books about shapes and days of the week

The teachers and their director prepared a proposal for a grant from the district's Staff Development Center. The center accepted the proposal and awarded the applicants $1,500.00 to fund a pilot program.

PILOTING THE PROGRAM

The children were identified as being in need based on pre-kindergarten enrollment evaluations and a home language survey. The DIAL-3 was given to all of the children in the district as part of the school enrollment process in order to identify children in need of more specific diagnostic assessment and possible academic intervention. It was administered in the children's native language. Children scoring below the thirtieth percentile on the language subtest, who also had no school-based experiences such as nursery school or pre-kindergarten prior to kindergarten enrollment, were invited to participate in the K-PASS Program. These children demonstrated a lag in their native language (L1) development and it was theorized—drawing on the work of Cummins (2001) and Krashen (1981)—that this underdevelopment would make learning English (L2) challenging.

For the pilot of the K-PASS program, all twelve families attended three literacy training workshops, worked with the materials and the strategies over the summer months and completed a parent survey in the fall.

When comparing the May and June kindergarten enrollment screening administration of DIAL-3 scores prior to the program, and the September DIAL-3 scores after the program, 67 percent of the children improved their scores. One ESOL teacher commented:

> Most children seemed much more ready to participate in kindergarten. Based on classroom observation, even the children that did not show improvement in their age-normed scores on the DIAL-3 in actuality seemed more ready for the curriculum after the program than when we first met them.

In sum, more than half had very significant gains in their scores by fall and reached the district's benchmark on the Developmental Reading Assessment (DRA) in the spring. These results are significant and impressive given that students usually lose ground in their reading skills over the summer (Arlington, 2006).

The pilot resulted in improving children's academic performance and made an impact on the parents' on-going participation in their children's education as well. The outcomes of the parent survey revealed that a home-school connection was being developed. The parents remarked that they recognized the value of the program, saw their children's progress in literacy, were interested in attending more workshops, and realized that the community served as a stimulus to develop literacy skills.

With the documented initial success of the K-PASS pilot, the district administration has extended the program throughout the district. In the second year, the data continued to be impressive. For the second group of K-PASS students, 92 percent improved their raw scores on the post-administration of the DIAL-3. Ninety-six percent of the parents in the second group attended at least two parent workshops thus increasing the potential for building home-school connections.

TEACHER REFLECTIONS

The teachers shared a vision for teaching parents simple ways to nurture their children to be ready for school through every day activities such as noticing letters on street signs and talking about them, visiting the library and selecting books, labeling family photo albums, making books about family events and members, and so on. All of the teachers were impressed by the open collaborative network they were able to develop with parents. A dedicated K-PASS teacher shared about the power of this networking, "By partnering with parents early on, we are increasing the likelihood that their children will be successful in kindergarten and beyond." When reflecting on the program another participating teacher wrote:

> The parents [. . .] were very eager to learn and complete the activities we modeled. Each week we devoted some time before the session began to allow parents to share their feelings and ideas about the activities they tried at home. It was a pleasure to see how many parents had completed little books and projects with the materials we had provided.

To illustrate this reflection, let's return to the vignette at the beginning of the chapter:

> *After finishing the reading and discussion of the bus ride story, the children line up and go to another classroom to engage in a language-rich experience with the teacher's assistant while their parents remain in the library with two ESOL teachers. The topic for the previous week was "What's in a Name?"*
>
> *Teacher: Compartamos las actividades que hicieron durante la semana. (Let's share the activities that you did this week.)*
>
> *Mother 1: Preparamos los libritos. Me dijo, "mami, otra vez!" (We made the little books. She said to me, "mami, again!")*
>
> *Mother 2: La mía también. Les preguntó a toda la familia cómo escribir sus nombres." (Mine, too. She asked the whole family how to spell their names [to put them in her little book].)*
>
> *Many of the parents nodded their heads in agreement. One of the teachers continued with the question, "Encontraron problemas?" (Did you encounter problems?) There was some chatter in English and in Spanish among the parents and one mother dared to share, "No sabe cómo agarrar el lápiz." (He doesn't know how to hold the pencil.) The teacher smiled and provided a simple solution, a homemade pencil grip. She demonstrated how to turn a rubber band into a pencil grip. The parents' faces shone with an "aha moment look."*
>
> *The teacher proceeded to discuss this week's topic, the community. Each parent is given teacher-made materials to take home and use with his or her child. The contents of the folders were computer-generated pictures in color of the commercial logos and recognizable signs found in the community with their initial letter. Some examples include: A with an Applebee's sign, S with a stop sign, F with the fire station, D with a Dunkin Donuts sign, and H for a hospital. In fact, there was a whole set of alphabet cards with pictures taken around the community that illustrated and depicted each letter.*

K-PASS parents and teachers worked together to ensure school success prior to kindergarten entrance. A K-PASS teacher voiced, "I felt the participants created a community of learners. They brainstormed ideas, and worked together to solve issues that came up when they practiced the activities at home. They were supportive of each other." She was convinced that this community building made the program seem increasingly accessible to parents who were initially reluctant to participate. Similarly, it created a bond between the teachers and parents that facilitated honest and open dialogue about American schooling and the transition to kindergarten.

CONCLUSION

Ultimately, this program engaged immigrant Spanish-speaking parents in workshops that helped them understand what American schools and teachers would expect their children to know upon arrival in kindergarten. K-PASS empowered parents to help their children command an array of information, skills, and concepts, which in turn tremendously improved their children's kindergarten readiness. Further, the positive supportive engagement of the parents formed a community of learners who created *avenidas nuevas* for themselves, their children, and district educators. Suzanne Lasser, the district's director of K-12 Programming for ELLs, sees the program "as transforming the whole school experience for ELLs who have not attended pre-school or other such programs. Kindergarten-Providing Academic Skills and Strategies is worth every penny we spend because we are creating opportunity and avoiding the need to bridge an achievement gap in kindergarten and first grade."

REFERENCES

Adams, M. J. (1995). *Beginning to read: Thinking and learning about print.* Cambridge, MA: The MIT Press.

Arlington, R. L. (2006). *What really matters for struggling readers: Designing research-based programs* (2nd ed.). Boston: Pearson Education.

Cummins, J. (2001). *Negotiating identities: Education for empowerment in a diverse society.* (2nd ed.). Los Angeles: California Association for Bilingual Education.

Gutierrez, C. D., Larson, J., Enciso, P., & Ryan, C. L. (2007). Discussing expanded spaces for learning. *Language Arts, 85*(1), 69–77.

Krashen, S. (1981). *Second language acquisition and second language learning.* Oxford: Pergamon.

National Institute for Literacy. (2009). Developing early literacy: A scientific synthesis of early literacy development and implications for intervention. *National Early Literacy Panel.* Retrieved April 10, 2009, from http://www.nifl.gov/nifl/early_childhood.html

Chapter 18

High School Redesign in New Hampshire: Follow the Child

Mary Ellen Freeley and Richard Hanzelka

The goal, then, is to attempt substantial reform and do it by persistently working on multilevel meaning across the system over time.

—Fullan, 2001, p. 80

Given the state motto, "Live free or die," it seems appropriate that New Hampshire has adopted a statewide initiative entitled *Follow the Child,* which focuses on encouraging personalized learning in a flexible environment. Through the efforts of the state board, the legislature, educators, and friends of education, New Hampshire has succeeded in initiating what many people perceive as the best high school redesign plan in the U.S.

The New Hampshire plan is in alignment with the Whole Child Initiative in the New Compact introduced by the Association for Supervision and Curriculum (ASCD) in 2007. The initiative also serves as a response to calls such as the one from Eisner (2002):

The kind of schools we need would make it possible for students who have particular interests to pursue those interests in depth and, at the same time, to work on public service projects that contribute something larger than their own immediate interests. This twofold aim—the ability to serve the self through intensive study and the desire and ability to provide a public service—is like the head and tail of a coin. Both elements need to be a part of our educational agenda. (p. 583)

The bold steps taken by the state of New Hampshire represent a powerful new direction for schools. In *Personalizing the High School Experience for Each Student,* DiMartino and Clarke (2008) listed problem areas for high schools and identified six matters in which high schools are often failing their students: depersonalization, lack of adult support, unresponsive teaching, imperceptible results, invisibility, and isolation. They went on to ask how public schools can create experiences intended to develop individual capability and often simply make students feel they are stupid.

BACKGROUND

How did New Hampshire go about addressing the problems identified by DiMartino and Clarke and other critics? In 2003, the state board began work on a new set of school approval rules focused on what they initially called *real world learning.* Among the driving forces in the board's deliberations were the ideas that the emphasis had to be on each student and on the concept of the engaged and successful learner. By March 30, 2005, a final draft of the new rules went to the legislature and was adopted within two months. *Follow the Child* became law.

The new rules did not set out to force schools to follow a timeline, and there was also no dangled carrot in the form of special funding. Instead, the emphasis on personalized instruction and the needs of the child have allowed a kind of "I'll see it when I believe it" approach. The legislature and the state board appeared to be willing, as Fullan (2001) suggested, to work persistently on multilevel meaning across the system over time. Much attention is being given to helping educators create and develop curricular structures supporting the new school approval rules.

The New Hampshire decision to keep the approval rules as participatory, not mandatory, is clearly in keeping with the 2006 *ASCD High School Reform Proposal* that was developed in collaboration with experts who created a plan with five key components:

- Multiple assessments
- Personalized learning
- Flexible use of time and structure
- Professional development for teachers and school leadership
- Business and community engagement

As summarized in *High School Reform: Key Components* (n.d.) on the ASCD Public Policy Web site:

> This voluntary program is guided by the knowledge that today's high school needs greater innovation, increased student engagement, and a rich and rigorous curriculum that is more educationally meaningful for students. It is

flexible to ensure that schools have the choice to participate and that those that do will receive additional resources to support these efforts. *It is not a mandate.* (para. 2)

Schools had three years to move to a greater focus on competencies. There is also a move toward more *power sharing* to help personalized learning become a reality; the school, parents, and students can determine together how the state competencies can be met.

PROFESSIONAL DEVELOPMENT FOR SCHOOLS

The approach being followed in New Hampshire suggests that the goals of *Follow the Child* will be realized when educators have had sufficient opportunities to reflect on the degree to which their schools are meeting the needs of the students and when they have had sufficient opportunities to learn about ways to assess the success of the state wide initiative. This focus on professional development will serve to strengthen the efforts of educators to provide the very best curriculum for students.

It is important to note that schools are working to create the best environment for the *Follow the Child* goals to be accomplished. The state board has not, and will not be, dictating the particular approach that must be followed. As one would expect, the school redesign efforts are more evident in some places than they are in others, and in addition, there are some questions and concerns about implementation of the new rules.

What is Happening Across New Hampshire?

According to Laura Rogers, principal at Oyster River High School, the expansion of independent studies and the advent of internships at the high school are two initiatives for grades 9–12. Students at Oyster River also have the option of doing charitable projects as alternatives to final exams in some courses. Such Extended Learning Opportunities (ELOs) are available to students in Oyster Bay for two elective courses in the junior year and two courses in the senior year. The ELOs take the form of internships at radio stations, the fire department, various businesses, and other aspects of the community. In Oyster Bay, ELOs are not available in core courses because in most cases the particular business or other intern placement requires that some competencies should be in place.

Principal Rogers points out that during student internships, students journal, self assess and are evaluated by their supervisor in the field. The guidance outreach counselor visits the workplace every two weeks, meets with the student, and provides the final evaluation of the intern's achievement.

In addition to the ELO opportunities, in the ninth-grade Oyster River World Cultures class, during a project entitled Power of One Voice, all students choose a cause, research it, create a fundraising initiative, and then report back to the community during an Open House. Guests at the Open House use a rubric to assess the students' level of achievement. Guest evaluators include parents, community members, teachers outside the department, and older students who have already graduated. The World Cultures projects have had great impact. As pointed out in an on-line article by Claffey (2008):

> Had ninth-graders at Oyster River High School taken final exams instead of doing an end-of-the-year project for their World Cultures class, the National Breast Cancer Foundation wouldn't have received a $1,000 donation. Dozens of letters written by second-graders wouldn't have made their way to American soldiers serving overseas. And the Cross Roads shelter in Portsmouth wouldn't have been given boxes of soup and quilts. (para. 1)

Feedback from New Hampshire high school students shows their strong motivation and passion for programs like Power of One Voice. Several students wrote to the authors with their stories of how they were energized by how they were learning. One student noted:

> This project was a turning point for me—both in a personal and an educational way. The Power of One Voice experience showed me that I wanted to do something to support AADI (an educational institution in India created to help children with severe disabilities, both mental and physical), but had never really known if it was possible until completing this project. This project proved that young people really can make a difference in the world they live in.

John Rist, principal of Central High School in Manchester, New Hampshire, is pleased with the flexibility that personal learning plans offer because they create a learning pattern that is unique to the student and interests them.

In the same vein, Steven Beals, principal of Laconia High School, says that personal learning plans can aid all students in an effort to build ownership and say in their program. Students who are engaged are capable of far greater rigor and do it without feeling overwhelmed by the expectations. The goal is to find the item of interest or hook for each student's learning. Beals states that assessment is conducted through teacher check-ins, reflections, and student exhibitions.

At Laconia High School, ELOs are used at the discretion of the teachers with a limit of four although that number can be moved higher for students who show they are capable of operating well with the ELO option. The ELOs are available to students from grades 9–12, but in reality there have not been freshmen or sophomores at Laconia who have been ready yet. It was the willingness on the part of Laconia High School to include the possibility of additional ELOs and a variety of other innovative steps that resulted in Laconia being awarded a state "Light the Lamp" award for its approach to change.

In Swanzey, New Hampshire, another iteration of the new approach is the Monadnock Community Connections (MC2) known as a Public High School of Choice. This small public school is showing a great deal of evidence of the personalized learning vision intended for all schools by the legislature and the state board. Under the direction of Kim Carter, MC2 has become a competency-based school where a student meets competency checklist requirements rather than time requirements. MC2 students document their learning and present it for assessment.

The design principles for MC2 are learner-centered, knowledge-centered, assessment-centered, and community-centered. The school is organized around four phases rather than the amount of time in particular grades. Expectations for each phase are detailed in a graduation checklist. Students are able to move from one phase to the next phase by preparing a portfolio and presenting and passing a Gateway. Since a student can declare intent to gateway at any time during their time at MC2 and enter into the gateway process, it is possible for students to complete high school in less time than usual. Students must also show progress in the mastery of seventeen habits of lifelong learners.

CHALLENGES AND CONCERNS

It is clear that New Hampshire is moving toward the idea that "the new vision of high school is schooling that puts students at the center of their learning" (DiMartino & Clarke, 2008, p. 5). At the same time there are some concerns related to the loss of the Carnegie unit as the focus of credit. The Carnegie unit measures the amount of time students study a subject, and therefore, it is often difficult to understand the change to competency-based learning that may take less, or perhaps more, time to accomplish. In other words, some of the certainty available in a Carnegie system is lost.

There is a need, in some cases, to provide additional rationale for the competency-based programs to institutions of higher education. Since it will no longer be possible to point to four units of English and other subjects as evidence of mastery of content, it has been necessary for schools to work with colleges and universities to help them see the advantages of competency-based programs such as those that use ELOs. In the opinion of some principals, there appears to be less and less concern about that issue among colleges and universities in New Hampshire. There is still work to be done with institutions outside New Hampshire to assure them of the value of the approach.

The idea that schools would move away from the Carnegie unit has also raised concerns among parents who see such a change as changing the quality of education away from its traditions. At Laconia High School, for example, the Carnegie unit still exists even as the school moves to establish programs that implement the competency-based approach. In fact, it appears likely that for the immediate future, most high schools will need to provide a dual system of Carnegie units and competency-based approaches.

CONCLUSION

There is great optimism in New Hampshire about the *Follow the Child* initiative and success stories are beginning to be more frequent as educators become more informed about the possibilities. The New Hampshire initiative is still on track because educators are being supported and encouraged. All parties recognize the need to allow time for the new rules to be understood and for the philosophy and pedagogy needed for its success to become part of the approach of educators in the state. New Hampshire is succeeding by "persistently working on multilevel meaning across the system over time" (Fullan, 2001, p. 80). Change is not easy in a building, let alone in a district, let alone in a region or a state. New Hampshire is attempting to have statewide impact by making it possible for districts to have the time and the support to *Follow the Child.*

REFERENCES

The ASCD High School Reform Proposal. (2006). Retrieved September 22, 2008, from http://www.ascd.org/ASCD/pdf/newsandissues/High%20School%20Reform%20One%20Page%20Summary.pdf

Claffey, J. (June 17, 2008). The power of one: Oyster River students do charitable projects as alternative to final exams. *Fosters Daily Democrat.* Retrieved September 22, 2008, from http://www.fosters.com/apps/pbcs.dll/article?AID=/20080617/GJNEWS_01/822474929

DiMartino, J., & Clarke, J. H. (2008)). *Personalizing the high school experience for each student.* Alexandria, VA: Association for Supervision and Curriculum Development.

Eisner, E. W. (2002). The kind of schools we need. *Phi Delta Kappan, 83,* 576–594.

Fullan, M. (2001). *The new meaning of educational change* (3rd ed.). New York: Teachers College Press.

High School Reform: Key components. (n.d.). Retrieved September 22, 2008, from http://www.ascd.org/public_policy/High_School_Reform/High_School_Reform _Summary.aspx

Part IV

Community Involvement
and Support

In a recent interview, Darling-Hammond (2009) stated that:

> There has to be a process by which people have the opportunity to come to learn, to see children, to connect with them and their families and parents, to see them as partners and as capable, to understand what the resources are that kids bring with them and what the community offers, to understand that there is not only one way to be in the world. (p. 55)

Schools have the challenge of being part of a social structure that is not always fair or equitable. The role of families and the participation of communities at the school level are widely recognized as essential for school success. It is with this understanding that we set out to find innovative stories based on strong community involvement and powerful examples of local change.

This section of the book focuses on opportunities which are created to maximize community involvement and support for the schools. Mavis G. Sanders focuses on the role of community in school, family, and community partnerships with emphasis on district leadership practices. Linda Kantor Swerdlow describes a program called *Operation Day's Work,* a student-run service program highlighting student leadership and global understanding. Nora E. Hyland and Furman Brown invite us into a Generation School in Brooklyn, which is a model of urban high school reform designed to increase students' opportunities for electives and careers. In another chapter, Charles F. Howlett uses a local history journal project as a means for students to examine their community and enhance their understanding from a historical perspective. Next, Michael Pezone and Alan Singer take their readers (as they did with their students) on *a Slavery Walking Tour* to demonstrate the power of an engaging political and social learning activity. Finally, Zoila Tazi introduces a program called *First Steps,* which aims to raise literacy levels and offers an equitable early learning foundation for children from birth through age four.

REFERENCE

Darling-Hammond, L. (2009). We must strip away layers of inequality. *Journal of Staff Development, 30*(2), 52–56.

Chapter 19

District Leadership and School-Community Collaboration

Mavis G. Sanders

Who is responsible for the education of children and youth? While much of the debate surrounding this critical question centers on schools and families, theory and research suggest that schools, families, *and* communities have a role to play in children's learning. When schools, families, and communities work collaboratively, students' learning, and social and emotional development are enhanced. Moreover, school climate is improved; families become more actively engaged in their children's education; and businesses and other community agencies and organizations have greater opportunities to connect with and influence future employees and citizens (Blank & Berg, 2006; Sanders, 2006).

While research and policy support school, family, and community collaboration in theory, practice often falls short of this goal. Successful collaboration requires strong district and school leadership. Through such leadership, educators are given the support, tools, and time needed to effectively reach beyond the school walls to engage students' families and communities in the learning process. This chapter provides a definition of school-community collaboration and describes leadership practices that support such collaboration in one public school district in the Midwest.

DEFINING COMMUNITY COLLABORATION

Within the school improvement literature, community involvement is viewed as an extension of or supplement to family involvement. Adults and agencies in students' communities are seen as significant others in the lives of children and youth. As such, they can provide additional human and material resources to support the intellectual, social, and emotional development of children, especially given dramatic changes in family demographics and greater demands placed on schools during the last two decades. Much of the literature and policy on family involvement thus includes references to community volunteers and community-based student support programs. This is one reason that family involvement has been largely replaced by the broader, more inclusive term—school, family, and community partnerships.

Schools' partnerships with community organizations can be student-centered, family-centered, school-centered, community-centered, or any combination of these. Student-centered activities include those that provide direct services or goods to students, for example, student awards and incentives, scholarships, tutoring and mentoring programs, after-school enrichment programs, job-shadowing, and other career-focused activities.

Family-centered activities are those that have parents or entire families as their primary focus. This category includes activities such as parenting workshops, GED and other adult education classes, parent/family incentives and awards, family counseling, and family fun and learning nights. School-centered activities are those that benefit the school as a whole, such as beautification projects or the donation of school equipment and materials, or activities that benefit the faculty, such as staff development and classroom assistance. Community-centered activities have as their primary focus the community and its citizens, for example, charitable outreach, art and science exhibits in community venues, and community revitalization and beautification projects.

Schools can collaborate with a variety of community partners to plan and implement partnership activities that address important goals. These partners include:

- Large corporations and small businesses
- Universities and educational institutions
- Government and military agencies
- Health care organizations
- Faith-based organizations
- National service and volunteer organizations
- Senior citizen organizations
- Cultural and recreational institutions
- Media organizations
- Sports franchises and associations
- Other groups such as fraternities and sororities
- Community volunteers who can provide resources and social support to youth and schools

Finally, the kinds of community partnerships that schools implement can vary from simple to complex. Simple partnerships are characterized by short-term exchanges of goods or services. Such partnerships require very little coordination, planning, or cultural and structural shifts in school functioning. Thus, they are relatively easy to implement, especially for schools that may lack the experience needed for more complex school-community partnerships. When well implemented, their impact is likely to be positive, albeit, limited.

As partnerships increase in complexity, they require more time and coordination. For example, complex community partnerships such as full service community schools or professional development schools are long-term arrangements that are characterized by bi- or multi-directional exchange, high levels of interaction, and detailed planning. More extensive benefits for students, families, schools, and communities can result from such collaboration (Blank & Berg, 2006; Dryfoos & Maguire, 2002; Sanders, 2003).

Schools that successfully collaborate with their communities share common features. They are a high-functioning schools, or in other words, schools that are goal-oriented and well organized with committees that are focused on defined areas for school improvement. Often they are student-centered environments that place students' academic achievement and personal success at the center of their improvement efforts.

They also have effective partnership teams that allow these schools to share the responsibilities for planning, implementing, and evaluating partnership activities among school administrators, teachers, family members, community members, and students in the higher grades. They have strong principal leadership and support for the partnership teams' efforts. They also have consistent district support in the form of team training and professional development; funding, planning, evaluation assistance, and recognition (Sanders, 2006).

The National Network of Partnerships Schools (NNPS) at Johns Hopkins University (see www. partnershipschools.org) was begun in 1996 to assist school, district, and state leaders in developing structures, processes, and climates that facilitate effective school, family, and community partnership programs. The case district has been a member of NNPS since the organization's inception and has developed and sustained an environment that supports school, family, and community partnerships at its elementary, middle, and high schools for over a decade. The following discussion of this NNPS award winning district is largely based on data collected during a multi-case longitudinal study on district leadership for school, family, and community partnerships. Because all study participants were assured anonymity and confidentiality, actual names of the district and featured schools are not used.

DISTRICT LEADERSHIP FOR COLLABORATION

The case district is a suburban school district in the Midwest with about twenty-one schools serving approximately 19,000 students. According to 2000 Census data, the district has a population of about 130,000 residents. The median family income is about $89,000 and the median home value is about $254,000.00. It would be easy to conclude that school, family, and community partnerships occurred "naturally" in this affluent, suburban school district. However, this conclusion would be incorrect, which is what school officials learned early on when a referendum to increase the Education Fund tax rate failed. The referendum asked voters for a $.35 increase to finance a technology plan, pay off a deficit in the Education Fund, reduce class size, and create a reserve fund. The referendum was defeated 17,943 to 8,233.

Through a series of focus groups, district education leaders found that families and communities felt isolated from the schools and that more meaningful collaboration was needed. The district then joined NNPS and has been working to improve collaboration since that time. The success of its efforts was evident when hundreds of parents, teachers, administrators, senior citizens, students, and community leaders worked collaboratively to ensure that another education tax rate referendum passed. The subsequent referendum passed with a margin of over 2,000 votes in an election that drew the biggest voter turnout of any non-primary election in the district's history.

The success of the district's partnership activities has not only been visible at the polls, but also at the district central office, in the schools, and in the community. Key changes that have produced greater school, family, and community collaboration include:

- The development of a District Core Partnership Team. The team is comprised of the superintendent, Central Office administrators, and representative principals, teachers, and parents. The Core Team is co-chaired by a parent leader and a principal. Initial start-up funding for the Core Team came through a $5,000.00 grant from the Japanese Chamber of Commerce. Now the Team's budget is a permanent line item for the Office of Community Relations.
- The development of School-Based Partnership Teams. The Core Team established guidelines that correspond to NNPS guidelines (Epstein & Associates, 2009) to direct the work of schools' partnership teams. These guidelines provide direction but are intentionally broad to allow each

school to develop partnership activities that reflect and respond to diverse school, family, and community needs.

- The provision of Professional Development. The district, as well as NNPS staff, have provided school teams and district leaders with professional development on NNPS guidelines, the significance of school, family, and community partnerships for students' success, different types of family and community engagement, implementing a team approach to partnerships; linking partnership activities to school goals for students; and other topics as needed.

To further facilitate community collaboration, the district's Office of Community Relations established a database of businesses and other community groups and agencies that schools can access when seeking partners. It also developed a multi-step process to guide schools through the development of school-community partnerships. These steps range from identifying a person or persons on the school partnership team to act as the main contact for the community partnership, to establishing an ongoing process of feedback and communication with the community partner, including examples of how to recognize and thank the partner.

As part of the process, schools are guided to conduct an informal signing ceremony with the community partner once the goals and activities of the partnership have been established. The Community Relations Office prepares a partnership certificate suitable for framing for these signing events, ensures that the events are photographed, and when appropriate contacts local media for coverage. Signing ceremonies are often used to kick off the first planned activity of the partnership.

In addition, the Office of Community Relations established a senior citizens volunteer group and the Business Community Education Partnerships Council (BCEPC). The senior citizens volunteer group matches the interests and abilities of mature, experienced adults in the community with the needs of students in the schools. This active group has increased volunteerism in the schools, as well as encouraged greater intergenerational communication and interaction within the district.

The BCEPC serves as a liaison between the business community and the school district. It has been instrumental in helping each to understand the other's needs, requirements, limitations, and responsibilities. Each spring, the BCEPC hosts a partnership awards breakfast where exemplary school-community partnerships and those responsible for their planning and implementation are recognized. The district's progress on school, family, and community partnerships and highlights from district and school activities are presented to the Board of Education annually.

MEETING GOALS FOR STUDENTS THROUGH
SCHOOL-COMMUNITY COLLABORATION

The mission of the case district is to produce students who are:

- Self-directed learners
- Collaborative workers
- Complex thinkers
- Quality producers
- Community contributors

The district's business and community partnerships help it reach these important goals for students. The following school-community partnership activities show the diverse partners with which schools and families in the district collaborate, the variety of activities that have resulted from this collaboration, and how community collaboration benefits not only students but the community as well.

Math Mates

Bank Street Elementary School's partnership team collaborated with BP Amoco to provide math tutoring for students needing extra support. Bank Street's parent organization bought math games and manipulatives for the tutoring program, and selected parents and staff members trained the volunteers—a vital component of the program. The volunteer tutors from BP Amoco were called Math Mates. Working in small groups or individually with Math Mates, students engaged in different activities to improve their math skills and understanding.

Math Mates also provided weekly feedback to the teachers about student progress in the program. This student-centered community partnership activity resulted in increased math achievement and confidence for participating students and more informed parent and community volunteers. Teachers also benefited. They appreciated the extra help and support for their struggling math students and were able to use the Math Mates materials with other students in their classrooms, increasing the benefits of the program (Maushard, Martin, Hutchins, Greenfeld, Thomas, Fournier, & Pickett, 2007).

Loaves and Fishes

Stevens Elementary School's partnership team conducted fall and spring food drives to help a local food pantry. During the fall drive, one child from each classroom, several teachers, and parent volunteers took a tour of the food pantry. The director spoke with the group about the pantry's mission, outreach activities, and needs. The students listened, took notes, and gave short reports about what they learned to their classmates, who were all involved in collecting food for the pantry. Through this bi-annual community-centered partnership activity, Stevens Elementary School donated over 4,000 food and non-food items to individuals and families in need, while learning more about themselves and others (Maushard et al., 2007).

Summer Internships

North High School's partnership team coordinated a summer internship to provide graduating seniors with a real world, hands-on learning experience that could not be achieved in the classroom. For six weeks in the summer, North High graduates worked at Citibank. Nearly two dozen mentors at the bank introduced students to the various departments, including finance, sales, operations, and human resources. Students met with secretaries, loan officers, and senior managers, and learned about interest rates, home mortgages, and the stock market. They worked at the bank's corporate office, as well as at several branch locations.

Students were required to keep a journal and portfolio of their experiences. At the end of the program, they gave short presentations to the partnership team and bank officials. This student-centered partnership activity increased students' understanding of the banking industry, and awareness of employment opportunities and requirements (Hutchins, Maushard, O'Donnell, Greenfeld, & Thomas, 2008).

CONCLUSION

While not an exhaustive account of the school-community partnerships in the case district, these activities illustrate how students' learning experiences can be enhanced through collaboration with community partners. The featured activities were made possible through the collective efforts of students, teachers, principals, families, and community members supported by district leaders who model, guide, and set high standards and expectations for collaboration. Who is responsible for the education of children and youth? In the case district, the answer is clear—schools, families, *and* the community.

REFERENCES

Blank, M., & Berg, A. (2006). *All together now: Sharing responsibility for the whole child.* Washington, DC: Institute for Educational Leadership. Retrieved March 10, 2009, from http://www.ascd.org/ASCD/pdf/sharingresponsibility.pdf

Dryfoos, J., & Maguire, S. (2002). *Inside full-service community schools.* Thousand Oaks, CA: Corwin.

Epstein, J. L., & Associates. (2009). *School, family and community partnerships: Your handbook for action* (3rd ed.). Thousand Oaks, CA: Corwin.

Hutchins, D., Maushard, M., O'Donnell, C., Greenfeld, M., & Thomas, B. (Eds.). (2008). *Promising partnership practices 2008.* Baltimore, MD: National Network of Partnership Schools.

Maushard, M., Martin, C., Hutchins, D., Greenfeld, M., Thomas, B., Fournier, A., & Pickett, G. (Eds.). (2007). *Promising partnership practices 2007.* Baltimore, MD: National Network of Partnership Schools.

Sanders, M. G. (2003). Community involvement in schools: From concept to practice. *Education and Urban Society, 35*(2): 161–181.

Sanders, M. G. (2006). *Building school-community partnerships: Collaboration for student success.* Thousand Oaks, CA: Corwin.

Chapter 20

Operation Day's Work: Developing Student Leaders for the Global Era

Linda Kantor Swerdlow

On Sunday afternoon, March 1, 2009, a storm—a *Nor'easter*—was predicted for the Boston area. One hundred middle-school students and their families braved the weather to attend the Make a Difference Award Ceremony at the John F. Kennedy Presidential Library and Museum. The Library's award honors middle-school students from the state of Massachusetts who have made a difference in their communities through their participation in unique community service projects. Thirty sixth–eighth graders, from Broad Meadows Middle School in Quincy, were recognized for their participation in Operation Day's Work (ODW), the school's student-run service club.

BEGINNINGS

ODW originated in Norway in 1964. It is based upon the premise of *youth helping youth*. Its goal is to develop student leadership and increase global understanding and community involvement by raising money for projects to help youth in developing countries. Fifteen middle and high schools from nine states across the United States participate in ODW annually. Each year, students in ODW schools review grant proposals from Non-Governmental Organizations (NGOs) and vote on one project to fund. At the beginning of the year, the focus is on team building, leadership, developing an awareness of the problems faced by the world's youth, and proposal review and voting. Once the project has been selected in December, students learn about the project country's history and culture. They devise an advocacy and fundraising campaign for their project. The project culminates in a day's work where students are sponsored for doing a day of service work in their local communities.

147

Broad Meadows was one of ODW USA's founding schools. The work of Broad Meadows students served as the catalyst that brought ODW to the United States. It began on December 5, 1994, to be exact. According to the ODW faculty sponsor, seventh-grade English teacher, Ron Adams, "That was the day that everything changed in our school."

A SCHOOL FOR IQBAL

Iqbal Masih, a twelve-year-old, Pakistani children's rights activist won the Reebok Human Rights Award. At age 4, Iqbal had been sold as a bonded laborer to a carpet factory owner for $12.00. He escaped at age ten and became an anti- child labor activist. When he came to Boston to receive his award, he asked to meet other students his age. Broad Meadows was selected because of its Human Rights Curriculum. On December 5, 1994, Iqbal Masih, age 12 and barely four-feet tall, met with Ron Adams' 7th-grade English classes and told them about his life as a child laborer in a Pakistani carpet factory. Three months later, Iqbal was assassinated as he was riding his bike to his grandmother's house in Pakistan.

The Broad Meadows students were outraged and decided to build a school in his memory. Ron Adams agreed to serve as faculty advisor. He said, "When Iqbal was shot and killed, the kids wanted to send a message. Adults may accept the status quo . . . that there will always be poor children, but children won't accept it. They'll say 'how would you like it if you were bought and sold?' There is this empathy and the thinking is that this has got to stop. That is the first step to action."

This step led to "The Kids Campaign to Build a School" for Iqbal, which took the students on a two-and-a-half year journey. They raised $150,000 and opened a school for former child laborers in Iqbal's hometown in Kasur, Pakistan. They also established a fund so that Pakistani families could buy back their children from bonded labor. Throughout the process, they acquired invaluable life skills. They learned how to develop and organize a project, advocate for a cause, raise funds, seek outside political support from their elected officials, including Senator Edward Kennedy, write speeches, present at public gatherings, and work collaboratively with representatives from governments and NGO's from other countries.

A week after the school was launched, Ron Adams received a call from Brian Atwood of the United States Agency for International Development (USAID). He had heard about the Kid's Campaign from Edward Kennedy and asked if Broad Meadows would be willing to be a pilot school for ODW USA. Broad Meadows became one of the eight founding schools.

OPERATION DAY'S WORK USA

Operation Day's Work is a student-run organization. In keeping with this premise, over one hundred student leaders and advisors from the eight pilot schools met in Philadelphia from July 18–23, 1999, to write the *ODW Constitution.* Twenty-two students from Broad Meadows Middle School attended. The *ODW Constitution's Preamble* (2000) captures the spirit of ODW and its emerging leaders.

> We, the youth of the United States of America, strongly believe that every child deserves the opportunity to choose his or her own path to success. We believe that knowledge and understanding are maps that lead down these paths. Operation Day's Work strives for local, national, and universal unity among all youth through friendship, service, and global financial support. After educating ourselves about our chosen culture and project, we work for a day to raise funds for this cause. We are youth helping youth to help themselves. (para 1.)

In addition to establishing the organization's structure and operating procedures, the students developed their own criteria for project selection. According to the *ODW Constitution* (2000), for a project to be funded by ODW, "it cannot promote a government or religion, it must have an education base, and it must be sustainable after our funding. We must consider a country's basic needs and current overall status" (para. 13). For Ron Adams, seeing his students convene in Philadelphia to write a constitution was "a teacher's dream come true."

Since its inception in the United States, ODW schools have raised funds for educational projects in Haiti, El Salvador, Nepal, Ethiopia, Bangladesh, Sierra Leone, Vietnam, Rwanda, and Burundi. The fifteen member schools' annual goal is to raise $30,000. This year ODW schools will be funding two programs, one in Haiti and another in Gambia.

In Haiti, the students have selected to fund a project submitted by Partners in Health, (PIH), the public health organization developed by Dr. Paul Farmer. The program is geared to help victims of the 2008 hurricanes by providing school fees, money for textbooks, and uniforms to 2,000 children whose parents are HIV positive and unable to afford their children's education. It will also provide money for HIV/AIDS prevention and treatment through therapy, tests, and medical care in the clinics developed by Partners in Health as well as Aids Education Awareness.

The students also voted to raise an additional $1,900 for the Salikenni Scholarship fund in Gambia. The money will be used to provide Internet access to poor children. In Gambia, high school classes are taught in English and Internet access is needed for them to acquire English language texts and grammatical exercises.

DEVELOPING LEADERSHIP, COMMUNITY,
AND GLOBAL UNDERSTANDING

Quincy is located south of Boston. A colonial town and home of such notables as John Hancock, John Adams, Abigail Adams, and John Quincy Adams, it was named after Abigail Adam's grandfather, Colonel John Quincy.

Quincy began as a residential area adjoining Boston that provided reasonably priced housing. Its proximity to Boston and its mixture of privately owned homes and rentals has made it attractive to immigrants. According to the Census Bureau's 2005–2007 American Community survey, the city has an estimated population of 84,368, 73.7 percent of which is Caucasian (the majority being Irish American, followed by Italian American), 19 percent Asian, (Chinese and Vietnamese), 4 percent African American, and 2 percent Latino (Puerto Rican and Dominican). This diversity is also reflected at Broad Meadows and in ODW.

From the beginning of the school year, leadership and community are developed at the ODW club's weekly Friday after-school meetings. Prior to the meeting, the veterans (returning ODW members who are now 7th- and 8th-graders) met with Mr. Adams and the students to plan recruitment and organize the first meeting. Forty-five students showed up for the meeting. Ron Adams ushered them into the auditorium and immediately introduced the day's theme: team building. He said, "A lot of big-hearted people have come here today. They are sixth, seventh, and eighth graders. You might not know everyone, but you are all here because you want to help other kids around the world get some of the things that you have. Our goal is to become a team over the next year."

Ron told them that they all had to sit in the first three rows in the center so they would feel like a team. Two veterans, an eighth-grade boy and girl, ran the meeting. They introduced themselves and Ducky the ODW mascot, a huge stuffed toy duck wearing an ODW T-shirt. Each student was instructed to rise, introduce her or himself, and explain why he or she was at ODW. After each student spoke, the rest were asked to try to clap in unison to show they were a team.

Ron introduced the second theme of the orientation: pride in the school's tradition of global social activism. An eighth-grade boy wearing an ODW T-shirt turned around. The years and names of the countries that they have helped are listed on the back. Students read the names of the countries and the veterans described the projects and the numbers of youth who were helped over the past ten years by ODW. They then watched a video about the birth of ODW. After the film, Ron and the older students told the new students about Iqbal's life as a bonded child laborer. The meeting ended with a call to action.

The next ODW meeting was devoted to empathy building through participation in a simulation World Class created by Net Aid. The simulation is part of the ODW tradition and is referred to as *the game* by the veterans. The veterans ran the simulation and initiated the newbies. The purpose of the game is for students to understand that schooling is a privilege denied to many of the world's children. At the beginning of the meeting, the students were first asked to identify their dreams or what they would like to do when they are older. Next, they adopted the identity of an actual child living in Tamil Nadu, Southern India. They received an identity card that described the details of the child's life, the child's dream, and how many years of schooling are required for the child to reach his or her dream. Players then selected cards which presented obstacles or opportunities for the child to reach his or her dreams. Both veterans and newbies play the game each year.

Empathy is reinforced by analysis of hard evidence as the students begin to research the state of the world's children. At the next meeting, students were given a copy of "The World in Focus: Fast Facts on 194 Countries" (2006). The newbies were asked to sit at tables in cafeteria the in groups of six. Eighth-grade veterans joined each table to help them find information. Ron introduced the concepts of literacy rate, Gross Domestic Product (GDP), death rate, and the Human Development Index (HDI). The veterans showed the newbies how certain concepts are broken down by gender.

Each table was given a world area to research. They were asked to determine the top three countries in their region of the world where the children will need the most help. A huge world map was placed on the cafeteria wall and the students were given stickers. Each group was asked to place stickers on the map that represented their choices and explain their choices based upon evidence. At the tables, the eighth graders became teacher coaches as they helped the new students interpret the data and think about the choices. Once the blue dots had been placed on the maps and the evidence discussed, it became apparent to the students that there were areas where poverty was concentrated. The activity laid the foundation for evaluating future proposals and developing a community where decisions are made based upon inquiry, evidence, and debate.

A MESSAGE OF YOUTH

ODW also provides students with the opportunity to make public presentations about the program. Over the years, students have presented in the General Assembly of the United Nations to three hundred children of UN Delegates, before a Congressional Roundtable on Child Labor in Washington, DC, at Wellesley College, Regis College, the University of Massachusetts, the Harvard Graduate School of Education, and public schools in Minnesota, Washington, DC, Vermont, Massachusetts, and New York. When an invitation comes, students vote and elect members who they agree would best represent the group. The presenters work collaboratively to write and design the presentation. They learn how to analyze an audience and develop public speaking skills.

MAKING A DIFFERENCE LOCALLY

Toward the end of the school year, students perform a day's work, an event that Ron Adams describes as "empowering." Students design the day themselves. They are asked to address something that is missing, wrong, or broken in their community. They can select reading at a day care center, cleaning the grounds at museums, serving a meal at a senior center, or planting flowers at a library. The kids nominate jobs and once they are listed, anyone can sign up. They have one month between April 15 and May 15 to perform this community service and find adult sponsors. The workday at the local level connects the idea of service that is both local and global. They improve their own community while making the world better for youth around the world.

REFERENCES

Corporation for National and Community Service. (March 2006). *Educating for active citizenship: Service learning, school-based service, and civic engagement.* Retrieved November 8, 2008, from http:// www.nationalservice.org
ODW Constitution. (2000). Retrieved February 24, 2008, from http://www.odwusa .org/GenWeb/odwconst.html
Stoneham, D. (2002). The role of youth programming in the development of civic engagement. *Applied Developmental Science, 6*(4), 221–226.
The world in focus: Fast facts on 194 countries. (2006). Retrieved April 25, 2009, from http://www.thefreelibrary.com/The world in focus: fast facts on 194 countries-a0153706680
Youniss, J., Bales, S., Christmas-Best, V., McLaughlin, M., & Silbereisen, R. (2002). Youth civic engagement in the twenty-first century. *Journal of Research on Adolescence, 12*(1), 121–148.

Chapter 21

Generation Schools: A Comprehensive Urban School Reform Model

Nora E. Hyland and Furman Brown

After years of working in dysfunctional urban schools in which students are failed by an inefficient, poorly organized, and terminally troubled school systems, one is forced to believe that there must be a better way to do this—to educate urban school children from communities that have been historically failed by schools and marginalized by society. Creating a better way for urban schools to operate is difficult enough, but bringing that model to life within a system as politically complex and deeply internalized as New York City's public schools presents an even greater challenge. This chapter tells the story of a school reform model designed to address the shortcomings of schools in a holistic, rather than piecemeal and reactive way, and describes some of the ways that the model's founders, Furman Brown and Jonathan Spear, brought this innovative design to life in a large urban district.

Generation Schools was co-founded by a former teacher and school reform worker, troubled by the intractability of school systems within which he had worked. Many successful school reform initiatives aimed at improving education for urban youth have focused on some combination of curricular reform, shrinking schools, offering intensive support for freshmen, and preparing students for college (Quint, 2008). Others have extended the school day and school year for both teachers and students, requiring funding beyond what is publicly allocated and creating high levels of teacher attrition (Farbman, 2006). In fact, historically, each new reform of the American High School has sought to rectify a problem with a previous reform (Ilg & Massucci, 2003). As such, most U.S. urban high school reforms have been piecemeal attempts at changing part of a behemoth structure. In fact, what is needed is a revamping of the entire system, not just minor alterations (Ancess & Darling-Hammond, 2003).

THE ORIGINS OF GENERATION SCHOOLS

Generation Schools is designed to go against the grain of disjointed and reactive attempts at change. It is based on the idea that whole-school reform must happen intentionally and systematically. Furman Brown, the founder of Generation Schools, began with the fundamental assumption that this type of school redesign could be done. By pulling apart all of the features and critical resources of a school and re-imagining how they could be rearranged allowed him to invent a comprehensive school reform that incorporated the best of the singular reform efforts. Moreover, he believed that it was possible to make this type of reform happen without additional school funding and additional work time for teachers. Brown decided to reinvent public schooling in a way that was focused on efficiency, collaboration, achievement, wellness, and choice.

Brown started this process by taking the elements of school reform that were deemed important and useful for student success and school sustainability. He identified the following priorities:

- Expanded learning time for students, without expanding work time for teachers.
- Small class sizes to eliminate tracking, to increase flexibility, and to allow teachers to know students as individual learners and people.
- Expanded professional development and collaboration for teachers.
- Well-planned new teacher induction and retention.
- High academic expectations and opportunities for all students.
- Opportunities for all students to choose intensive non-academic (arts, technology) courses based on their interests.
- Opportunities for students to comprehensively learn in the "real world" about career and college opportunities.
- Inclusion and support for students with special needs and for English language learners.

In the planning process, Brown wanted to make certain that these priorities were more than just philosophical *beliefs* about how schools should operate, but central to the organizational model. Too frequently, schools believe in the value of small class size, or real life learning, or a commitment to the arts, but the typical school is faced with the pressures of a growing list of compliance mandates and test score expectations. Moreover, the conventional operation of these values do not always fit well with existing school structures and mandates; in fact, they can frequently disrupt the existing structures or require extra funding. Brown believed that schools could be reorganized to ensure that school reform priorities would actually become the more efficient way of operating and could be closely linked to the academic success of students.

THE GENERATION SCHOOLS MODEL

Brown tested alternative scheduling, staffing, and instructional technology strategies in a variety of New York City schools. He developed a comprehensive organizational model that included all of his priorities by leveraging resources of people and time innovatively. The Generation Schools model offers core academic courses in the morning in two consecutive 90-minute blocks. Students take math/science during one block and humanities during another block, for a total of 180 minutes of instruction. For example, in the humanities block the English and social studies teachers teach the same content to their students, meeting both curricular needs. In the math/science block, the educators are teaching the same content as well. In this way, all subject-area teachers are teaching the foundation courses in two consecutive 90-minute blocks in student-teacher ratios of 14:1.

In the afternoon, students take three one-hour studio courses. Every teacher teaches one studio class of twenty-two to twenty-eight students. The teachers' schedules are staggered so that each grade-level humanities and math/science group of teachers have common planning time for two hours each afternoon (this is in addition to a common lunch period). Studio courses may be used to meet foreign language requirements, to offer additional or advanced academic courses, remedial or ELL services, or even additional core courses. Teachers may also design project-courses so that students can intensively study a topic, such as sculpture or healthy cooking, for a month at a time. Because of the flexibility in the design, this scheduling feature functions as a credit-recovery strategy to prevent students from having to wait a full year to retake a course that they have failed. It eliminates at least one common reason that students often drop out.

Brown's model also incorporates a team of teachers, primarily English teachers, who teach Intensive Courses. Twice a year for a month at a time, all students at a Generation School participate in rigorous, credit-bearing courses modeled after intersession programs at many universities. At Brooklyn Generation School, these courses concentrate college with career. Taught by certified teachers in ratios of 15:1, working with the guidance counselor, the city becomes the classroom: students explore a wide variety of college campuses, corporate boardrooms, community organizations, and public services. Over the four years of high school students develop the academic skills and knowledge to enroll in post-secondary education and the life skills and experiences to succeed once there. They also gain English or math credit for these learning experiences, since they are academically, as well as experientially, rigorous.

These intensives function in several critical, organizational ways. First, by ensuring that the intensive teachers integrate the hands-on focus on career and college with academic work, the courses can function as an additional credit recovery option for students. Second, the intensives extend the school year for students and allow the Foundation and Studio teachers to use this time for one week of extended planning and professional development and for three weeks of vacation, which are staggered based on the intensive schedules for each grade level. Third, these intensives form the foundation of the professional development model described below.

Because the intensives offer a flexible schedule with a staggered work-year for teachers, students get an additional twenty days of schooling and teachers get extra opportunities for professional development. This innovative use of time and personnel allows teachers and staff to engage in a two-week long professional development session prior to the start of the school year, two weeks of professional development within their grade-level clusters during the time that students are in intensive courses, and an additional week each spring while students are on spring-break. The spring-break week is designed to become a professional conference for teachers at all schools that use the Generation Schools model.

The extensive professional development time for teachers operates within their allocated work time. That is, teachers at Generation Schools are not required to log more work hours than teachers at any other public school. Built into the work year, however, is substantially more planning and professional development time for teachers, whereas students in a Generation School receive up to 30 percent more learning time than students in other schools. Unlike other school reform models that increase student-learning time, Generation School teachers, according to Brown, "have work life sustainability, the ability to have a family life and still develop as professionals."

Clearly, this model addresses many of the challenges facing urban schools in innovative and cost-effective ways. Rather than reforming one aspect of public school, the Generation Schools team sought to rethink the model as a whole—particularly how to organize people, time, and space. The result is a sustainable and scalable public school model that leverages all existing resources more effectively.

Operating at below current per pupil funding levels, the model more than doubles the value of current public education funding by providing far more services with existing resources. As a result, each student benefits from the small-school setting while also accessing valuable opportunities typically offered at much larger schools. Highly competitive workplace-success strategies and comprehensive professional development are implemented to ensure that Generation Schools can recruit and retain an exceptional school staff.

OPENING A GENERATION SCHOOL

Once this model was fully developed, the challenge for the founder, Furman Brown, was to get it implemented as a real school. In 2003, this innovative model won a prestigious Echoing Green Prize for Social Innovation and was honored as one of the "world's best emerging social innovations." This award allowed Brown to devote his energies to finding a home for the model and gave him the credibility to propose this radical model of school reform to the educational community.

In order to bring the model to life, Brown needed a co-founder who had experience and knowledge about the operations and politics of schooling. Brown partnered with Jonathan Spear, a former New York City teacher, principal, and compliance officer for charter schools, to find a way to implement the model. They co-founded Generations Schools Network (GSN) as a nonprofit educational organization. Over the next three years, it became clear that the most viable opportunity for GSN to open a school was through the New York City Office of New Schools. This office was designed in response to the growing number of charter schools in New York City, to create a mechanism for innovative schools to open directly as part of the city system. Spear's comprehensive understanding of the New York City system, including budgetary and compliance issues, allowed the co-founders to describe the model in a way that made sense within the intense bureaucracies of an urban public school district.

After two years of discussions and negotiations with the New York City Department of Education and the Teachers Union (UFT), GSN was granted permission to open a high school, starting with grade nine, in the Canarsie section of Brooklyn. The school opened at the site of one of the most underperforming high schools in New York City, at the campus that was deemed "least popular" among students and that suffered from spiraling decreased enrollment.

Most remarkable about the negotiations to open the Brooklyn Generation School in the fall of 2007 was that the UFT and the DOE signed an agreement to amend the contract for Brooklyn Generation School teachers, which permitted the innovative school calendar with staggered vacation time, and agreed to approve the changes to the school day in which teachers work seven hours during instructional days and approximately five hours for professional development days. This agreement was essential to the opening of the first Generation School and allowed the model to be implemented with design integrity. Brown and Spear had met one of their key policy goals: to demonstrate that teachers' contracts need not be a barrier to innovation, but that the spirit and the key provisions of contracts could be upheld within a radical model of school reform.

THE MODEL'S SUCCESS

Since the opening of the Brooklyn Generation School, Brown and Spear have worked to support the school's success through their nonprofit status, which has operated with limited private funding. Their organization provides essential support to the district, the school staff, and the union as they transform from the long-established and deeply internalized current system to a new operational model. Helping the many professionals—at district and school levels—adapt to the new set of roles and structures requires high-caliber, ongoing technical assistance and training. Generation Schools is successfully providing these services.

The success of the model is evident in the initial outcomes of the school, including: (a) the UFT and DOE's independent evaluations of the viability and success of the model's execution; (b) strong school performance data in attendance, credit accumulation toward on-time graduation, and standardized test scores; and (c) the four hundred student applications for the ninety spaces in the freshman class of 2009.

It is clear that in order for radical change and radical improvement to occur in public schools we must have systemic change. That is, we must change the ways that schools operate and break the traditional mold. What this story demonstrates is that systemic change is possible and schools that operate with radically different organizational structures designed to better meet student needs can be created. The Generation School story also demonstrates that radical change need not cost more money, nor operate completely outside of existing systems. It is incumbent upon educational innovators to build bridges to the existing system and to demonstrate a path for bureaucracies to grow and change. Clearly, comprehensive school reform requires innovative thought and reinvention of how to better meet the needs of students, but also requires imaginative restructuring that meets the needs of teachers, bureaucracies, and unions.

REFERENCES

Ancess, J., & Darling-Hammond, L. (2003). *Beating the odds: High schools as communities of commitment.* New York: Teachers College Press.

Farbman, D. (2006). The promise of extended-time schools for promoting student achievement: A case study approach. *Teachers College Record.* Retrieved January 9, 2009, from http://www.tcrecord.org/content.asp?contentid=12274

Ilg, T. J., & Massucci, J. D. (2003). Comprehensive urban high school: Are there better options for poor and minority students? *Education and Urban Society, 36*(1), 63–78.

Quint, J. (2008). Lessons from leading models: What we can learn from talent development, first things first, and career academies. *Educational Leadership, 65*(8), 64–68.

Chapter 22

Writing Local History Journals Can Be Engaging and Educationally Worthwhile

Charles F. Howlett

There are many different ways to investigate a community's social, economic, religious, political, and educational history, as well as the lives of its more noteworthy inhabitants, but far too many of us fail to do so. Learning about the history of where we live is one of the best ways to develop a connection to the community, respect for the treasures of its past, and a greater sense of appreciation for how people once lived (Felt, 1983). How, then, are we to take local history seriously? How is it possible to engage younger people in researching and writing about the communities in which they live?

THE CHALLENGES

Let us start with schools, which need to begin teaching local history and recording it as vigorously as they do global and American history. In New York state, the teaching of community history begins as early as fourth grade. Yet little has been done in the way of encouraging students to look in their own backyards and write stories about what they find. Nor, as students advance in grade, is there any effort to promote the research and writing of local history. Unfortunately, the emphasis on the present–on how communities function–rather than on how they came to be still remains one of the more important barriers for an appreciation of the past. Where history is studied, most teachers take a *roots* approach, emphasizing such aspects as family histories, as opposed to a more meaningful investigation of the community and its traditions. Often, little effort is made to find out what resources are available and how they might be utilized.

THE RESOURCES

Clearly, teachers can do better in terms of the discipline of history by requiring students to use local sources and primary documents in order to stimulate their interest in research and writing. But, to accomplish this, teachers need to provide hands-on experiences in historical research and wean students away from textbook dependency. Students need to feel a tangible connection to the land and people where they live. This means shifting emphasis from the larger events and figures in history, which are recounted in school texts, to the smaller things, the less famous lives and events that are just as important in the ebb and flow of historical change.

When first teaching high school social studies some years ago, I was intrigued by the prospect of creating a local history journal with my students in American history. What I had found at the time was the sad realization that despite my own enthusiasm and love for history, it was not being reciprocated. What I began to realize was that for years, as students progressed from one grade to the next, the social studies taught to them came simply from the textbook and very often the material was just being spoon-fed. They had become bored, uninvolved, and detached.

I decided that if I was going to remain as a high school social studies teacher I had to create educationally worthwhile activities for my students to do in addition to the mandated state curriculum. For my students at Amityville Memorial High School on Long Island, NY—a culturally and linguistically diverse community—exploring the village government, the local historical society, and community newspapers dramatically sparked their interest in social studies with the creation of their own local history journal.

The first thing I did was to tell students that a research paper based on primary source documentation would be required. Next, I encouraged them to work with local history data. Simply going to the library and finding history books to copy material, reword it, and then claim that this was an original paper, no matter how much documentation was provided, was no longer acceptable. Instead, I guided them to feel and touch history by examining diaries, autobiographies, conduct oral history interviews, read personal letters, gather village board minutes, look at local archived newspapers, gather census data—to understand more vividly how Amityville residents lived at certain times and reacted to particular events. I also wanted them to think as aspiring scholars and successful writers.

THE ORIGINS OF A STUDENT-CREATED
LOCAL HISTORY JOURNAL

A local history journal was established! The editorial board was composed of students in my American history classes. All student-generated research papers were considered for publication in the journal. The cost of printing the journal—roughly two hundred copies—was borne by the school district and the cover, as well as all illustrations were developed with the aid of the art department.

Students read Barzun and Graff's *The Modern Researcher* (2003). The district purchased a large number of copies as a supplementary class text, as well as Strunk and White's *Elements of Style* (1999). Although computer programs have grammar and spell check, *Elements* remains an indispensable resource to grammarians and became the students' research bible.

The purpose for developing the history journal was so that students would learn to think critically and understand the effects of public opinion, prejudice, personal likes and dislikes, as well as the healing effects of time. The last aspect was particularly significant since the Amityville School District and community was the subject of civil rights activity and lawsuits in the 1950s and 1960s. So, it was only appropriate that students be encouraged to investigate such issues to see for themselves what has happened over time.

After pointing out that their research papers would be more enjoyable to write if they wrote *history close to home,* a timetable was then established during the first week of classes at the start of each school year. A comprehensive outline of their intended research project had to be submitted by the first week of January after students had time to do the initial research, a rough draft turned in the first week of March, and the finished product completed a month later.

After topics were selected and appropriate sources located, students visited—on their own—the local historical society, public library, families in the community recognized for their role in past events and issues, long-established business, school officials, village trustees, police and fire department officials, and church leaders (Kobrin, 1996). Students developed appropriate sets of questions to ask when interviewing local residents and officials. Thus, the skills of oral history gathering were also being developed and practiced in recreating their community's past. Finally, the students themselves placed a notice about their project in the local newspaper—*Amityville Record*—to obtain more information specific to their projects.

THE JOURNAL CONNECTS TO THE PAST

The results were pleasantly unexpected. Two energetic African Americans studied the relationship cultivated more than 100 years ago between Black and Native American families in North Amityville where they lived. Another student, who lived in the village proper, examined how historic homes had been preserved over generations.

Students went into the field with vigor, interviewing residents, visiting sites, and using materials at the local historical society. During a three-year period, successive classes of American history students produced a trilogy that covered the history of the Amityville community chronologically from the turn of the nineteenth century to the late-twentieth century. The research was reviewed, compiled, and edited by student editorial boards and subsequently printed in journal form. The student local history journals were then made available to the community as well as the historical society and the local public library.

The students chronicled among other subjects:

- Family life
- The African American experience
- Village politics
- The school system
- The experiences of overseas combat veterans
- The impact of hospitals in the community
- The history and role of the police and fire departments
- Bootlegging during the prohibition era
- How local residents coped with the Great Depression
- De facto segregation of the public schools during the modern civil rights movement
- The real story behind the *Amityville Horror* (1979)

The local history project expanded its focus after the first three issues as students occasionally reused source materials in new and exciting ways. A topical, as opposed to a chronological, approach was then developed. Students began taking a more in-depth look at local institutions and how they affected community life—churches and other religious places of worship, hospitals as sources of assistance to local residents and employment, and grand old hotels as popular summer tourist attractions in the pre-World War I period. In addition, they traced local connections to a larger slice of Long Island's life, including the civil rights movement, the Vietnam War, and the important role defense industries played in terms of economic employment.

One of the essential questions behind this project was the following: how can students achieve a sense of connectedness to local history and will the community respond in kind? Apart from the educational benefits of students developing better historical skills and marked improvement in their writing, once the project was in full swing, it became evident that the community embraced the idea of shared history. It turned out to be one way residents showed greater appreciation for the local school system. Senior citizens, moreover, were delighted to talk about what it was like growing up in Amityville. The local historical society sponsored a scholarship for the best student essay on local history. The mayor and village board of trustees instituted mock public meetings to stimulate students' participation in government. Even, prospective homebuyers and newly assigned clergymen consulted the history journals to get a feel for the community.

The crowning success of this project occurred when the school district sponsored a centennial celebration of the Park Avenue School—the oldest extant school building in the community and present home to the district administrative offices. Inspired by the students' history project, residents worked hand-in-hand with students and school district personnel to stage a series of commemorative events. These events not only linked school and community, but also past and present—a homecoming parade featuring high school graduates since 1920, a memorabilia exhibit, a twelve hour video of graduates' recollections, and burial of a centennial time capsule.

CONCLUSION

There is no question that this kind of hands-on, learner-centered, inquiry-based instruction is labor-intensive. However, teachers of social studies need to make history come alive. Writing a local history journal enables students to extend themselves, to understand what they have not experienced personally, and to bond with those from different times and locations. By bringing the past to life, students are able to forge a new and better understanding of the communities in which they live and work, as well as prepare them to meet their community's needs in the years to come.

REFERENCES

Arkoff, S. Z., Geisinger, E., & Saland, R. (Producers), & Rosenberg, S. (Director). (1979). *The Amityville horror* [Motion picture]. United States: American International Pictures (AIP).

Barzun, J., & Graff, H. F. (2003). *The modern researcher* (6th ed.). New York: Wadsworth.

Felt, T. E. (1983). *Researching, writing and publishing local history.* Nashville, TN: American Association for State and Local History.

Kobrin, D. (1996). *Beyond the textbook: Teaching history using documents and primary sources.* Portsmouth, NH: Heinemann.

Strunk, W. Jr., & White, E. B. (1999). *The elements of style* (4th ed.). New York: Macmillan.

Chapter 23

Time to Tell the Truth About Local History, New York Was a Land of Slavery: How Student Activism Promotes Leadership and Literacy

Michael Pezone and Alan Singer

Read the books and it's plain to see,
New York's the land of slavery,
If you thought the North was a freedom land.
You thought wrong — because here you could own a man.
From Francis Lewis to Fernando Wood,
Slave labor is what was happening,
They bought and sold human beings and made their millions,
Soon the whole trade was worth more than 60 billion!
Read the books, if you don't trust me,
New York's the land of slavery.
AT&T and Citibank, just to name a few
From the slaveholding ranks,
Slaves used to be brought in all the time,
So we wanna know, JUST WHERE ARE THE SIGNS?
They tried to cover up these Northern slaves,
And if you thought it was just the South, then you got played,
Read the books, and you'll surely see,
That New York's the land of slavery.

India Nelson, Junior, Law, Government, and Community Service Magnet High School

FORGOTTEN HISTORY IN NEW YORK

On May 23, 2008, over six hundred upper elementary, middle-level, and high school students walked the streets of Manhattan learning about the forgotten history of slavery in New York City. It was the largest group to participate in the three-year history of the New York and Slavery Walking Tour.

There are no markers at the locations where enslaved Africans rebelled in 1712, where they plotted to win their freedom in 1741, where they were publicly executed—hanged or burned at the stake—or at the seaport where slave traders and bankers met to plan trans-Atlantic voyages. People, places, and events have been erased from the past. One of the purposes of the tour is to demand that historical markers be installed.

The New York and Slavery Walking Tour is organized by juniors and seniors from Law, Government, and Community Service Magnet High School, Queens, NY. The population of the school is overwhelmingly African American, Caribbean, and Hispanic. Many of the students come from troubled communities and have academic difficulties. They are the survivors of less than adequate schools. They are also leaders who have chosen to take ownership over their educations.

Each year, a new group of students chooses to take part in the project that they learn about from students who participated the previous year. They choose to become involved because they want to study their history and learn the truth about American history. They also take part because they want to teach about it to the public and to other students from around the city.

Preparation takes a full school year, although the intensity picks up during the last three weeks before the tour date. The tour is in May each year, because that is when the 1741 freedom plotters were executed in what is now New York City's Foley Square (Singer, 2008). The square is surrounded by courthouses, but as one tour guide explained to a group of elementary school students, "In colonial New York, there was no justice for Blacks who wanted to be free."

HOW STUDENTS BECOME INVOLVED?

Each September, one of Michael Pezone's upper-level history classes is invited to organize the tour. Because they know about it already from friends, not much persuasion is needed. But there is a lot of work to do. The class uses the *New York and Slavery: Complicity and Resistance* (n.d.) curriculum guide to research the history of African Americans in New York City, and Mr. Pezone organizes the United States history course to place African American and local history at the center of what they will study. This year, a senior English class wanted to be part of the tour as well. Many of the students had been in Mr. Pezone's class the year before and wanted to be part of the project.

During the course of the year, students continually do research, organize information, and make oral presentations in class. For them, oral and written literacy are not just academic exercises, but part of their training to become historical interpreters and tour guides. These skills prepare them to become student community leaders and activists.

Oral presentations in class are essential for encouraging student engagement, democratic dialogue, and classroom community. Having the stage to yourself and the ability to speak your mind engages the emotions as well as the mind and promotes ownership of the final product. Oral presentation also increases attention, improves cognition and memory, and improves the ability of students to listen to and learn from others.

Three weeks before the tour, preparation begins in earnest. The sixty students in the two classes design and create historical markers that they will display at each of the eight sites. During the first tour in 2006, the markers were hung on lampposts, but a local business development group ripped them down and complained that attaching posters to public property was illegal (Pezone & Singer, 2006). Now, students stand at the sites and hold their signs aloft so passers-by can read them. Using computers and iron-ons, students make t-shirts explaining the purpose of the tour and designating them as official tour guides.

The most important part of the preparation, however, is writing and practicing presentations for the start of the tour and for each of the sites. Students are given decision-making power to choose what they want to present and how they will do it. The only requirement is that all statements be historically accurate.

THE DAY OF THE TOUR

Two students volunteered to greet classes arriving for the tour. They wrote and performed hip-hop raps on the history of slavery in New York. One student at City Hall and another in front of Citibank—which still has offices on the site where its predecessor bank organized to finance the illegal nineteenth century slave trade—gave speeches reminiscent of powerful church sermons and aroused their audiences with their chant and response format. At the African Burial Ground National Monument, a student-led class group sings *Amazing Grace*. Other presenters gave more traditional explanations.

At each site in the New York financial district, students finished their presentations by leading the assembled students in a chant: "Time to tell the truth, our local history, New York was a land of slavery!" or "Resist! Resist! Resist! Time to be free! Resist! Resist! Resist! No more slavery!"

Alberta Martin, a social studies teacher who brought sixty sixth-grade students on the Slavery in New York Walking Tour reported that before the trip she conducted a background lesson to get them thinking about the topic, but did not offer them too much because she wanted the high school students to provide much of the new information.

> I was not disappointed. The poetry and chants and slogans made the experience very interactive. My students were still reciting the chants hours later. Seeing physical sites where events took place, even though those places don't look the same, was a very important element for bringing history to life. The high school students who taught and guided the tours were excellent. Each one conducted themselves as professionals, and their enthusiasm infected the kids. This was a fantastic way to bring history alive and make it interactive. I am going to recommend this trip to the seventh and eighth grade for next year. I will definitely do the trip again next year. If elementary, middle, and high school students had more learning experiences like this, they might be more enthusiastic about learning history.

According to Vance Gillenwater, a high school social studies teacher who brought over one hundred tenth-grade global history students,

> The immediate feedback from the kids was overwhelmingly positive. They got a kick out of seeing fellow students doing the presentations, and just being outside on a beautiful day put everyone in good spirits. In my classes we had just completed lessons on the Atlantic Slave trade; this event not only reinforced the lessons but brought the abstract notion of slavery to life in their own backyard.

CONSTRUCTING KNOWLEDGE

Projects such as the New York and Slavery Walking Tour enable students to become organizers of their own learning experience: students create both form and content, with maximal freedom. The tour helps to undermine the ways in which the culture reduces people to passive and atomistic spectators of history by engaging students in political/social activity and by allowing them the opportunity to make history collectively. It is a form of social speech promoted by the Brazilian educator Paulo Freire that enables students to engage in public action to transform society (Freire, 1970). In addition, it models such activity to hundreds of other students on the tour.

Instead of strained motivational activities that attempt to relate abstract curriculum to the real world, the tour is in itself an authentic learning opprtunity. Instead of preparation for a future task, the learning is engaging and the learning *is* the doing. Journaling after the event, one student wrote:

> Being at New York City Hall, I believe we educated the individuals that passed by with a piece of erased history. We were next to a subway station, and every

time people came out, we would start our chant and people would be attracted by it. Every time a tour bus would pass, we would sing even louder so they could hear us.

Other student tour guides discussed how they were proud of the way the younger students looked to them as leaders, how they had "gained the courage to stand in front of people" and learned that students will "find history very interesting if it is presented in a fun environment and in a language they can understand." They were amazed that adults who were "walking by stopped to listen to us and were shocked to know that slavery had existed in New York City."

We believe the New York and Slavery Walking Tour builds on the theoretical work of a number of contemporary educational thinkers. Giroux (1989) called for teachers to open new spaces of critical discourse to help students criticize master narratives. McLaren (1989) wrote of schools as sites and agents of social empowerment. Barthes (1977) urged educators to use a strategy of *disappropriation*—to give up their typical authoritative roles. Fine (1989) and Delpit (1988) described how minority student voices are typically silenced or neutralized, and how real issues are psychologized and privatized, instead of opened up for examination. We especially support the impulse to empower students highlighted by Ladson-Billings' (1995) notion of culturally relevant pedagogy.

WHO BENEFITS FROM THE TOUR?

Teachers who brought their classes to the New York and Slavery Walking Tour learned about it over the Internet or at staff development activities. The first two years, teachers and students who followed the historical path were almost all Black and Hispanic. However, by the third tour, the classes that participated were much more multiethnic and interracial. This is a significant development because slavery and racism are a central part of American history, not just the history of African Americans.

Because of the work of the Law, Government, and Community Service High School students, many teachers are planning to involve their classes in similar projects in the future—not just as participants, but as leaders and community activists. Pictures and a map of the 2008 tour as well as updates about future activities are on-line at http://people.hofstra.edu/alan_j_singer/ slaverywebsite/slaverymain.html.

In her journal, one young woman summarized the feelings of most of the students from Law, Government, and Community Service Magnet High

School about the New York and Slavery Walking Tour and the entire project. She wrote:

> I think the slavery walking tour was the best educational activity I have ever had. I felt like I was making a difference in the world. It opened my eyes to many more possibilities. My favorite part was the chanting; the younger kids even started chanting with us. I wish to take part in next year's tour because I feel like I'm doing something good with my life by educating others on something unknown that's not even in our textbooks. During our chanting, some guy said it's the year 2008, so why are we doing this? We replied that it's a part of our history and people should know it. This is true, because if we don't know our history, how can we shape our future?

REFERENCES

Barthes, R. (1977). *The grain of the voice: Interviews.* New York: Hill.

Delpit, L. (1988). The silenced dialogue: Power and pedagogy in educating other people's children. *Harvard Educational Review, 58*(3), 280–298.

Fine, M. (1989). Silencing and nurturing voice in an improbable context: Urban adolescents in public school. In H. Giroux & P. McLaren (Eds.). *Critical pedagogy, the state and cultural struggle* (pp. 152–173). Albany, NY: State University of New York.

Freire, P. (1970). *Pedagogy of the oppressed.* New York: Seabury.

Giroux, H. (1989). Schooling as a form of cultural politics: Toward a pedagogy of and for difference. In H. Giroux & P. McLaren (Eds.). *Critical pedagogy, the state and cultural struggle* (pp. 125–151). Albany, NY: State University of New York.

Ladson-Billings, G. (1995). Toward a theory of culturally relevant pedagogy. *American Educational Research Journal, 32*(3), 465–491.

McLaren, P. (1989). *Life in schools: An introduction to critical pedagogy in the foundations of education.* New York: Longman.

New York and Slavery: Complicity and Resistance. (n.d.). Retrieved February 15, 2009, from http://www.nyscss.org/resources/publications/new-york-and-slavery. aspx

Pezone, M., & Singer, A. (2006). Reclaiming hidden history. *Rethinking schools, 21*(2). Retrieved February 15, 2009, from http://www.rethinkingschools.org/archive/21_02/hidd212.shtml

Singer, A. (2008). *New York and slavery, time to teach the truth.* Albany, NY: State University of New York Press.

Chapter 24

Preventing the Gap in Preschool: A Suburban Community Model

Zoila Tazi

The nostalgic notions of American life—a private house for one's family, ample outdoor space, and sufficient community resources—conjure up images of living in the suburbs. This representation of American life is tied to traditionally middle class values about what children should experience growing up. While every parent in every community may have the same desires for their children, the suburbs retain the illusion of breaking away from the problems of urban poverty or crowding to a more homogenous, predictable place.

The suburbs along the Hudson Valley, in the immediate ring beyond New York City, feature quaint villages with historic homes and shops. Often set within the panoramic backdrop of the Hudson River, these villages are as beautiful as they are charming. Driving through distinct neighborhoods within the villages, however, begins to paint a different picture. Scenes of poverty emerge in dilapidated homes, broken concrete sidewalks, and bare storefronts. These scenes exist in out-of-the-way streets, at a distance from the imposing Victorians with river views. The stark contrast of neighborhoods within villages begins to tell a story of segregation and poverty in the suburbs.

Ossining Village is a suburban community about thirty miles from New York City, in the northern corner of Westchester County along the Hudson River. Its nearly 22,000 residents might enjoy the conveniences of suburban living such as parks, scenery and a pervading *small town sensibility*. The proximity to a commuter railroad, a major hospital, and a substantial nature reserve add to the appeal of the village and draws many families from the city. According to the 2005–2007 American Community Survey census data, the median income in the village is $65,420, substantially greater than the national figure of $50,233 for the same period (U.S. Census Bureau, n.d.). It would seem that Ossining Village is a desirable place to live.

The first time that residents from different neighborhoods might encounter one another is upon entering the public schools. The Ossining Union Free School District serves approximately 4,200 students pre-kindergarten to 12th grade. Demographic figures about the school population reveal that once residents from all parts of the community come together in the schools, Ossining is actually a place of great diversity.

The population of the schools mirrors national trends and changes indicating that communities across the country are becoming increasingly diverse, both socioeconomically and ethnically. As in many parts of the country, immigration patterns have influenced these trends at a growing rate. Many immigrants, as well as native-born people of color, struggle with crippling poverty. All the issues that accompany poverty, such as overworked parents, decreased literacy rates, underemployment, and stress related illness, make Ossining *a suburb with urban problems* but with far fewer funding resources than their urban counterparts.

Even as children enter schools as early as pre-kindergarten, it is possible to observe great disparities in their early childhood experiences that portend future achievement. For some, the effects of poverty and inexperience are evident in their school readiness skills, language development, and parental involvement. The first and most obvious challenge in the early grades is to *catch up* those children who have entered school less prepared or disadvantaged. The earliest intervention, before any academic failure, sets the strongest foundation for learning and contributes directly to eradicating the achievement gap threatening to widen.

Confronted with a problem occurring before children even begin school, educators in the Ossining School district accepted the challenge to impact learning well before pre-kindergarten, but the question remained—how? How would the school district find those children that needed support during early childhood?

BUILDING A MODEL

The idea to enter the lives of very young children and their families with the hope of preventing a possible future of academic struggle seemed both generous and optimistic. So much research supports the benefits of an early intervention. However, how would a school district describe its goal to perspective families? Would this program become a way to label infants and toddlers as *deficient* according to some academic paradigm?

The Schools as Safe Harbor

Research on the childrearing practices of groups of American families helped to orient the rationale for a program model. In her book, *Unequal Childhoods: Class, Race and Family Life,* Lareau (2003) unmasked some of the differences in raising children that ultimately interact with academic achievement. The children of more affluent families enter schools more prepared because of the classes, activities, and experiences that comprise the *concerted cultivation* of the young in these families that Lareau describes. By contrast, poorer families, with less resources to accomplish such cultivation tend to assume a more relaxed or naturalistic approach to developing their children's potential, but this represents a cultural mismatch with school. Clearly, schools favor the more experienced child. Rather than contend that these differences are predetermined, Lareau's insights suggest a possible role for schools to assume that mitigates the alienation of poor families in favor of the more affluent.

The model of this new program would position the schools as an open, more neutral resource of enrichment. It would overtly represent itself as accessible to all families with young children, not as an obligation for the poor or a *correction* to anyone's parenting. As such, the schools would not be looking to identify needy children, but would instead look to offer the kinds of services that would be unanimously beneficial to the age group.

Focused on Language

Assuming the schools could attract young families with a new program, what would be the fundamental element in their experience to influence with services? What characteristic is evident as children enter school that sounds immediate alarm for their future achievement? Hart and Risley (1995) conducted an ethnographic study of language use in families of diverse socioeconomic groups. In their book, *Meaningful Differences in the Everyday Experience of Young American Children,* they chronicled the results of years of observation and reported some alarming discoveries about the first four years of life:

> In 4 years of such experience, an average child in a professional family would have accumulated experience with almost 45 million words, an average child in a working-class family would have accumulated experience with 26 million words, and an average child in a welfare family would have accumulated experience with 13 million words. (Hart & Risley, 1995, p. 198)

Entry-level assessments of Pre-Kindergarten and Kindergarten children in the Ossining schools demonstrated proportionate catastrophic gaps in language use and vocabulary, which often translated into later gaps in reading and math scores. Hart and Risley's work suggested a course for the program model that would place the stimulation and enrichment of language use in the early years as the primary focus of all services.

The First Language

Hart and Risley (1995) only studied monolingual English-speaking families. The population in Ossining was becoming increasingly diverse with growing numbers of Spanish-speaking immigrant families. The volume of research on bilingualism—that is perhaps a challenge to English-dominant schools but also an invaluable asset to individuals—suggested a dual language structure to the program model. In order to prevent the subtractive practices that enforce the acquisition of English at the cost of the native language, the program would actively promote using the first language in the home for activities such as reading, singing and talking. Parents would be encouraged not to *worry* about their children acquiring English but to focus on providing them the richest possible experience in the native language.

Many immigrant parents, receiving mixed messages about English acquisition from educators or from the media, sacrificed the child's first language so as not to hinder learning English. Sometimes the tragic result was that the child could speak neither to his or her parents at home nor to the teachers at school. As Gándara and Contreras (2009) made explicit in their book, *The Latino Education Crisis: The Consequences of Failed Social Policies,* Spanish-speaking children need introductory school experiences in the native language in order support their cognitive development.

Transformative Pedagogy

The idea of bringing together a socioeconomically, ethnically, and linguistically diverse community within any program is laden with notions about belonging and power. A model that would interrupt rather than reproduce the cultural mismatch with the schools still upholding the validity of a family's values, would emanate from a deep commitment to inter-cultural understanding and a fundamental belief in egalitarian principles. The term "transformative pedagogy" appears in the literature to describe practices that link education to equity. Cummins (2001) explained, "Transformative pedagogy explicitly aims to prepare students to participate fully in the democratic process and to uphold principles of human rights and social justice that are enshrined in the constitutions of most western industrialized countries" (p. 218). Both the philosophy and the culture of the Ossining School District validated the ideas of transformative pedagogy.

The heart of the innovation to prevent an achievement gap for preschool children in the Ossining School District are the beliefs undergirding the program model. From these beliefs grew the concept for a program entitled "First Steps". Once the underlying beliefs were explored, it was possible to consider services.

DESIGNING SERVICES

Reaching very young children in the community, before their parents have even approached the schools, could only be conceived as collaboration with the community. From funding to services, "First Steps" sought the commitment of the Ossining community to create a program for all its young children.

Funding

Funding for "First Steps" resulted from collaboration between the Superintendent of Schools, the School Board President, and the Town Supervisor. Together these individuals lent their support and expertise to forging a partnership between the School District and a local family who had formed a charitable foundation. First Steps became a model of neighbors helping neighbors in a suburban village. Eventually, three local families would lend their support, donating nearly $300,000 to the School District for this fledgling program which was launched in the fall of 2002.

Collaboration

First Steps approached service providers in the community to enlist their support for this new idea. The nearby Phelps Memorial Hospital where Ossining babies were born, the local health clinic, the public library, and the town government all joined the effort to reach young families and deliver a message about early experiences and emergent literacy. Joining with other service providers represented combined benefits of reaching more people with stronger support.

Personnel

The early design for services included four staff members:

- A program coordinator who would structure the collaborations with other organizations, schedule events, monitor progress and supervise staff
- A family specialist who would conduct outreach, referral for services ,and offer ongoing support to parents

- A nurse who would interface with the local hospital and pediatricians, offer families home visits and well baby visits
- A literacy facilitator who would plan and implement Mommy/Daddy and Me events

These four individuals would launch the First Steps program, never anticipating the remarkable reception and immediate growth the program would experience.

Outreach

The only restriction placed on the First Steps program is limiting services to Ossining residents with children up to four years of age. Upon enrollment in First Steps, the family specialist meets with the family and offers anticipatory guidance in child development, family dynamics, discipline, and introduces the concept of literacy from birth. Since its inception in 2002, First Steps has experienced dramatic growth in its reach of community members; every year it has maintained a list of approximately five hundred participating families.

Program Components

Monthly mailings to the entire roster of registered children outline the program offerings for that month, which include activities within the following program components:

- Weekly parent-child classes in art, music, read-a-thons, movement and exercise, and bilingual nursery rhymes.
- Parent workshops. The topics addressed include typical child development, parenting, play-based learning and others.
- A playgroup for two-year-olds offering stimulation and socialization.
- Adult education classes in ESL and literacy.
- Home visits to families with newborns to launch their participation in our program. We provide *blankets and books* to help stimulate the infant.
- A community-wide reading campaign entitled A Book a Day.
- A nursery program called Little School. Parents attend along with their children to learn more about stimulating learning and cognitive development. Little School serves sixty three-year-olds.

In response to the growing Spanish-speaking population, First Steps offers all services in Spanish as well as English.

Program Impact

First Steps is committed to a longitudinal study of its effectiveness that has only just begun. Collecting and analyzing data that links program participation to subsequent achievement may demonstrate empirically what is evident socially. To date, First Steps can document the following gains:

- Over 1,200 children in our community have registered with the program since it began.
- There are over one hundred interactive events per academic year each averaging fifty families.
- Over six hundred children have participated in the "Book a Day" reading campaign.
- Over three hundred children have obtained library cards; circulation of children's books has increased by many thousands.

While First Steps is just beginning to demonstrate how to prevent an achievement gap between ethnic and socioeconomic groups, the benefits of increased parental involvement and improved school readiness is already evident. First Steps has become a powerful answer to the School District's challenge to prepare children before they reach the schools.

BENEFITS TO THE COMMUNITY

Providing services for an entire community yields the added benefit of bringing families together to improve conditions for all children. This creates a positive dynamic between diverse members of the community who may live under very different circumstances. In January 2009, 10 percent of the First Steps children were identified as Caucasian; by contrast, 80 percent of the children were Latino, and the remainder was other ethnicities. The population served through First Steps redefines the small, suburban community of Ossining Village as a new American phenomenon. Diverse in so many ways, the community sometimes struggles with its new identity.

Today, driving through Ossining Village, it is difficult to miss the old stone buildings, the narrow streets, the steep hills, or the dark blue river. Ossining is a beautiful place. Families of every ethnicity, some transplanted from distant parts of the world, walk along the streets with their children. Looking at their little faces it is possible to imagine all their potential. Undoubtedly, one or two will be wearing a tiny t-shirt that says, "I took my 'First Steps' in the Ossining Schools."

REFERENCES

Cummins, J. (2001). *Negotiating identities: Education for empowerment in a diverse society* (2nd ed.). Los Angeles: California Association for Bilingual Education.

Gándara, P., & Contreras, F. (2009). *The Latino education crisis.* Cambridge, MA: Harvard University Press.

Hart, B., & Risley, T. R. (1995). *Meaningful differences in the everyday experience of young American children.* Baltimore: Paul H. Brookes.

Lareau, A. (2003). *Unequal childhoods: Class, race, and family life.* Berkeley, CA: University of California Press.

US Census Bureau. (n.d.). *2005–2007 American Community Survey 3-year estimates: Ossining Village, New York.* Retrieved March 14, 2009, from http://factfinder .census.gov/servlet/ADPTable?_bm=y&-qr_name=ACS_2007_3YR_G00 _DP3YR3&-geo_id=16000US3655530&-ds_name=&-_lang=en&-redoLog=false

Part V

Building and Facility Design

Winston Churchill is attributed the saying "We shape our dwellings and afterwards our dwellings shape us." How about school buildings and facilities where learning takes place? Do schools shape us as educators? In 2002, Nair claimed that we spend more than $20 billion a year in the United States to build and renovate schools without closely examining whether these funds would be improving learning or not. In a similar *Education Week* commentary in 2009, Nair cautioned not to just rebuild schools, but to reinvent them. This section of our book offers a selection of such reinventions: successful design, building, and renovation projects that each focused not only on physical improvements to a building but also on student learning and community building.

Margaret S. Parsons describes what happens when a district invests in an old building and transforms it to match twenty-first-century learning needs. Washington Technology Magnet Middle School in St. Paul, Minnesota is such a place: a school that honors the history and fabric of the neighborhood. Irene Nigaglioni takes learning outside the classroom and explores a traditional school's corridor system and its possibilities to support the learning experience. When corridors are no longer considered to be merely utilitarian in nature, used only for circulation or for storage, they are expanded to incorporate learning spaces that, in concert with the classrooms, become teaching and learning spaces. Michael A. Malone explains how Westview Elementary School in Michigan redefined *school* for the community. Its flexible design and assortment of learning environments along with dedicated and passionate educators offer students enhanced opportunities to succeed. James Capolupo, Douglas Carney, and Robert Pillar take us to the Springfield Literacy Center in Pennsylvania. The Literacy Center not only illustrates how to create a space that supports differentiated literacy instruction, but becomes the intervention itself. On Nantucket Island, Massachusetts, Philip J. Poinelli shows us around the new *community* high school, which serves the local population from pre-schoolers to senior citizens. He discusses how the community focused on early programming, savings calculations, dedicated space allocations, schedule coordination, and commitment and, as a result, successfully co-located facilities.

REFERENCES

Nair, P. (2002). But are they learning? School buildings: The important unasked questions. *Education Week, 21*(29), 42–43, 60.

Nair, P. (2009). Don't just rebuild schools—Reinvent them. *Education Week, 28*(28), 24–25. Retrieved June 8, 2009 from http://www.fieldingnair.com/press/Education _Week_Dont_Just_Rebuild_Schools_Reinvent_Them.pdf

Chapter 25

How to Teach an
Old School New Tricks

Margaret S. Parsons

On a hill overlooking a field sits an old high school. The red brick structure has been a landmark in its inner city neighborhood for over eighty years. Many of the folks who live nearby went to school in this building. Or their parents did. Or their children do. This school has a history and is an important landmark so there was never any discussion about tearing it down to build a new school better suited to today's education. But, like many schools of this vintage, it was not suited to the current students or program. This is the story of the transformation of Washington Technology Magnet Middle School in Saint Paul, Minnesota, from an architect's perspective.

BUILDING VERSUS DESIGNING

The story starts long before our first meeting with the principal and staff in 2004. The story of the building is written in its structure and on its walls–literally. While the original school was built in 1924, over the course of the twentieth century there were multiple additions, each adding to the confusion of the building. The changes over the years showed no obvious consideration for unifying the disorder. Similar to remodeling a house, one always wants more than one can afford. At times of enrollment spikes, districts worry about space for students first and how the space looks and feels second. It is more about *building* schools than *designing* places for learning.

This was true at Washington. When a new gym was added in the 1970s, the original gym was split horizontally to create two floors in the height of the old gym space. Walking into the media center—where we held our planning meetings with staff and community members—the original trusses of the old gym loomed directly overhead, huge in a room that had no natural light and was off a half level from the building's main floors. Saint Paul Public Schools recognized that this was a school in need of more than a new roof or carpet; their vision was to transform it for today's students. As we deciphered the history of the structure with its multiple additions, antiquated systems, and seventeen levels, we also uncovered the teaching and learning constraints of the building. The list was long.

CONFUSION AND DISORDER

Arriving at the school that first day, our initial problem was finding the unlocked entry. While the main entry of the old building was clear from the architecture on the east side overlooking the field, the entry that was monitored during the day was at the 1970s gym addition on the west side. The awkward 1970s-era haunches over the solid metal doors as an entry were not welcoming or obvious to first-time visitors.

Once in the building, after signing in at the metal desk in the lobby, we navigated up a half flight of stairs, crossed to the east side of the building through a narrow ten-foot corridor that passed in front of the media center, and then down a half flight of stairs to the second level office overlooking the field to the east. Because the building was built on a hill, the east entry allowed access to the first floor (had it been unlocked), and the west-side accessed the second level; however, with the addition of the floor in the old gym, there was a half level between the main levels of the school's two sides. This first impression was only the beginning of the challenges of the physical building.

The entry, corridor, and office are not the first concerns for student learning. They are necessary and important to the security and function of the school, but the primary concern to the District was the students. While Washington Middle School is a technology magnet school, nowhere was there evidence of technology. The classrooms, typical of the vintage, were smaller than what might be built today. In addition to student desks, classrooms contained a teacher work area and often had items stored around the perimeter creating an even smaller workable area. They had chalk boards, wood floors, and built-in wood casework with paned-glass doors. What they did not have was space for hands-on, project-based work, computers, projectors or interactive whiteboards.

Except for the addition of a TV monitor, the classrooms, for all practical purposes, resembled a classroom in which current students' grandparents might have been taught. And not only did these modern amenities not exist in the classrooms, they were nowhere to be found in the building except for computers in two large, dimly lit, cave-like labs below the media center, hidden a half level down from the office area.

FACILITIES DO MATTER

There are some who would argue that teaching and learning are not really about the facility. Education is about the teachers and the students. Consider this: if a teacher struggles to find the room's one outlet under the desk and behind shelves, he or she is less likely to use teaching methods that require electric power. Ventilation, daylighting, temperature and humidity, acoustics, lighting, aesthetics, and class and school size all contribute to how people feel in a space. In *Savage Inequalities,* Jonathan Kozol notes that, "all the school reforms on earth are worthless if kids have to come to school in buildings that destroy their spirits" (as cited in Lackney, 1999, para 4.).

Numerous studies have tied environment to achievement. For example, a study of 139 Milwaukee Public Schools facilities concluded that the "measures of school facilities explain more of the differences in test performance across schools than indicators of the family backgrounds and attendance/behavior patterns of students" (Lewis, 2000, p. 3).

THE VISION

The committee we collaborated with for this project clearly recognized the connection between the physical environment and learning. At our first meeting with the committee—comprised of school and district staff, parents, community members, and a city parks and recreation department representative—we talked about their visions for Washington and for what the school would be like when the project was complete. What we heard surprised us. They wanted a *wow* space.

As we listened further, we understood. The *wow* space was important because they wanted a school where students were eager to come each day. As an inner city school, the student population included a large proportion of free and reduced lunch students. To create a stimulating learning environment where students felt honored was an important part of this project. Other components of the vision for Washington included making technology and learning visible and creating an open and welcoming environment. When we asked the students what they wanted, they talked about having access to the school in the evenings and on weekends. The students also wanted access to computers, to be able to play basketball, to sing, and to have a lounge for reading after school hours. They talked about wanting a school that did not look so "schooly."

Saint Paul Public Schools has a history of partnering with community and city groups to provide opportunities for their students and families. There has been a long-term partnership with the City of Saint Paul Parks and Recreation Department and, at Washington, the District has been leasing space in the building for offices and providing access to the gyms. In addition, the school has community partnerships that provide programs for students after school. A representative from the City's Park and Recreation Department was part of the committee, and, as solutions were discussed, after-hours use became an important design consideration.

THE DESIGN SOLUTION

The process of design, in many ways, is as important as the resulting design. Creating a shared vision at the beginning of the design process is critical: it is a way of creating a filter by which decisions about the project can be analyzed. At Washington Technology Magnet Middle School, the vision created by the committee included creating spaces that did not, nor could not, exist in the old building. For example, there was a desire for project labs that contained both computers and worktables to allow a variety of uses and hands-on learning opportunities. As we worked with the committee, decisions about the project were discussed in relation to the shared vision and, as a result, while not everyone agreed with all decisions, they understood why they were made.

The vision served the building well. The design solution was not the easiest. The center of the building—the area with the half levels—became the target. This area—the connection between the two halves of the building—held the key to making the building functional and beautiful. We had to demolish the center of the existing structure and rebuild it, carefully knitting the new construction into the old. The challenges we faced included keeping the school functional during the year and constructing the new building over the existing boiler room.

The result was a three-story, day-lit Technology Gallery that organized the circulation of the building and tied the east and west sides of the building together. This became the *wow* space. The heart of the building was lit from above, like a streetscape looking down through connecting hallways to an arcade alive with student interaction. The Technology Gallery allows students to interact in both casual and formal settings. Circulation paths pass through the heart of the school and numerous floor levels create clarity from complexity. All spaces are now accessible.

Photo 25.1.   Interior Photograph of Washington Technology Magnet Middle School, courtesy of Dana Wheelock.

CREATING NEW SPACES FOR SCHOOL AND COMMUNITY

The new construction allowed us to create spaces not possible in the existing building. Larger activity spaces have been added to enhance learning flexibility. Three new project labs look out onto the Technology Gallery and allow students to have space to engage in project-based, hands-on activities; it is here that technology is celebrated and students are engaged in creative learning. Washington Middle School is also a place for the community to mentor and connect with students as the Technology Gallery can be made secure from the rest of the building after hours.

Safe and Secure

In the design of the new construction, a secure entry on the east side of the building was created. The school's administrative office was moved to the entry across from a newly remodeled Parks and Recreation office. Visitors are required to enter the school through one of these offices which flank a secure vestibule. Safety and security are enhanced with openness and visibility. The openness of the space allows office personnel to see into the Technology Gallery and provide passive security. Teacher resource areas also look onto the Technology Gallery, allowing observation of common spaces while promoting collaborative work and professional space for staff. Having eyes on a space is more effective in creating a secure environment than any number of security cameras. Passive security creates an environment that promotes respectful behavior while also respecting the students in the school.

Respect is a word that resonates with this project. Saint Paul Public Schools deserves credit for creating this respect—for the students and staff, for the neighborhood and alumni, and for the old building. At the opening ceremony for the renovated school, alumni who graduated from Washington High School were amazed at the transformation. On the first day of school, students and staff navigated through the new heart of the school, the Technology Gallery, looking up in surprise at the color and light. The decision not to tear down the existing building not only served to reduce the project's impact on the environment, it preserved the school's place in the fabric of the neighborhood.

A STORY OF TRANSFORMATION AND INNOVATION

Textbox 25.1. Comments from the Principal and a Student about the Renovated Space and its Impact

Our goal in this project was to turn a 1924 high school into a twenty-first-century middle school. The Washington building has had a proud history in the North End neighborhood of Saint Paul for generations, but to be honest, the building was "tired." The building has had a number of additions since it was built resulting in many half stories and hallways and stairways that led to nowhere. The result has been nothing short of spectacular! Every student, parent, and visitor says, "Wow!" as soon as they enter the building.

—Mike McCollor, Principal

The new Washington building feels like a place to excel and discover new ideas and technology; it feels like the building was built yesterday. At the first sight of our new building I gasped and just wanted to explore how it changed. I feel like this is where I belong and the teachers and faculty want what's best for your education and future life. Washington is like a new home to me. Washington's architecture makes me feel safe and secure and at the same time able to seek the future.

—A student from Washington Technology Magnet Middle School

Washington Technology Magnet Middle School exemplifies what can happen when an investment is made in an older building. There is a chronic problem in funding school facility needs, estimated to be more than $250 billion (Crampton & Thompson, 2008). Nationally, urban districts spend less per student on their facilities than suburban or rural communities or towns (Vincent & Filardo, 2008). This may be due in part to enrollment gains, particularly in the suburbs, that require building new schools to accommodate the pressures of increased enrollment. As families move from urban districts to the outer tier suburbs for the newer schools, a cycle of less spending to modernize older urban schools is created. This lack of reinvestment in urban neighborhoods ultimately leads to a loss of vitality and school facilities in poor condition (Vincent & Filardo).

The choice Saint Paul Public Schools made to invest in this school and go beyond merely fixing physical deficiencies was an investment not only in the school but in the vitality of its urban neighborhood. Most importantly, this project took care of the physical needs of the school while further addressing the greater educational needs of students. It is a place where students and teachers are respected and want to be: learning is transparent and visible, technology is integrated and celebrated, and the school honors the history of the neighborhood. It is a story of transformation—a success story.

REFERENCES

Crampton, F. E., & Thompson, D. C. (2008, December). *Building minds, minding buildings: School infrastructure funding need.* Retrieved March 10, 2009, http://www.aft.org/topics/building conditions/downloads/BMMB_Funding.pdf

Lackney, J. A. (1999). *Reading a school building like a book: The influence of the physical school setting on learning and literacy.* Paper presented at the Program of Research and Evaluation for Public Schools conference, Jackson, Mississippi. Retrieved March 10, 2009, from http://schoolstudio.engr.wisc.edu/readingschool.html

Lewis, M. (2000, December). *Where children learn: Facility conditions and student test performance in Milwaukee Public Schools.* Retrieved March 10, 2009, from http://media.cefpi.org/issuetraks/issuetrak1200.pdf

Vincent, J. M., & Filardo, M. W. (2008, June). *Linking school construction investments to equity, smart growth and healthy communities.* Retrieved March 10, 2009, from http://citiesandschools.berkeley.edu/reports/Vincent_Filardo_2008_Linking_School_Construction_Jun2008.pdf

Chapter 26

Learning Environments Matter: Taking Learning Outside the Classroom

Irene Nigaglioni

What is a learning environment? Is it the rectangular space traditionally known as a classroom, or is it any space where learning can occur? When asked to describe positive learning experiences, children and adults share stories and anecdotes of places and settings that were welcoming, safe, and exciting. Whether the settings were inside or out, they were key components of the learning experience. These places and settings are true learning environments—diverse, stimulating, and no two are alike.

LEARNING ENVIRONMENTS

Successful learning environments offer a variety of settings and experiences that foster the instructional process. These environments are crucial to the learning experience, and when not designed properly can be detrimental to a student's success. Increasingly, research shows that there is a direct correlation between the built environment and academic performance.

Classroom spaces have not traditionally been described as welcoming, safe, and exciting. According to Fielding (2008), "mention the word 'classroom' and many students think of long days of captivity, waiting for the bell" (p. 4). Most spaces used as classrooms lack the correct physical and environmental components to improve student performance: natural light, adequate ventilation, good acoustics, and flexible furniture (among others). The space where students spend the majority of their school day could be greatly improved if these attributes were carefully examined and upgraded to respond to published research.

LEARNING STYLES

Each individual person, child, or adult learns and works in different ways. Therefore, each is affected differently by external and internal stimuli. These unique attributes are called learning styles. Based on Dunn and Dunn, Rundle (2006) noted that "learning style pertains to the different ways humans learn new and difficult information and includes environmental elements (classroom stimuli) preferences for sound, light, temperature and seating, a few of the many elements that affect student achievement"(p. 18). In order to maximize learning potential, it is imperative that classroom design and organization also respond to individual learning styles. However, equally important to the classroom is the rest of the building. Spaces where students eat, read, talk, exercise, and walk can all affect their educational performance.

Learning styles not only respond to environmental qualities, but to other equally critical elements as well. Dunn and Dunn characterize these additional elements as physiological, psychological, sociological, perceptual, and emotional (as cited in Rundle, 2006). Research has shown that the students' ability to learn is improved when teaching methodologies cater to individual learning styles (Dunn & Griggs, 2007). Furthermore, learning styles change as students grow older, so instruction must respond accordingly in order to maximize student performance.

According to Dunn and Dunn, there are additional, nonenvironmental elements that affect learning styles (as cited in Rundle, 2006), such as:

- Physiological: the way we learn and retain new information
- Psychological: our preferences for processing new information, making decisions and solving problems
- Physiological: biological preferences that affect the way we concentrate and focus
- Emotional: how we tackle and how quickly we complete complex assignments
- Sociological: our preferred ways of learning and working with others

Given the diversity of stimuli that constitute each of these elements and understanding the impact they can have on learning, it is important that every space in the school be designed with students' learning needs in mind. The design of a cafeteria influenced by learning styles invites and entices students to pursue the necessary nourishment they need to be healthy. Nurturing our bodies with healthy food and water helps nurture brain activity, increasing our ability to perform successfully. Hannaford (2005) described water as "the magic elixir for learning, the 'secret potion' if you will" (p. 150).

CORRIDORS AND HALLWAYS

Some of the often neglected spaces in school design are circulation spaces. Any given school day, students navigate the campus through a network of corridors and hallways. These spaces—usually host to the most common security and discipline problems—are often a planning afterthought. Considered entirely utilitarian, these spaces are typically poorly planned and feel institutional. Yet, they can represent up to 40 percent of a building's total gross area.

Some experts believe that corridors in schools should be eliminated because they are *leftovers* from schools designed long ago. Most schools are built with a clear separation between the hallway and the classroom, which results in distinct uses between each: the hallway's main role is travel, whereas the classroom's main role is for learning.

According to Gott's (2007) interview with learning consultant Stephen Heppell, corridors should be completely removed from schools. Heppell stated that a problem with so many schools is that "we come to the end of a lesson—we ring a bell, we stop them doing what they are doing and then we take them into another box" (para. 12).

In many university and college settings, interaction outside the classroom is considered equally (or more) important than interaction inside the classroom. Although traditional in its implementation of schedule and time (students still report to class at a predetermined time and leave after a predetermined period of time), experiences outside of the classroom are enhanced by spaces that foster social interaction and exchange of ideas. O'Donnell (2007) described a recent renovation to Pennsylvania's Swarthmore College as follows, "the halls feature spaces that let students to step out of the path of travel, pause, and converse with a classmate or teacher" (para. 6).

So why has this concept been ignored in the K-12 setting? The notion of unsupervised students in a social setting has often been rejected by many who believe the only proper place for learning is in the classroom. The opportunity to enhance learning by enhancing common/circulation spaces has been overlooked in the past, as the focus has been on other strategies to improve student success.

Given today's limited school funding, it makes sense to focus on circulation/common spaces and enhance them to offer a broader spectrum of school learning environments. The challenge is to find a way to blur the line between the traditional classroom space and the utilitarian spaces used for circulation. Understanding that no two students are the same and using learning styles as a platform, we can take learning outside of the classroom and into the corridors. Transforming circulation spaces into learning environments ensures a presence of constant learning and affords the opportunity to create more diverse and varied learning settings in a school building.

A SUCCESS STORY: A SUBURBAN HIGH SCHOOL

Using learning-style theory as the basis of design, we applied it to a new suburban high school organized around the concept of small learning communities. Each such community accommodated three hundred students and offered self-supported administration spaces, as well as collaborative spaces including teachers' workrooms and conference rooms. By locating classrooms along the exterior walls of the building, natural light permeates each classroom environment.

Hallway spaces have been expanded into triangular shapes, a notable departure from the traditional corridor with rooms on both sides, commonly known as a double-loaded corridor. This alternative layout allows for the creation of unique activity spaces that enable both formal teaching and active learning to take place. In lieu of dimly lit, utilitarian hallways, now centers of activity serve as the heart of each community. This change enhances learning by improving student-to-teacher, as well as student-to-student relationships. The varied learning-style elements—sociological, physical, physiological, perceptual, emotional and environmental—are incorporated by the effective use of furniture, color, lighting, acoustics, temperature, and human scale.

Located within the new hallways are spaces such as a large group instruction room, a learning node, a coffee bar and computer lounge, and small informal learning areas. These areas each become learning environments that support the overall community, each with unique characteristics:

Large Group Instruction

A multi-tiered space with fixed seats that is introduced to corridors via folding partitions works best for large groups. It can be left open during and in between classes. The depth of the steps in this space allows students to sit. It also provides an informal dining setting where students can engage in conversation. The technology includes large plasma screens and a sound system that helps make the space an exciting classroom where more than one class can be assembled for learning. The use of indirect lighting and the introduction of natural light through windows provide a flexible environment. This learning space can be dimmed, bright or natural, affording teachers and students a space that is engaging, and that can change as needed to best respond to the learning activities.

Coffee Bar/Computer Lounge

Abandoning the concept that computers must be locked up and access limited, this space creates a relaxed environment that enables students to work on their own or in teams. The student-operated coffee bar and adjacent computer lounge allows students access to nourishment, and provides an environment that fosters individual study or team discussions.

Learning Node and Informal Learning Areas

Located in the heart of the newly expanded corridor, the node is a private space that can be used by one or more students. Circular in shape, it provides soft, comfortable furniture, indirect lighting, and technology upgrades including multimedia screens and portable media players. This area accommodates small lectures, small team meetings, or offers a private space for individual reflection.

The node is flanked by unique spaces that encourage serendipitous learning. These areas allow for individual study separated by a bookcase. Group viewing of a multi-media wall can display current events for an entire class to experience. Soft materials and undulating shapes improve the acoustics and invite movement, which is highly encouraged by Hannaford (2005). She explained that "movement and play profoundly improve—not only learning—but creativity, stress management and health" (p. 18). Applied in concert with different lighting schemes and naturally lit clerestory windows, a combination of bright and neutral colors make the space stimulating yet comfortable for students.

SAFETY AND SECURITY

In order to ensure the functionality and usefulness of auxiliary spaces, we also considered their impact on safety and security. Corridors have traditionally been associated with discipline issues and most teachers consider them difficult to monitor because of the location of lockers. Fielding (2008) commented that

> We all need to feel connected to the people immediately around us, and we want to be able to visually survey who is coming and going. Long rows of metal lockers along corridors fail to meet our most basic needs for territory and space. It's uncomfortable to have one's back facing a corridor while digging into a locker. (p. 5)

The expansion of the corridor into a large, open space with different activities and settings provides an enhanced feeling of safety and security. O'Donnell (2007) explained this change in perspective as we "consider circulation systems not as corridors but as public places. Once we have elevated their status beyond circulation, our task becomes one of designing great places that foster positive interaction, not just movement" (para. 7). Lockers become activities within this public space, not obstacles in the flow of student traffic.

The expanded corridors also enhance supervision. Glass walls and operable walls serve as dividers between the more traditional classroom spaces and the enhanced corridor. This shift in design allows for observation between the two spaces and a real connection between activities inside and outside of the class-room. O'Donnell (2007) referred to this observation and connection as *subtle security*. He defined it as "great public places in which adults in surrounding program spaces can unobtrusively observe activity in non-program spaces. This casual observation invites participation and enables proactive rather than reactive intervention when necessary" (para. 21). The transparency between spaces also enhances the opportunity for unanticipated learning, team projects, and professional collaboration between teachers and students alike.

A CHALLENGE WORTH TAKING

To improve the learning environment, we must first consider the students. Armed with an understanding of differing learning styles, coupled with the ultimate objective of improving students' opportunity to succeed, this challenge is easy to tackle. Regardless of the intended functional objective (classroom, gymnasium, or corridor), our schools must comprise spaces that create positive learning environments. A student's school day should include experiences that are nurturing, exciting as well as impacting; and school buildings should provide this.

Engaging in the design of a school project should start with the students. Ask students of all age levels to describe their perfect learning environment. The answers, as diverse as they may be, will provide the right artist's touch to the blank canvas that is school design. Years from now, the anecdotes and stories that students share may be of the times they spent studying, talking, reading, singing, running, eating, and learning in the corridors of their school.

REFERENCES

Dunn, R., & Griggs, S. A. (Eds.). (2007). *Synthesis of the Dunn and Dunn Learn-ing Styles Model research: Who what, when, where, and so what?* Jamaica, NY: St. John's University.

Fielding, R. (2008). Designing personalized spaces that impact student achievement. *Council of Educational Facility Planners International Educational Facility Plan-ner, 43,* 33–37.

Goff, H. (2007). The shape of schools to come? *BBC News.* Retrieved March 13, 2009, from www.bbc.co.uk/1/hi/education/6276055.stm

Hannaford, C. (2005). *Smart moves: Why learning is not all in your head* (2nd ed.). Salt Lake City, UT: Great River Books.

O'Donnell, S. (2007). *Place-making: How the out of classroom experience can foster social and emotional learning.* Retrieved March 13, 2009, from www .learningbydesign.biz/2007/feature2.html

Rundle, S. (2006). Planning for learning space in existing structures. *Council of Educational Facility Planners International Educational Facility Planner, 41,* 18–21.

Chapter 27

Liberating Learning and Its Environment

Michael A. Malone

Student reactions to well-designed and thoughtfully planned school buildings are overwhelmingly positive. Studies have shown that students are more apt to excel in a learning environment that they are comfortable in and that accommodates their individual learning styles (Dunn & Griggs, 2007). Educational facilities directly and measurably influence critical student success factors including attendance, behavior, health, on-task time, information recall, and academic outcomes. Student comfort is attributable to factors including color, lighting (natural and artificial), room temperature, acoustics, spatial adaptability, accessibility, flexible furniture, ability to move, familiarity of surroundings, and sense of safety and security (Earthman & Lemasters, 1998; Schneider, 2002).

Since research findings unequivocally reveal that learning environments significantly contribute to the overall educational success of students, these considerations served as a planning preface for the design process that resulted in the new Westview Elementary School built for the Fitzgerald Public School District located in Warren, Michigan. A mission statement created for this new facility served as a litmus test for the myriad of design decisions to be made throughout the process. The design team—including administration representatives and members of the Fitzgerald School Board—committed to creating an educational facility built around its purpose: to be a learner-centered environment focused on opportunities to increase student achievement and student engagement.

FACILITY OVERVIEW

The new 98,500 square-foot learning environment was designed with diverse learning and teaching styles in mind. Differentiating instruction requires teachers to be creative and flexible in their approach to teaching and to adjust the curriculum and presentation of information to learners, rather than expecting students to adapt themselves to the curriculum (Hall, Strangman, & Meyer, 2003). Westview responds to this principle by offering educators limitless physical and environmental choices that result in a flexible environment.

Each day, Westview's pre-kindergarten through fifth grade students look forward to attending their school—an inspirational place that supports exploration, discovery, and team-based learning. The building, which has an 800-student capacity, is broken down into small, grade-level learning communities that support student comfort, as well as disguise its large size to its users.

The design team kept in mind what several studies have revealed: learning-style-responsive environments—facilities designed to match individual preferences for light, sound, temperature, seating, grouping, movement, audio, verbal, visual, and tactual learning—increase student academic achievement (Schneider, 2002; Earthman & Lemasters, 1998). Thus, the assortment of spaces for student engagement has become a hallmark of the facility. Small and large, formal and informal, indoor and outdoor environments provide unique opportunities for educators to implement differentiated instruction.

PRE-PLANNING OBJECTIVES

Aspirations for the new Westview Elementary School were set extremely high at the onset of the project. The district staff and the community intended to make the most of this opportunity and sensed the need to redefine *school* within their community. Thus, the Fitzgerald Public School District and its planning team established a list of objectives that best defined their ideal school. These objectives supported their purpose of increasing student achievement and their vision of redefinition. The key objectives were to provide a learning environment that:

- Satisfies today's needs while remaining adaptable to future educational demands
- Is a place where students want to be
- Promotes socialization, exploration, and interaction
- Allows opportunities for community involvement
- Incorporates sustainable design principles and technologies
- Is easily navigated by young students and contains simple way finding measures
- Incorporates small-scale learning communities

- Is unique, stimulating, and inspirational
- Fosters creativity
- Complements and enhances the surrounding residential properties

During the planning phase, these objectives were incorporated into the design of the building in an effort to engender them in the everyday thought processes of the children and adults—who would eventually use it. Each design decision was tested against the established objectives. If a proposed design direction did not support the objectives, it was re-evaluated and altered. This process helped the designers adhere to the district's overall vision.

BUILDING ORGANIZATION

We found that organization is what really matters! The new Westview Elementary School is organized around a central entrance lobby and main corridor spine. The facility includes both single and two-story components. In view from the entrance lobby are access points to the main administrative office, the outdoor classroom, the media center, gymnasium, cafeteria, and early childhood center. The circulation spaces are wide as well as bright and provide opportunities for interaction, displaying student work, and other informal learning. Circulation spaces are used to create gentle transitions from different locations within the school, taking advantage of turns and bends to create unique areas for learning (Tanner & Lackney, 2006).

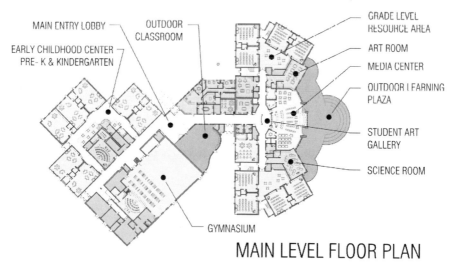

MAIN ENTRY LOBBY

OUTDOOR CLASSROOM

EARLY CHILDHOOD CENTER PRE- K & KINDERGARTEN

GRADE LEVEL RESOURCE AREA

ART ROOM

MEDIA CENTER

OUTDOOR LEARNING PLAZA

STUDENT ART GALLERY

SCIENCE ROOM

GYMNASIUM

MAIN LEVEL FLOOR PLAN

Figure 27.1. Main Level Floor Plan of Westview Elementary School, Warren, Michigan. Courtesy of PARTNERS in Architecture, PLC.

Each grade level is organized into individualized learning communities—the first and second grade students are located on the first floor, and the third through fifth grade students are located on the second floor. Each of the learning communities has its own identity with its classrooms grouped around a separate, centralized resource area. The two-story academic wing also houses the media center, art gallery, computer lab, and the art and science rooms.

AN ENHANCED LEARNING ENVIRONMENT

Aside from being an inviting, enjoyable, and inspirational environment for developing young minds to grow, the new Westview Elementary School is a functional, learner-centered community. It holds the students' needs as a top priority, showcased by the assemblage of learning areas both inside and outside of the school.

Prior to entering the school, students are drawn to and inspired by the color, texture, shapes, and scale of the building's playful exterior design. Its lively collection of sloping metal panels, textured and glazed brick veneer, vertical and horizontal metal siding, and metal roofing all equally contribute to a dynamic appearance. This stimulating imagery engages the children and conveys a message of excitement and livelihood, preparing their young minds for a day of open discovery. The exterior aesthetic remains complementary to the surrounding residential properties while taking on its own identity. The result is a distinguishably welcoming facility.

This energy and excitement is continued inside the facility as well. Each of the small grade-level learning communities reflects the over-all design principles of the building and allows for the development of the character of each particular group. By promoting individuality in these areas, students develop a sense of place and inherently are more comfortable among their peers. Personalization of space is an important factor in the formation of an individual's identity and sense of self-worth (Bredekamp & Copple, 1997). These informal, grade-level resource spaces provide opportunities for both small and large groups, as well as individualized instruction, and are planned to accommodate future distance-learning activities. The proximity of the resource areas to the classrooms also encourages teacher collaboration and teaming. These areas have become the most popular spaces within the building due to their flexibility, accessibility, and layout.

For ease of identification and to aid in defining their place, each learning community is designated with its own color. The same color is used as an accent throughout the grade-level resource areas as well as in the associated classroom spaces. The use of color further defines the spaces and becomes part of the wayfinding system. Such familiarity increases young students' comfort and easily allows them to confirm if they are in the correct location or not.

The early childhood area consists of eight classrooms that serve pre-kinder-garten and kindergarten students. The rooms are approximately 1,200 square feet in area and contain both carpet and linoleum flooring to accommodate wet and dry activities. The size of the rooms provides sufficient space for age appropriate, developmental learning to occur. The flexible furniture supports teachers' personalization of the learning environment as well as the creation of differentiated settings for instruction. In addition to the large classrooms, the early childhood section is organized around a central resource area similar to the communities of grades 1 to 5. As well as providing space for circulation and further accommodations for diverse groups, this space houses an early childhood library, several activity tables and provides space for indoor play during inclement weather.

LEARNING OUTDOORS

One of the most exciting educational spaces within the facility is immediately discovered when first time students, staff, and visitors enter the warm, open, and bright lobby. The outdoor classroom greets students, staff, and visitors and interjects energy and excitement into their day. Its purposeful placement also enhances visual interaction between the spaces. Most innovatively, the readily visible outdoor classroom provides an educational environment for hands-on life science lessons like no other.

This dynamic learning arena offers a pond, built-in seating, lecture area, several teaching platforms, butterfly and hummingbird gardens as well as an abundance of vegetation. The twelve-foot-high glazed brick serpentine wall adds an interesting backdrop and is a welcomed and inspiring surprise to visitors, onlookers, and users of the space. The outdoor classroom provides a cohesive learning environment focused on the school's learner-centered philosophy and addresses various learning-styles. This enriched and diverse environment provides the necessary inspiration and excitement children desire. Evidence suggests that experiential, inquiry-based outdoor learning reinforces the text-based curriculum and deepens students' understanding of core academic concepts. It fosters excitement about learning and helps accommodate students with different learning styles or diverse linguistic and academic needs (Corson, 2003).

Photo 27.1.   Outdoor Classroom at Westview, courtesy of Michael A. Malone.

MORE UNIQUE SPACES INDOORS AND OUT

As one approaches the media center and the two-story academic area, a most unique space opens up—the student art gallery. This oval-shaped node provides an opportunity for informal learning. It has been thoughtfully placed at the intersection of two corridors. The lively space has a direct view into the media center and contains wall surfaces and display cases for showcasing student artwork. A built-in seating area is large enough for a single class to use for a brief presentation or discussion, as well as the facilitation of student interaction. Student-created art, as well as handwritten poetry, have been permanently incorporated into a laminated glass installation in the center of the gallery. All first- through fifth-grade students are inspired by this space each day.

With its separate instructional, seating, and computer areas, the media center allows for the flexible use of its space and can easily accommodate two classes at one time. Upon entering this warm and inviting environment, students and teachers alike are exhilarated by the thirty-five colored-glass windows that highlight the tiered seating of the story-telling area. Low-height book shelving units allow ease of student access as well as the clear supervision of students. Windows are provided into the adjacent art and science rooms that allow students to visually engage with the adjoining activities. Natural lighting pours through the abundance of exterior windows, allowing the students to see the second outdoor learning space—the outdoor learning plaza.

The outdoor learning plaza is accessed directly from the media center, as well as from the adjacent art and science rooms. The learning plaza contains both hardscape and landscape areas, as well as tiered, amphitheatre-style seating. This accommodating environment provides endless opportunities for outdoor art and science projects, student activities, student performances, and lesson delivery. More than a place to burn off energy, the natural environment's potential for hands-on and project-based learning is being tapped (Tanner & Lackney, 2006).

The gymnasium and cafeteria are accessed from the main corridor and entrance lobby, which doubles as an excellent pre-function space for large gatherings or simultaneous student events. Their placement near the main entry is logical, which allows ease of access for the community. These spaces are divided by a large, electrically operated folding partition which, when opened, creates a large group assembly space. Combine this large space with the raised platform stage adjacent to the cafeteria—which is also separated with a folding partition—and you have a perfect example of shared, multi-use space. The raised platform stage can also be used as a classroom space as it includes all of the functional elements of a typical classroom.

CONCLUSION

Westview Elementary School's flexibility and assortment of differing learning environments contribute to enhanced opportunities for students to succeed. It has become evident that consideration of individual differences and diverse learning styles can truly alter the outcome of school design. All those who share Westview daily believe that the comfortable, inspirational, and flexible learning environments have led to increased student engagement and will lead to increased achievement. Westview has indeed redefined *school* for the Fitzgerald Public School District and hopes to serve as an example for years to come.

REFERENCES

Bredekamp, S., & Copple, C. (1997). *Developmentally appropriate practice in early childhood programs.* New York: National Association for the Education of Young Children (NAEYC).

Corson, C. (2003). Grounds for learning: Hope for America's derelict schoolyards. Retrieved March 18, 2009, from http://www.cherylcorson.com/Pubs/groundsforlearning.pdf

Dunn, R., & Griggs, S. A. (Eds.). (2007). *Synthesis of the Dunn and Dunn Learning Styles Model research: Who, what, when, where, and so what?* Jamaica, NY: St. John's University.

Earthman, G. I., & Lemasters, L. (1998, February). Where children learn: A discussion of how a facility affects learning. Paper presented at the annual meeting of the Virginia Educational Facility Planners, Blacksburg, VA.

Hall, T., Strangman, N., & Meyer, A. (2003). *Differentiated instruction and implications for UDL implementation.* Wakefield, MA: National Center on Accessing the General Curriculum. Retrieved March 10, 2009, from http://www.cast.org/publications/ncac/ncac_diffinstructudl.html

Schneider, M. (2002). *Do school facilities affect academic outcomes?* Retrieved March 10, 2009, from http://www.edfacilities.org/pubs/outcomes.pdf

Tanner, C., & Lackney, J. (2006). *Educational facilities planning, leadership, architecture, and management.* Boston: Pearson.

Chapter 28

Re-Writing the Rules for a New Design Literacy

James Capolupo, Douglas Carney, and Robert Pillar

What prompts change? Many suggest that elections lead to change; others believe change occurs only in a crisis. Our story begins in 2000 when dramatic change occurred in Springfield, near Philadelphia, Pennsylvania. Responsible public officials teamed with diligent and gifted administrators to face an all-too-common issue in our educational system: student failure. In this chapter, we show how the Springfield School District made a bold shift in traditional thinking that would *turn a new page* in how literacy and a purposeful facility design can work in concert.

STRUGGLING WITH THE SYSTEM

Sean was—and remains—a bright boy with excellent intellectual and interpersonal skills, but he simply could not learn to read. Despite working with an Instructional Support Team (IST), having an Individual Education Plan (IEP), participating in an Extended School Year (ESY), and receiving private summer reading interventions, Sean entered 5th-grade reading at the pre-primer level. Sean's father, School Board President Douglas Carney was concerned! With parental urgency, Carney searched for the *silver bullet* that most parents of struggling readers seek.

It became clear that one-on-one reading instruction for a significant part of the school day was the only solution that might help his son to catch up. After a struggle with the District on many levels, Sean started to receive services: he made his goals with the help of a reading specialist and exited the IEP process in 9th grade to complete his high school experience and go on to college.

Why is Sean's story relevant? Because it offered the context for change. After his fight for services, Carney felt that the educational system was broken: no child should ever get to 5th-grade reading at a pre-primer level. Not only was change needed, it was a moral imperative to restructure literacy instruction in the district. No one knew how many other Seans there were.

RECOGNIZING THE CHALLENGES

The leaders in Springfield realized two critical dimensions needed to change: the instructional methods and the acceptance of anything less than 100 percent success, the latter being significantly more challenging. Recall that this was before the No Child Left Behind Act became law, so the concept of *zero defects* was foreign to most educators.

An essential question asked of all stakeholders was, "Do you really believe that every child can read?" The answer that most said was, "No, not every child." Certainly, everyone wanted to say yes, but there were no examples of other schools or districts that had successfully taught *every* child to read. The zero defect mindset challenged the educational culture to its core. Springfield's slogan soon evolved into, "We believe every child can read," which was and still is at the heart of Springfield's philosophy. This bold thinking would change the instructional model forever.

Springfield set out to find the context that would support their new-found belief to make significant changes in their reading and literacy program. The Board insisted on a measurable, research-based starting point that would give direction to the program. A salient study was the Tennessee STAR Project, a large-scale, longitudinal study of the effects of class size on student-learning outcomes and one of the most authoritative publications on the subject (Word et al., 1990). One of the key findings of the STAR Project was that a student's development and achievement are greatly improved if the student is in a small-class environment (13–17 students), particularly in Kindergarten and 1st grade. Incremental benefit is derived from maintaining small class size throughout the K-12 academic experience, but the majority of benefit is achieved in just the first year.

This was a significant finding and a public policy jewel hidden among thousands of pages of data. Springfield educators realized they could provide this at a modest cost, but they also noted this one research study did not go far enough. Little compelling research existed on the subject, so the district would need to create its own evidence. Then Director of Teaching and Learning, Dr. James Capolupo, was charged with turning dreams into reality.

The public policy stage was set. Due to an ebbing K-1 population, a window of opportunity existed to establish smaller class sizes with no more than

15 students in 1st grade for 2001–02. (Previous class size guidelines set the limit at 25 students.) The Board announced that resources would be committed in an effort to get 100 percent of Springfield children reading at grade level by the end of 4th grade. If a student does not read independently by then, academic difficulties increase exponentially when moving forward. It was a pilot program; if measurable results were not seen, it would not continue.

HOW CHANGE BEGAN

To get started, the first step was fostering a change in culture. All stakeholders agreed to focus on this singular goal with a laser-like beam. The administration, faculty, parents, and students embraced the program and breathed life into it every day.

The next step was to look at the leadership component. Who would administrate and hold the organization accountable? The principals had to ensure that their attention was focused on literacy in terms of observations, supervision, and even daily walk-throughs of the building. A literacy coordinator linked the two, somewhat independent elementary schools together unlike ever before. Curriculum coordinators became liaisons between the Director of Teaching and Learning and the staff. Two elementary-level literacy coordinators already serving as advisors to teachers—started to work directly with students, and so did all other support staff.

TALLYING THE RESULTS

A critical issue that concerned the Board and administrators was how they were going to define success. Borrowing from business process models, the Board established measurable goals as a criterion. The elementary guided reading levels (Fountas &Pinnell, 1999) were proposed as an appropriate benchmark for measuring student progress and achievement since they are widely recognized and clearly reflect the growth a student makes within one year. Naturally, the general expectation was that other test results would also indicate improvement.

Our goal was to achieve 100 percent grade-level reading skills, regardless of students' regular, gifted, IST, or IEP status. Soon the notion of status became significantly less relevant as every child received a customized education plan that was discretely tracked for longitudinal progress. Springfield calls this process *mass customization,* a term originally coined by Davis (1987) in his book *Future Perfect.*

Interventions and assessments were placed into a matrix with a basic and below-basic list or *recipe card.* Teachers followed it in a sequential format to standardize their interventions. Additionally, the curriculum was aligned to formative assessments, benchmarks, and monthly goals and targets. Quarterly reports on progress were presented to district teachers, the Board, and the community. By the end of the fifth year, only two students were below basic level and seven students were at basic level out of a cohort of 175 students in the pilot study. The program was so extraordinary in its success that the superintendent guaranteed parents that if they brought their child in Kindergarten, he or she would be reading at grade level by the end of 4th grade.

After five years—when 99.2 percent of the students reached the goal of reading at grade level—it became a challenge to see if the results were replicable or not. The following year brought similar results: Springfield schools continued to improve students' literacy strategies and institutionalized the program and processes. These interventions are among the most exciting reforms happening in differentiated instruction today.

SUSTAINING THE SUCCESS THROUGH A NEW FACILITY

The Design Process

After eight program years with consistent results in the high 90th percentile, it was easy to engage in a public discourse on how to ensure that future generations would benefit from the same successes. Due to the underlying need for more classroom space and belief in the program's continuous improvement, the District examined the physical building itself and how it could support both the program and the vision. Soon after, the idea of designing a purpose-built *reading machine* was born.

As an architect himself, Carney knew it would be exceptionally challenging to grasp the nuance and complexity of this assignment. Dr. Capolupo, now superintendent, also knew this would be a tall order. Springfield was looking for an architect to design a building that would give form to the very curriculum, the intervention strategies, and pedagogy that were the essence of their literacy program.

Burt Hill was the firm hired as the project architect based on its team's creative, out-of-the-box thinking. A concept for a K-1 Literacy Center was developed, drawing upon the expertise of a facilities committee consisting of parents, administrators, outside consultants, and school board members. The building's function would be entirely focused on literacy—from its classroom design to its playground and to all of its systems. The building itself would become an intervention.

In most cases, architects are agents of change, especially in the K-12 educational design context, and Burt Hill had a wealth of knowledge to offer related to innovative curricula. Burt Hill architects often challenged their school-affiliated clients to think of a building construction project as an opportunity to examine the teaching and learning process. This was not the case with the Springfield School District. When work began, it was *Burt Hill who was challenged* to design a new facility for a curriculum that provided mass customization of literacy education through the application of interventions aimed at teaching each child according to his or her own learning style.

Furthermore, the challenge required that every dollar of investment and every square inch of the site and the building would aid in the literacy process. In other words, the building and site had to become a teaching tool, which required a change in traditional thought. For example, corridors and lobbies were typically used as a means of circulation through a building. However, in order to meet the district's challenge, these spaces were transformed into text-rich, engaging educational spaces.

The Springfield Literacy Center

As students and visitors approach the Springfield Literacy Center, they are immediately immersed in the teaching and learning of literacy. The building entrance begins on a covered front porch where faculty, students, and visitors are encouraged to write on the exterior chalkboards or on the sidewalk. Here, they begin to understand word and sentence formation as they read the greetings written each day by the principal and faculty. They also experience the tactile differences of writing on slate chalkboard and the rough sidewalk.

The building entrance opens directly into the library and media center—intended to be the heart and focal point of the facility. Students are invited to select reading material on their way to class. Crucial to the success of this design was the abandonment of the traditional Double-loaded corridor model. To create a more accommodating space, the circulation function was minimized so that the instruction function could be maximized.

Classrooms are arranged along a single-loaded educational space that also provides a circulation path. Expanded areas along this path create an extension of each classroom, and folding glass partitions allow for additional configuration. Each pair of two classrooms shares a common small-group instruction zone. This zone can be divided into four individual small-group

Figure 28.1.   Outdoor Hallway Rendition, courtesy of Burt Hill.

spaces for one-on-one instruction and is separated from the classroom by a sliding barn door with a writing surface.

Additionally, there are several floor-to-ceiling writing surfaces and interactive white boards located in the classroom, a small group space, and a classroom extension that provides opportunities for movement and the opportunity to meet the needs of kinesthetic learners. The design supports the literacy intervention curriculum by incorporating flexible spaces for individual learning styles, different groupings of learners, and variety in instruction.

To meet the challenge of utilizing the site to support literacy education, Burt Hill made sure to take advantage of the facility's location on a wooded site with a natural ravine. In today's digital society, it is common to see children playing basketball on a four-inch screen rather than on the court. Although it is exciting that a child in Pennsylvania can play with a child from Singapore, over-dependence on technology is causing a crisis in interpersonal skills, which are necessary for collaboration and exchange of ideas. The over-stimulation of graphically rich television and computer games has drawn our children away from the outdoors. This has become so prevalent that author Richard Louv has determined it is causing what he has termed *nature-deficit disorder*. In his book, *Last Child in the Woods,* Louv (2005) writes: "As the young spend less and less

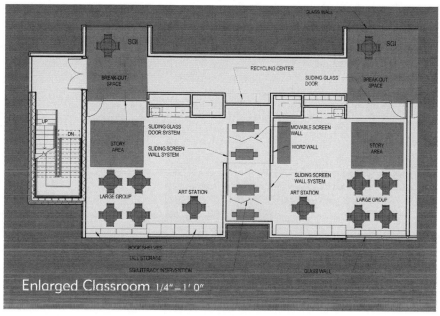

Figure 28.2. Classroom Floor Plan, courtesy of Burt Hill.

of their lives in natural surroundings, their senses narrow, physiologically and psychologically, and this reduces the richness of human experience" (p. 3).

To counter this phenomenon, the site was designed to maximize social interaction and support differentiated instructional opportunities by providing an outdoor amphitheater and a treehouse classroom. There are separate playground areas for Kindergarten and 1st-grade students. Ribbons of text from children's literature are woven into playground surfaces. Climbing walls with hand holds that spell words like *courage* and *adventure,* as well as an alphabet walk, help students learn as they discover and explore literacy *and* their natural environment.

CONCLUSION

All building and site features complemented the fresh, bold, and necessary thinking and practices applied by this innovative school district. With visionaries who are passionate about a common goal, it seems the story of change can unfold like a thrilling page-turner. The tremendous momentum the program gained from its supporters and its results means that the book will not soon be closed on Springfield School District.

ACKNOWLEDGEMENT

The authors wish to acknowledge the support of Emily Chiodo in preparation of this manuscript.

REFERENCES

Davis, S. (1987). *Future perfect.* Reading, MA: Addison-Wesley.

Fountas, I. C., & Pinnell, G. S. (1999). *Matching books to readers: Using leveled books in guided reading, K-3.* Portsmouth, NH: Heinemann.

Louv, R. (2005). *Last child in the woods: Saving our children from nature-deficit disorder.* Chapel Hill, NC: Algonquin Books of Chapel Hill.

Word, E., Achilles, C. M., Bain, H. P., Breda, C., Folger, J., & Fulton, B. D., et al. (1990). *The State of Tennessee's Student/Teacher Achievement Ratio (STAR) Project: Final summary report 1985–1990.* Nashville, TN: Tennessee State Department of Education.

Chapter 29

Still Hoping for that Cradle to Grave High School

Philip J. Poinelli

New high schools are among the single largest (and most expensive) infrastructure projects most communities undertake. Because of the wide variety of spaces required by educational programs, school buildings have the capacity to touch and serve a much larger segment of the community. When planning committees and funding agencies think beyond high school curricula, school facilities can become community resources serving children in day care through senior citizens. When doing so, a high school transforms its role from a building open 8 a.m. to 3 p.m. while serving only high school students, to a facility that might open at 6 a.m. and close at 10 p.m. or later while serving a wide spectrum of community needs.

Most high schools today have some community component; incorporating more community facilities within a single school rather than building separate facilities can save money and enhance the overall community experience.

SERVING ALL GENERATIONS

Early Childhood Centers

It is not unusual for a high school to include some type of early childhood center or family science curriculum covering the subjects of child growth and development, early childhood education, and family living. In Massachusetts, high schools in such diverse communities as Quincy, Nantucket, Wellesley, and Hudson integrate early childhood centers into their daily activities.

Nantucket High School hosts a parent cooperative for day care and Pre-Kindergarten from ages 0 to 5. Hudson High School and the soon-to-be-completed Quincy High serve the children of teachers and students through curriculum-based early childhood programs. Other schools accept children from the community through a lottery process.

Teen Centers

A thoughtfully designed high school facility is a particularly efficient venue for teen activities and services beyond the academic day. A dedicated space where kids can relax, interact informally, and experience as *theirs* is substantially enhanced by access to the numerous facilities within the school that host after-hour, weekend, and summer programs. Computer rooms, art, music, photography and performing arts spaces could all serve teen center programs. Supervision of shared spaces can be addressed through the community's formal or volunteer organizations.

Adult Programs

Adult education is probably the most universal use of high schools after hours with programs ranging from hobbies and travel to new skill training and career development. Traditionally, many adult education programs have been offered by local school districts. More recently, there are examples of community colleges establishing satellite campuses in high school buildings. These partnerships can unburden school districts, ensure high quality education programs, and provide rental income for school systems.

Gymnasiums across the United States have been the home for adult basketball leagues for years. More recently, high schools have added fitness and weight rooms and dance studios to promote lifelong fitness for all. These spaces can now serve before-school and after-hours programs for adults for fitness, dance, and yoga for a fraction of the cost of fitness clubs. At Wellesley High School, private funding ensures high quality fitness equipment and lots of it!

Hudson and Quincy high schools include elevated walking tracks around the perimeter of their gymnasiums. Available to their townspeople, the tracks are popular with senior citizens. Nantucket High School's swimming pool opens at 6 a.m. and closes at 10 p.m. In addition to lap swimming and family swim programs, the community offers courses from beginning swimming to lifesaving, aquacise, and hydrofitness.

Senior Centers

The Town of Swampscott set a precedent for eastern Massachusetts. Its new high school facility incorporates the town Senior Center as a distinct facility, while it shares many high school resources. The decision to co-locate the

Town's Senior Center with the new high school resulted in benefits that no one originally envisioned (Poinelli, 2008).

When the architects first met with the Council on Aging (COA) to understand its program requirements, they quickly realized that many of the spaces and features requested were already part of the new high school program. Once the COA and the school administration agreed that facilities could be shared, planning moved ahead quickly.

The dedicated space for the Senior Center is only 7,500 square feet, but when built as part of the 200,500 square foot high school, construction cost was significantly lower than if the Center were a stand-alone building. Co-locating offered a real economy of scale. The high school building provides the utility infrastructure. The 3.5 percent additional building area added little to the school's utility equipment sizing. By simply sub-metering the utilities, the Center pays for its own utility services.

Initially, seniors were very concerned that co-mingling in the school might cause them harm because of the physical size of students. They took a leap of faith, however, and both seniors and students have benefited from the cross-generational teaching and learning experiences stimulated by physical proximity and shared facilities. Students conduct computer and other technology classes for seniors. Seniors teach cooking classes and assist with staffing

Photo 29.1. Living room at the Swampscott Senior Center, courtesy of Symmes Maini & McKee Associates (SMMA).

the school library. The seniors use a wide range of school classrooms and specialty spaces for their programs. Culturally, the shared facility has helped transform the community, bringing generations closer together. The COA director, a former high school principal, and the school administration continue to explore additional cross-generational opportunities.

A SUCCESS STORY: THE COMMUNITY SCHOOL AT NANTUCKET HIGH SCHOOL

The 2.5-hour ferry ride to Nantucket from the mainland isolates inhabitants on this island located thirty miles off the southeastern coast of Massachusetts. If it is not on the island, it is not readily accessible. Prior to the creation of a Community School within the new Nantucket High School facility, schools were for children. The new building changed that thinking. The Community School is considered the fourth school in the Nantucket system after the elementary, middle, and high schools. It employs five full-time administrative staff members and dozens of part-time instructors and staff.

The school is used by the public until 9:30 p.m. in the evenings and on weekends as well. When Nantucket High School closes for the summer, the demand for the Community School surges. The year-round town population swells from 10,500, to a tourist and summer resident population of over 50,000. The Community School is now formally designated "for the purpose of providing year round educational enrichment for adults and children outside the traditional school day" (*Mission,* Nantucket Community School, n.d., para. 1). The Nantucket Community School Web site lists its major activities and components as:

- Adult education
- GED preparation
- Literacy training
- Community pool
- Parent enrichment programs
- Community network for children
- Summer camps
- After-school programs

The Community School offers adult education courses through the Work-force Education Resource Center/Cape Cod Community College, with approximately one hundred and twenty courses at the high school facility in dozens of interest areas, as well as access to over three hundred online courses. The director, Pauline Proch, estimates that the Community School serves approximately 2,500 people in a typical year, approximately one quarter of the island's year-round population.

MERGING EDUCATION AND COMMUNITY

Communities vary in their needs; the marriage of community resources and education facilities reflects local needs and priorities. When discussions begin among seemingly diverse groups within a community, each states that its space requirements are unique and could not coexist with those of other constituencies or age groups. In fact, each does require some dedicated space, but the number and types of possible shared spaces may surprise almost everyone. These include:

- Health and fitness rooms, gymnasiums, walking or running tracks, dance and aerobics rooms, pools
- Computer rooms
- Lecture halls, auditoriums
- Language labs
- Art rooms, ceramics, kilns, photography labs, and darkrooms
- Libraries
- TV studios and community access TV

Town Municipal Uses

It is not unusual for town halls or other facilities to remain open late at night for a range of committee meetings or school board meetings. All these activities could be aggregated to a high school that likely remains open after hours. Auditoriums and large group instruction rooms are ideal for public hearings. Conference rooms and classrooms can easily serve the needs of many committees. The result is substantial savings of financial and energy resources.

Revenue Stream

Many communities have discovered that after-hour uses become important revenue sources to supplement school operation costs. Community college offerings, recreational user fees, auditorium rentals, and other performance spaces to outside non-profit institutions are just some of the revenue possibilities. These rentals are often a win–win for all parties. The outside organizations can rent the school facilities less expensively than they could commercial facilities, and the rent supplements operating expenses for the school.

Environmental Benefit

Shared facilities result in less building area, fewer buildings, less energy consumption, and reduced impact on the environment than stand-alone facilities. Making broader use of high school buildings follows the tenants of smart growth, mixed-use development, and sustainability through avoidance of redundant facilities.

Voter Support

Many communities and school districts require voter referendum ballots to approve major capital projects. Offering programs for generations of voters who do not have school-age children is one of the best ways to encourage a positive vote for both capital investment and ongoing maintenance and operation costs. Voters of all ages recognize the value that a multi-use facility offers.

KEYS TO SUCCESS

In approaching the concept of shared facilities, a community needs to focus on five factors:

- Early programming—an understanding of all needs will yield the most shared space opportunities.
- Savings calculations—the savings gained by not constructing and maintaining redundant spaces need to be shared with the community.
- Dedicated space allocations—each facility partner will need space it can call its own, including a separate entry.
- Schedule coordinator—this key person must be responsible for scheduling to avoid conflicts.
- Commitment—a shared consensus and commitment to the final preferred concept helps maintain energy and focus through project completion and program implementation.

A combination of well-defined stakeholder needs, a collective vision, and a collaborative approach allows communities to achieve a much greater return on their investment in public facilities. High school buildings stand for fifty, sixty, seventy years, or more. They can, and should, provide active learning, meeting, recreational, and cultural environments for residents from cradle to grave.

REFERENCES

Mission, Nantucket Community School. (n.d.) Retrieved on April 24, 2009, from www.nantucket.k12.ma.us/~cnc/ncs/

Poinelli, P. J. (2008). Mixing generations: New high school enriches senior/student life: Community benefits emerge from a multi-generation, shared space model. *CEFPI Educational Facility Planner, 43*(1), 21–23.

Part VI

Educational Innovations from Around the World

In a recent *Newsweek* interview with Garland (2008), Darling Hammond looked to countries in Europe, Asia, and Australia to explore the strengths of their educational system and compare their successful practices to U.S. instructional approaches. Our intention with this section is to showcase lesser known examples of successful, innovative practices from diverse countries in the world.

Monisha Bajaj opens up the section by ushering us into Umutende, a private school in Zambia, Africa. Freedom from the government system—both its pressures and its conventions—enables many innovations, such as longer school days, unique incentives for teachers, and consistent and on-going teacher training. Alan Cooper takes us to St. George's preparatory school in Wanganui, New Zealand, where students are explicitly taught meta-cognitive skills and processes to develop and appreciate self-management. While still in New Zealand, we take a short trip to Christchurch with Fleur Harris, who allows us to witness a Whānau (family) classroom. Here, the teacher scaffolds the children's learning within a bilingual and bicultural context—using a holistic approach to the curriculum, including daily waiata (singing), utilizing tuakana/teina relationships (older or more experienced teach younger and less experienced), and creating and saying chants. Mária Molnár, József Braun, and Judit Kováts take us to Budapest, Hungary, where young adults in turmoil (YATEs) may attend a second-chance high school. It is an ethos-oriented organization that builds on the notion that students may not be at risk because they lack something—knowledge, relationships, or experience—but because they have a surplus and a need for autonomy. Unique innovations such as student mentoring, restorative conflict resolution, and teacher peer assessments are described.

With Ingvar Sigurgeirsson as our guide, we enter Laugar Comprehensive, one of the smallest high schools located in a rural community in the northern part of Iceland. In Laugar, a flexible approach to teaching allows students to work individually, according to their own pace, based on their needs and interests.

REFERENCES

Garland, S. (December 18, 2008). *Reform school: An Obama education advisor thinks U.S. schools could take a lesson from Finland and Singapore.* Retrieved June 7, 2009 from http://www.newsweek.com/id/175894

Chapter 30

Innovation and Transformation at a Zambian School

Monisha Bajaj

While most in the Western industrialized world are bombarded with images of out-of-school and undernourished children in Africa, and while these realities demand international attention, a small, low-cost private school in northern Zambia offers some interesting lessons for educational scholars and practitioners worldwide. The Umutende School was started by two retired African educators committed to character education, peace and human rights, and a brand of pan-African self-reliance and cultural empowerment formed by their previous involvement in liberation struggles during the mid-20th century. The school's unique structure and curriculum are the main focus as I illustrate the impact on students amidst a larger social context characterized by corruption, widespread poverty, and unemployment.

This chapter is based on eleven months of fieldwork in Zambia (2003–2004), where I spent considerable time at the Umutende School carrying out interviews, observations, surveys, and participating in the life of the school by living in the teachers' compound, teaching as a volunteer, and attending daily school assemblies and special events. Since then, I have maintained contact with many students and teachers, as well as collected information through an in-depth follow-up survey with 20 former students of the school. In order to set the stage for discussing the innovations—in both curricular content and school structure—it is important to provide some background on the central African nation of Zambia and some of the challenges facing its educational system. Selected practices that the school employs and how they appear to be transforming students' educational experiences will be addressed.

Zambia boasts a relatively high literacy rate (81 percent) as compared to other African countries, which is largely due to government programs that prioritized increasing educational access since independence from British rule in 1964 to the present day. The educational system, however, faces tremendous challenges including class sizes of over 100 students in many schools, run-down facilities, infrastructure for only 30 percent of eligible students to go on from primary to secondary school, and the devastating impact of HIV/AIDS on teachers, students, and families (an estimated 15 percent of Zambian adults are infected with HIV [UNAIDS, 2007]). In order to accommodate as many students as possible, the school day in government-run schools is split into different sessions such that students go to school either in the morning or afternoon, resulting in a day shortened to five hours, thereby limiting the instructional content.

It is amidst this context that an unusual school opened in 1992 and sought to create a high-quality and low-cost educational environment for marginalized children in Zambia. The Umutende School, which offers grades one through twelve, differs from public schools in many ways. While I have written more extensively about the school elsewhere (Bajaj, 2005; 2009), the following sections highlight the areas in which students responded most favorably to the school's innovations related to school structure, policy, pedagogy, and content.

STRUCTURE AND SCHOOL POLICY:
SETTING THE STAGE FOR INNOVATION

Since Umutende is a private school and does not face the same pressures that public schools do to educate as many students as possible, there is greater flexibility to set limits on admissions and class sizes (500 students in classes of 15–25 on average in the high school). The freedom from the government system—both its pressures and its conventions—enables a range of innovations. It is worth highlighting three areas related to structure in which the school's innovations seem to be resulting in the greatest benefit for Zambian students, particularly given the prevalent realties at most public high schools in the country: (a) the longer school days, (b) incentives for teachers, and (c) regular and on-going teacher training.

First, the Umutende School offers students longer school days and school weeks: the school day for high school students at Umutende is from 6:45 in the morning to 5:00 in the evening Monday to Friday and a half day on Saturday. Students in grades 7, 9, and 12 who are preparing for competitive national exams also have two to three extra hours of preparation a week. Given this rigorous schedule, offering nearly double the contact hours of public schools, there is also time for environmental studies, community service, character education, and daily hour-long assemblies that are not present in public schools. The longer school hours also result in stronger bonds between students and teachers when compared with the more superficial bonds noted in large classes with fewer contact hours at public schools in Zambia.

Second, the Umutende School offers teachers greater incentives. While the salaries are comparable for teachers at Umutende and in public schools in Zambia, salaries are paid more regularly at Umutende versus public schools where economic crises mean that, oftentimes, teachers are not paid on time. Additionally, the Umutende School provides teachers housing for their families—which is a significant incentive—and small plots of land, where teachers can grow food to eat or sell to supplement their incomes. All of these incentives make teaching at the Umutende School—despite its longer hours and additional training requirements—attractive to many teachers.

The last aspect, in terms of school structure, is the Umutende School's provision that teachers go through a six-month course that meets weekly focusing on their approach to character education. In addition, there are monthly day-long in-service trainings for teachers to share lessons and experiences. By contrast, in other Zambian schools, there is little training beyond the two-year teacher training course. The monthly in-service days provide an opportunity for teachers to get together, be recognized as professionals, and renew their commitment to the school's unique approach. The structure of the Umutende School provides the scaffolding for its unique pedagogical content.

CURRICULAR CONTENT: MAKING EDUCATION RELEVANT

The hallmark of the Umutende School's approach is its distinctive curricular content focused on *moral, academic, and environmental excellence*. The approaches used to promote academic achievement are largely related to its structure, namely longer school hours, dedicated teachers (who are constantly trained and regularly evaluated), and relatively small class sizes. In addition, the school uses strategies that distinguish it from other schools in three areas: school as a family, cultural pride, and environmental education. These three areas are the most distinct vis-à-vis government schools in Zambia and are the areas which present lessons for educators worldwide.

School as a Family

Students and teachers consistently refer to the Umutende School as a family and note the significant impact that this atmosphere has on their educational or professional experience. Long hours and small class sizes (structural elements of the school), combined with daily assemblies where children and teachers partake in role-plays, receive advice from senior administrators, and sing songs in the local language, offer students the chance to build familial-like bonds. In interviews and focus groups the notion of *school as a family* repeatedly came up.

Some high school students refer to their teachers as elder siblings, while other students refer to teachers and administrators as parents. This type of camaraderie is encouraged from administrators and even discussed in monthly in-service trainings. A senior teacher, who had previously worked in a public high school, commented on the way the unique curricular approach contributed to the family-like atmosphere of the school:

> The one thing I've observed in this school when compared to the other school I was at, [is that] there's this apparent, observable spirit of brotherhood [and] sisterhood. The pupils tend to relate to one another in almost like a family way I think because of what they learn here. They are so friendly with each other. I haven't really experienced a fight in the seven years I've been here, which was not the case where I was [previously].

There are rarely fights among students. Students and teachers often share food with one another at lunchtime, are affectionate with one another, and teachers often make efforts to ask about and intervene in any problems that are occurring in students' homes and communities.

Cultural Pride

Despite the social problems students face, the Umutende School encourages a sense of cultural pride that is manifested in various ways throughout the school's operations and practices. First, students greet teachers before every class in the Bemba language, which requires a call and response. This is in contrast to government-run schools where children reported being punished (in some cases being beaten, although corporal punishment was legally outlawed in Zambia in 2000) for speaking any language other than English in school (Sibanda & Gama, 2000). Instruction at Umutende, however, is carried out in English, as it is in all other high schools throughout the country. Second, students have daily assemblies to start the schoolday where they sing and drum songs in Bemba. By comparison, in public schools, assemblies occur twice a month and are mainly for announcements. While Umutende emphasizes the students' culture, it does not hold a rigid conception of culture, as evidenced by its permitting female students also to drum, a practice that is not common in Zambia. Third, students are often reminded of their role in building their country and Africa as a continent, rooted in the pan-African vision of the founders. This results in students' expressing a desire to enter into public service and serve their country, whereas public high school students mostly articulate a desire to earn money or go overseas.

Two areas related to cultural pride at Umutende are specifically for female teachers and students. Women in Zambia are targeted by many industries related to skin lightening and hair straightening—both of which involve products that contain chemicals that have been found to be harmful to young women. Through assemblies, young women are discouraged from seeing themselves as inferior if they possess dark skin or kinky hair and are instructed not to utilize products that endanger their health in pursuit of socially constructed beauty standards.

Additionally, students wear uniforms made of local *chitenge* cloth with African print, and female teachers are asked to wear traditional African clothing two days out of the week. This practice is not observed at any other school in Zambia where young men and women wear uniforms consisting of button-down shirts, blazers, and ties rooted in the colonial tradition. An additional component of pride in the students' culture is related to their relationship to agriculture, which is historically the mainstay of most Zambians.

Environmental Education

The Umutende School promotes environmental education by having all students engage in hands-on environmental work around the school's large campus and by integrating concepts related to environmental conservation into the school's curriculum and assemblies. While paid workers supervise the maintenance of the grounds of the school, which is too large for students alone to manage, students are scheduled for environmental periods weekly. Depending on their age and skill, they pick fruits or vegetables, water plants, plant seeds, carry hay, or participate in other activities related to agricultural production. In classes and assemblies alike, students learn about water conservation through writing and performing songs, doing role-plays and skits, and creating awareness campaigns through posters and badges that they wear.

Given the meanings associated with education and the consideration of agricultural work as inferior to office or white-collar jobs by most Zambians, it is unusual to find a school that values and emphasizes agricultural labor. In government-run schools, this notion of agricultural work being menial is reinforced with the common practice of students who misbehave being sent to tend the school-grounds as a punishment. The declining state of the Zambian economy is perhaps one incentive for youth to learn agricultural production skills, aside from the more ideological ones associated with the school's mission. Thus, while students are all required to partake in the agricultural activities as part of their education, a positive outcome of such activity is the provision of skills for the future that may allow greater access to income generation in an uncertain economy.

UMUTENDE'S IMPACT:
FROM INNOVATION TO TRANSFORMATION

The explanations of how structural and curricular innovations are implemented at the Umutende School in Zambia necessitate some mention of how students are responding to them. The vision of the founders and administrators is juxtaposed in Table 30.1 with students' responses in journals that they completed for my original research study and individual interviews carried out during the eleven months I spent in the school.

Table 30.1. Administrators' and Students' Voices on School Themes.

Theme	Administrators' Words	Students' Words
Cultural Pride	"Having come from a colonial background where our culture was disregarded, and we faced cultural alienation, we were made to feel inferior, to copy the white man, and [to feel] that all the white man did was good and all that the black man did was bad. Coats and ties represent the dress of Europeans. We want to make our students and teachers feel proud of being African, of being black". (School Director)	"At assembly, [the Director] was talking about how he passed through a lot of difficulties when he was a boy; he had no shoes, but he went to university. He was simply telling us about his life; that's the subject I most enjoy. He was telling us that we can also do it. We are Africans just like him. In every African home, there are problems. He was simply telling us to work hard and we can achieve our goals like him." (Emmanuel, 12th grader)
Environmental Education	"We feel children shouldn't just learn book knowledge. When they finish, even if they live well, even if they can afford things, they should be able to… love the soil, love to look after their environment, and… not to feel that 'I'm too good to touch the soil.'" (Senior Teacher)	"In secondary school, I've learned a lot of production work like when we go farm. I've learned how to just to stand on my own two feet, to take up farming as one of my careers so to say, if things go bad." (Nicholas, 12th grader)

(Continued)

Table 30.1 *(Continued)*

Theme	Administrators' Words	Students' Words
Future Goals and Leadership	"Focus your attention on your studies; you will become good and great in this country. You, like many other boys and girls, will become the leaders of this nation, become the leaders of Africa, become the leaders of the world. You will be addressing the United Nations, the Councils of the world. Every human being must have a focus, must have a goal. Set your mind on that goal. Nothing is impossible. So think big." (School Administrator)	"As for Zambia, in my imagination, I really believe and trust that in the upcoming years, a great deal of changes will take place. We are the leaders of the next generation and I believe that we will be good leaders who will lead Zambian people in a friendly way and manner. I always thank the teachers for taking care of me and making sure that I become a responsible person in the future." (Annie, 8th grader)

CONCLUSION

The Umutende School offers one example of how innovation can transform student experiences, particularly amidst an educational system in which problems—such as overcrowded schools, limited resources, and poor quality—abound. Set against such a backdrop, innovation that engages students and provides them a distinctive and high-quality educational experience can provide meaningful instruction and direction as young people discern how to navigate their uncertain futures.

The school's challenges include sustainability given that it is donor-driven and does not receive government funding. Another key concern is its scope, since the school's impact is limited to those students fortunate enough to attend. Finally, it cannot effectively shelter students from the often-harsh social realities beyond the school gates. Despite these limitations, for those students who have passed through this unusual educational institution, it is certainly an experience they remember well beyond graduation.

Continued contact with many students as they enter higher education and the world of work offers a modicum of hope about the role of innovative schooling amidst wider social problems. While some encountered problems, especially related to rampant corruption in Zambian society that their idyllic school environment had not prepared them for, most students are involved in higher levels of academic study, working in public service, or employed in other professional capacities throughout Zambia and beyond.

Umutende offers lessons about schools as spaces for engendering transformative possibilities regardless of the larger social context. By participating in a school culture that differs from other schools as well as the larger society, students imbibe a sense that social change is possible and that alternatives exist to a wide range of unequal social practices (be they related to gender inequality, racism/marginalization, environmental degradation, or the myriad other forms of disenfranchisement). School innovations, particularly when driven by a larger democratic vision, offer the promise for a gradual shift in the direction of greater social equity and justice in all corners of the globe.

REFERENCES

Bajaj, M. I. (2005). *Conceptualizing agency amidst crisis: A case study of youth responses to human values education in Zambia.* Doctoral Dissertation, Columbia University, New York.

Bajaj, M. (2009). 'I have big things planned for my future': The limits and possibilities of transformative agency in Zambian schools. *Compare, 39(4)* 551–568.

Sibanda, N., & Gama, H. (May 10, 2000). *Colonial era punishment scrapped in Zambia.* Retrieved February 12, 2005, from http://www.ugandaruralcommunitysupport.org/2000/05/10/colonial-era-punishment-scrapped-in-zambia-10-may-2000/

UNAIDS. (2007). *Zambia. Country Data.* Retrieved January 26, 2009, from http://www.unaids.org/en/CountryResponses/Countries/zambia.asp

Chapter 31

At St. George's, It All Begins with Self-Management: Getting to Know Yourself

J. Alan Cooper

Think hard. If you still don't get it, think harder.

—Jen Savage

Although there is a national curriculum for New Zealand—which all schools must teach—and although schools are centrally funded by the New Zealand government, each individual school has its own Board of Trustees. These Boards have substantial autonomy in impacting how the curriculum is taught and what practices are to be implemented. Where there is a proactive principal acting as the educational advisor to the Board of Trustees, innovation can flow. Thus, while many schools may take a traditional path, there are many opportunities for those who wish to take a more innovative approach.

This chapter presents the practical, innovative steps that St George's Preparatory School in Wanganui, New Zealand took to give the students the skills that fostered self-management. Case studies using Dunn and Dunn's Model of Learning Styles (Dunn & Dunn, 1992) serve as exemplars.

PHASE 1: SELF-MANAGEMENT WITH THE TEACHER AS FACILITATOR

The Student as Novice

In the initial stages, the teacher is the facilitator for the novice, self-managing student. Underlying this concept is the importance of relationships, in particular, collegial relationships that engender feelings of efficacy. Such relationships are many and varied: teacher to student, student to teacher, teacher to teacher, teacher to parent, parent to teacher, student to parent, parent to student, and more. In all cases, it is a matter of working *with* not doing *to*.

A Kinesthetic Learner

There is no success for Greg learning his multiplication tables. It is his homework task, and his mother has been standing over him as he alternately recites and writes each multiplication table, but without success. He is putting in time and effort, but to no avail. Frustration is building in both mother and son.

Aware of this learning difficulty, his teacher intervenes. The record shows the student is kinesthetic, so the advice to him and his mother is to chant/recite his tables as he bounces a basketball on the patio. Capitalizing on his kinesthetic learning style, he at last learns those tables. There is a great deal of rejoicing at home when he repeatedly gets everything right when his mother quizzes him.

However, while he knows them at home, at school the multiplication recall eludes him. Again, Greg's teacher acts. This time the suggestion is that he taps his index finger on his thigh during a multiplication test. He taps and his math recall at school rapidly increases to 100 percent. Success and satisfaction come at last to a struggling learner.

Metacognitive Reflection: The Key to Self-Management

This is an opportune time—the teachable moment—to further grow Greg's capacities and capabilities by guiding him to reflect metacognitively on what happened in his learning experience. Inviting him to *analyze* and *evaluate* and, therefore, to understand his own learning process is critical: Because he is a kinesthetic learner, it was the process of bouncing the basketball as he recited the tables that stored those tables in his procedural memory.

Greg benefits from knowing that procedural memory is activated by movement, and that this memory lane equates to his kinesthetic learning style. Using the wrong retrieval process and failing to find the right match may result in forgetting or not being able to perform academically. That is exactly what he had been doing in class until he started tapping and allowed the right retrieval process to open up the procedural memory lane for him.

How about episodic memory? What is a possible connection there? Episodic memory relates to a specific location. The tapping on his thigh allowed Greg to visualize or feel the action on the patio, so a second memory lane is opened, making retrieval easier. Greg's experiences give an important insight into how the body and brain work in unison as a system, creating a more detailed schema for both storage and retrieval.

Overall, by raising all these experiences to Greg's conscious level, the teacher is developing the executive function of his student's brain. The area of the brain—situated in the frontal lobe—is being programmed and prepared to plan and prioritize when future action is required. Through these processes, new capacities and capabilities are being added to the student's intrapersonal intelligence, thus his ability to self-manage and self-learn is enhanced.

Rehearsal

The more information is processed, the more the material is manipulated and reviewed, the better it is secured into long-term memory and the more the student ends up knowing and understanding. This is especially so when meaning can be created. In the scenario above, Greg is engaged in a process of *analyzing* and *evaluating* to see what method of rehearsal will best cement his learning. He needs to be encouraged to articulate these experiences at the consciousness level as a form of rehearsal.

PHASE 2: SELF-MANAGEMENT WITH TEACHER AS COACH

In the scenario above, Greg's metacognitive reflection has been teacher facilitated, largely through an external voice. The shift in this phase is to a greater internal voice, aided by interdependent thinking that comes with the coaching role of the teacher. This is a key progression. Not only does the teacher move from facilitator to coach but also the demands on the student increase. Greg transitions from straight-forward remembering, understanding, and applying to the more sophisticated skills of analyzing, evaluating, and using the criteria to plan creative solutions (*Beyond Bloom: A new version of the cognitive taxonomy,* n.d.). Moreover, the student must do this consciously through a deliberate, purposeful, and meaningful process. It will not *just* happen.

Initially, most students might not understand why they are reflecting metacognitively and will need to be taught explicitly why and how to do so. Until this happens, they are caught in a dilemma between a feeling of relief from completing the work and incomprehension, bewilderment, and even resentment at having to think further about it. Therefore, initially, student reflection most often will be little more than a safe comment, done quickly and without thought, such as, "I enjoyed the lesson."

Shifting the Initiative from the Teacher to the Student

The starting point for more insightful, more significant, and more growth-oriented metacognitive reflection is to provide the students with a self-monitoring guide or list to use as a scaffold on which to build their thinking and, beyond that, their self-management. Thus, the goal is to have them ask themselves:

- What they do
- Why they do it
- What are the results
- How they feel about it

The above is not a definitive list but is merely representative of what teachers may use. Regular journal writing is one of the most effective approaches to achieve this. At the start of the school year, various rituals are recommended to be in place such as:

- Appropriate use of language: the need to use *because* as a key conjunction
- The need to explain where they *clicked* with the lesson and where they did not
- An agreement that what is written is their own thoughts, honest and forthright
- A regular set time to write, such as the last ten minutes of Friday, to summarize the week

As the year progresses, the personal, practical knowledge of the journal writers grows as they become more aware of what their learning styles and their other learning idiosyncrasies are. As their collegial trust in the teacher and the other students becomes defined, they tend to write more; thus, the time limit may need to be extended. Over time, the written reflection becomes more revealing, indicating to the teacher the diverse ways in which students learn and how they self-manage their own differentiation.

Global and Analytic Processing

The Dunn and Dunn (1992) model has a subset of the main processing styles, which include global and analytic styles. The global learning style focuses on the overall understanding—often referred to as the big picture—where the learner wants the freedom to learn in their own way without detailed direction. The other approach to learning is the analytic approach which is often interpreted as the opposite of global. The learner requires a detailed task structure and likes to be told exactly what to do.

An analytic learner writes:

> I worked from 1–9 because I prefer to do things in order. I preferred the fact sheet because the information was clearly visible, the key words were in bold and were easily seen and, therefore, I could see the information that explained about the key sentence. I am doing this analytically because I am following what we have to do in order.

By contrast, a global learner records her thoughts and a different procedure:

> I worked by starting at number 9 because I had so many feelings. I wanted to get them out quickly on paper. After that though I went back to 5 and worked down the list. This is because I wanted to remember more detail for the poem. I am doing WWII globally because I like to choose where to start.

Note the use of *because* in each answer. Conjunctions, such as because give direction, requiring the student to go beyond the general and select specific, practical evidence to support the assertion that has been made.

Coaching by Oral Conferencing

The relationship that is developed between teacher and student throughout this process is crucial. Feedback—which takes the students from where they are and moves them on in their own unique style—requires empathetic listening and a warm and supportive, collegial voice. The teacher needs to be adept at playing the appropriate role. Some students will require a nonauthoritarian approach with a conversational tone, whereas at the other extreme will be those who want to be directed with an imperative voice but still make their own decisions.

An effective way of achieving this is by the teacher conferencing with students as he or she moves about the classroom, or at times when they sit quietly together at a desk. For some students, it is better to converse in their own space (at their desk); for others the teacher's space is best (at the teacher's desk).

The results of such conferences may be documented in the next round of journal writing. In the following example, the student directly addresses the teacher in a collegial way that indicates much about the relationship between the two.

> Before I spoke to you I never really knew what persistence meant in learning styles, but now I know that I am very persistent for example, when I work and

do hard things like this essay. I stick at it until I am finished, rather than do it bit by bit.

Teachers are Learners, Too

Another advantage of such ongoing narrative is to give both the teacher and the student an invaluable insight into their personal progress. Such qualitative information has so much to offer beyond the narrow confines of the quantitative knowledge from a test score.

PHASE 3: SELF-MANAGEMENT WITH TEACHER AS MENTOR

In the previous stage, the students had to be coached and guided by the teacher/coach. In Phase 3 of the process, they are able to self-manage the process comprehensively. Affirmation from the teacher is needed to acknowledge student success. Marie is an analytic learner. She understands this well as she states in her journal:

> I feel I am analytical because I like Math and lists. My room is like a filing system, I know where everything is and it is very tidy. I hate noise and I love structure.

Her ability to self-manage is thus challenged when she gets global directions from the producer of the school's operetta to create a programme. There is no detail, just a brief instruction. The first problem is to interpret the instruction—recognize that it is a global instruction—and then to find a solution. She first finds the problem; it is a global instruction:

> This year Mrs. R. and Mr. E., who I'm sure are globals, asked me to do a programme for the operetta. I wasn't sure what they wanted so I went home and sat down and wrote out a list of all the things that should be in a programme. Now I think I can do one.

And Marie could and she did!

Empathy for Other Styles

In solving the problem above, Marie demonstrates another important aspect of her growing maturity. She is not just egocentric. She has become not only aware of other people's learning styles, but also how they can impact her and what to do about them. This recognition gives her an empathy, which, in turn, enables her to manage her relationship with others.

THE SCHOOL AS A LEARNING ORGANIZATION

By continually expanding the students' capability and capacity to self-manage, as detailed above, mental models are developed. These models—by being articulated through regular written and oral metacognitive reflection—are thus raised to the conscious level in a way which constantly challenges the status of each individual student's current learning processes.

If teachers mindfully provide feedback to the students' metacognitive reflection, either in writing or by individual conferencing, they are also practicing higher-level thinking skills themselves. When this is a schoolwide initiative, as it has been at St. George's, the development of collegial relationships among the faculty is inevitable (Ball, Vossler, Gibbs, & Broadley, 1999). As one teacher wrote:

> We kept piggy backing off each other's ideas and innovating. I learnt so much about learning, children's learning, and me.

At St. George's, teachers and administrators alike believe that we need to develop mindful students and mindful teachers. We need to develop efficacious students and efficacious teachers. We need to develop schools as learning organizations—teaching students to self manage is an innovative way of doing all that.

REFERENCES

Ball, T., Vossler, K. Gibbs, C., & Broadley, G. (1999). *St George's School: Teaching thinking: An evaluation of the process involved in innovative curriculum development.* Unpublished research report. College of Education, Massey University, Palmerston North: Massey University.

Beyond Bloom: A new version of the cognitive taxonomy. (n.d.). Retrieved December 18, 2008, from http://www.uwsp.edu/education/lwilson/curric/newtaxonomy.htm

Costa, A., & Kallick, B. (2000) *Habits of mind: A developmental series.* Alexandria, VA: Association for Supervision and Curriculum Development.

Dunn, R., & Dunn, K. (1992). Teaching elementary students through their individual learning styles. Boston: Allyn and Bacon.

Dweck, C. (2006). *Mindset.* New York: Random House.

Gardner, H. (1999). *Intelligence reframed.* New York: Basic Books.

Kohn, A. (1996). What to look for in classrooms. *Educational Leadership, 54*(1), 54–55.

Sprenger, M. (2003). *Differentiation through learning styles and memory.* Thousand Oaks, CA: Corwin.

Chapter 32

Successful Teaching Practices in a New Zealand Whānau Classroom: Enhanced English Reading Learning for Māori Children

Fleur Harris

In New Zealand, the whānau (extended family) class environment is one way in which Māori (the indigenous people) have established an effective bilingual, bicultural learning context supporting Māori children as high-achieving learners. These classrooms are among a variety of Māori immersion contexts that have surfaced during the past thirty years. They have emerged, in part, to change the deficit thinking about Māori as *at-risk* children in the mainstream educational system, especially in relation to speaking and reading English (Harris, 2008).

New Zealand, a former British colony is located about 1,000 miles southeast of Australia. In 2006, the 4.5 million inhabitants comprised of Pākehā (non-Māori, European) (70 percent), Māori (15 percent), Asian (8 percent) and Pasifika (7 percent) peoples. Since the 1840 Treaty of Waitangi, Māori have endured a Eurocentric domination of their lands, language, and culture.

THE WHĀNAU CLASSROOM FRAMEWORK

The whānau classroom framework reflects the parents' dreams for their children to be able to walk confidently in both Māori and Pākehā (non-Māori, European) worlds. This unique structure includes family groups of children ranging in age from five to twelve, where siblings are placed in the same class regardless of their age. Instruction is usually bilingual (Māori/English) or total immersion in Māori. Currently, the majority of Māori children are enrolled in the mainstream. A whānau class differs from the mainstream, where children are grouped according to year/age groupings, and the learning environment is monocultural Pākehā and monolingual English.

This chapter describes the bicultural/bilingual home contexts for eleven Māori whānau class children, (aged five to twelve years), who formed part of a study group in which I was a participant observer. The class was located in Christchurch, the South Island's largest city of 450,000 inhabitants. It presents the teaching and learning contexts within the classroom, illustrating how the teacher Whāea (Aunty) Kath taught in ways that intermeshed both Māori and Pākehā world-views. She provided a bilingual/bicultural environment that enhanced the language and English reading achievement of her students.

Bicultural and Bilingual Home Contexts

At home, at least one parent or grandparent spoke Māori and both parents spoke English. Some children had been to Kōhanga Reo (full immersion Māori language pre-school) before primary school. Most parents said that English was their first language and Māori their second, but they regarded Māori as the indigenous language and, therefore, their mother or native tongue.

Tikanga Māori (Māori practices) were visible in their homes where parents said daily karakia (a type of prayer), regularly attended meetings on the marae (community centre that is Māori-specific), and socialized with other Māori. Parents were employed with other Māori, worked in Māori organizations, and belonged to Maori dominated clubs.

It is well established that being bicultural and bilingual influences the way language is learned (Gee, 1985), and that pathways to learning to read English are different for those who are monolingual English and monocultural western. It can take several years (perhaps five to seven) for bilingual children to learn to read English fluently (Cummins, 1992). The teacher in the whānau class portrayed here used teaching practices that allowed the children to learn to speak and read English in ways that respected a bicultural/bilingual framework.

A VISIT TO THE CLASSROOM

Holistic Approach

Pere walks into the classroom with a newspaper article about the Crusaders (a Christchurch based franchise) winning the Super 12 (a rugby competition of 12 teams from New Zealand, Australia, and South Africa).

Pere speaks up, "Whāea, the Crusaders won the Super 12." "Āe, wasn't that awesome!" responds Whāea. Pere holds up the newspaper article showing

Whāea and she asks Pere if she can show the class. Whāea holds it up for everyone to see. She asks the children questions, "Why do you think the Crusaders won the Super 12? What makes them such an awesome team? The children call out their answers. Whāea hears an answer, repeats it, and writes the word on the whiteboard, then reads the word. Sometimes she says the first sound of the word and asks the children the letter that goes with the sound she made, before she begins to write.

This lesson was like many in which Whāea used a holistic teaching approach. She moved from the Crusaders being great rugby players to the importance of teamwork, caring about each other, enjoying the game, being prepared physically and mentally, and working hard. Then there was discussion about the ethnicities of players. She asked if there were any Māori players on the team. Whāea changed the conversation into a history discussion, talking about the Crusades and where the name Crusaders came from.

The holistic approach was evident in the way Whāea linked a range of topics together and the children participated as active and interested learners. Whāea Kath liked these lessons because of the connections between relationships, history, and health issues. Further, Whāea's holistic approach to teaching was visible with her inclusion of vocabulary, developing knowledge of the written word, and scaffolding letter-sound correspondence. She asked her students for ideas, repeated the words they said, wrote them on the whiteboard, and repeated them as she wrote. The letter-sound correspondence teaching was always incorporated into the lesson, as if it were incidental.

BILINGUALISM

To promote the bilingual nature of the class, Whāea Kath enlisted Uncle Rewi, the school Kaumātua (community elder) for weekly Māori lessons. Uncle Rewi spoke only Māori and included listening, speaking, and writing tasks in his lessons. Whāea Kath spoke Māori for karakia (a type of prayer), greetings, instructions, daily waiata (song), and during shared-class book reading with Māori text, followed by comprehension questions in English and Māori. English was spoken at other times. Māori written tasks were completed by the children at different times during the week, and a combination of Māori and English words were incorporated during other lessons, as in Figure 32.1.

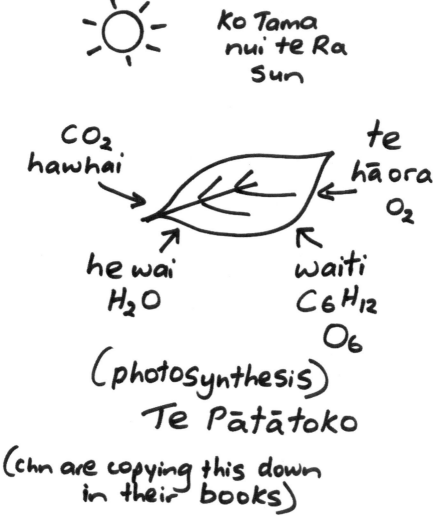

Figure 32.1. **An example of a lesson combining Māori and English words. After a discussion about photosynthesis, the children had to copy this diagram into their books.**

Words and Word Meanings

The emphasis on teaching words and their meanings is evident in the next class vignette, and according to Metge (1990) this tends to be given a central place in teaching by Māori teachers.

> *The children are on the mat. Whāea holds up a book, reads the title, "Sneezy Snatcher and Sammy Small," and says "It's about a giant. Who can tell me*

some words about a giant?" The answers come, "big ears," says Big JL and Whāea repeats "big ears." "Big feet," says Ariel and Whāea repeats "big feet." "Hairy," says Tama and Whāea repeats "hairy." (Whāea repeats all the words in this way.) "Scary," "mean," wide," "huge," "big body," and "unhappy." Whāea is reading the book and comes to the word "shortsighted." "What does that mean?" The children are silent. Big JL calls out "I don't know." Whāea explains the word and she asks, "When someone looks foolish, they look what?" She then says "s." "Silly!" call out some of the children.

These shared reading times were a typical daily learning activity. Whāea Kath's technique of repetition, her use of questions to scaffold comprehension of language, and her focus on expanding the children's vocabulary were all common practices. The next vignette illustrates Whāea's emphasis on words and meanings within a bilingual context.

Whāea speaks in Māori, telling the class that the day is cold and cloudy. She looks at her small whiteboard and says, "I want you to read this."

Te Maramataka.	*(The calendar.)*
Ko Mane.	*(It is Monday.)*
Ko Ngāhuru tō wa o te tau.	*(It is the season autumn.)*

Everyone reads together while Whāea points to each word. Some children read out loud and the other children join in at different times, saying some of the words in unison with Whāea and the older children, and some just after Whāea. Whāea speaks in English, telling the children it is autumn. How do we know it is autumn? Rata calls out "cold." Whāea repeats Rata's answer, writes the word on the board, and reads it. She looks at the class, "Leaves fall off the trees," says Mary. Whāea repeats Mary's answer, writes her answer on the board, reads it, and looks again to the class. Whāea does this with all the answers. Pere calls out "yellow leaves" and Big JL says, "red leaves."

Sometimes the younger children waited for the older ones to give answers before they did so. The whānau class concept allowed the older children to scaffold the younger children's learning. As a follow up task, the children wrote a poem together.

> *Ngāhuru*
> *Autumn.*
> *Is colder.*
> *Trees sleep.*
> *Trees are bare, clothless.*
> *Leaves drop.*
> *Leaves fall.*
> *All colors.*
> *Red, yellow, brown.*
> *Some stay green.*
> *Evergreen.*

This poem is rich in vocabulary and metaphor, the tree is sleeping and clothless. The use of metaphor in Māori is strong. The children were keen and able learners who participated in listening, answering Whāea's questions, and thinking about words. They were enthusiastic co-constructors in their learning with Whāea and the other children.

Chants and Cycles

The inclusion of chants in the education program aided learning of content, as in the example below.

> *The little girls are singing to the tune of "Head, shoulders, knees and toes, knees and toes." "Nose, mouth, windpipe, lungs and brain, lungs and brain. Oxygen, carbon dioxide, lungs and brain, lungs and brain." They are standing in front of each other, clapping their hands together. Sometimes they miss and laugh, but they keep going.*

The chant that the girls were singing was one that Whāea Kath and the children had created—including accompanying actions—when learning about the respiratory system.

Nose, mouth, windpipe,
Lungs and brain,
Lungs and brain,
Oxygen, carbon dioxide,
Lungs and brain,
Lungs and brain,
Diaphragm—controls it,
Respiration!
Ihu waha pu-korokoro
Pukahukahu—roro e
Whakaha!
Ha—kino
Pukahukahu—roro e
Whakaha e!

Teaching that promotes the learning of concepts in relation to a physical dimension, such as a word chart or actions, and the technique of verbal rhythms to establish a sequence, are typically used in a Māori educational context (Metge, 1990).

Daily Waiata (Song)

Rata is at the front holding up the waiata chart. The children are standing on the mat. "This one," says Rata. "Tahi, rua" (one, two). The children sing and Rata points to the words as they do so, "A e i o u. A ha ka ma. . . ." They sing.

The children participated in singing together every day, both songs in Māori and English. Daily shared singing is a way for Māori to be a group, "Frequent use of group recitation, singing and dancing reinforces the value of togetherness and group support" (Metge, 1990, 62).This waiata 'A Ha Ka Ma' made visible a Māori-specific consonant-vowel (CV) linguistic unit for the children, because the lyrics are the CV segments for every consonant and each of the five vowels (a), (e), (i), (o), and (u) in Māori. The CV structure is repetitive and portrays the Māori alphabet as consonant-vowel configurations.

The older students were involved in helping Whāea with teaching. In this way, they shifted their role from learner to teacher; a practice commonly used in Māori contexts and called 'ako' (Pere, 1994). Further, the older children were often involved in working with the younger children, in keeping with the tuakana/teina practice, in which the older person helps the younger. Pere wrote about the tuakana/teina relationship as bound in practices that "bond and strengthen the kinship ties of a whānau" (p. 26).

Reading Development

The standard reading assessments used in New Zealand, and in this classroom, are Running Records for word recognition in text and reading comprehension (Clay, 1998) and the *BURT Word Reading Test* (New Zealand revision; Gilmore, Croft, & Reid, 1981). According to these test scores, the youngest children (five to six years old) were emergent readers, the seven to nine year olds were developing proficiency, and the oldest students (ten and eleven years) were reading English fluently and comprehending text according to their age level. This contrasts with the mainstream, where the Māori children's performance is interpreted as poor and the students are thus labeled as deficient.

The developing proficiency of English reading over an extended time span in the whānau class is in alignment with the research that states bilingual learners can take several years to become fluent readers of English.

CONCLUDING COMMENTS

The ways in which Whāea Kath engaged with this community of learners incorporated an intermeshing of practices from the worlds of both Māori and Pākehā. Her teaching interactions were embedded in a holistic approach. She provided a bilingual/bicultural learning context aligned with the bilingual/bicultural lives of the students. Her focus on words and their meanings was richly interwoven within all class activities; chants were used to enhance content learning and were embedded in a cyclic approach to teaching; and waiata (songs) supported community togetherness.

The children were learning to speak and read English from a basis of bilingualism and biculturalism. They were following pathways for learning to read in ways supported by the research about how bicultural/bilingual children learn to read. The inclusive holistic context created by Whāea Kath ensured the enhanced achievement of language and English reading learning. It is important that teachers recognize the learning strengths of bicultural/bilingual children to ensure that classroom teaching practices support them to be learners *at-promise,* rather than at-risk.

ACKNOWLEDGMENTS

I would like to acknowledge the support of Drs. Baljit Kaur and Helen Hayward, University of Canterbury, Reverend Te Wharekawa Kaa, Kaumātua, Christchurch, and the Graham Nuthall Classroom Research Trust, Christchurch.

REFERENCES

Clay, M. (1998). *An observation survey of early literacy achievement.* Auckland: Heinemann.

Cummins, J. (1992). Empowerment through biliteracy. In J. Tinajero & A. Ada (Eds.), *The power of two languages: Literacy and biliteracy for Spanish-speaking students.* New York: McGraw-Hill.

Gee, J. (1985). The narrativization of experience in the oral style. *Journal of Education, 167*(1), 9–35.

Gilmore, A., Croft, C., & Reid, N. (1981). *BURT word reading test—New Zealand revision.* Wellington: New Zealand Council for Educational Research.

Harris, F. (2008). Critical engagement with the deficit construction of Māori children as learners in the education system. *Critical Literacy: Theories and Practices, 2*(1), 43–59.

Metge, J. (1990). *Te Kohao o Te Ngira. Culture and learning: Education for a multi-cultural society.* Wellington, NZ: Learning Media, Ministry of Education.

Pere, R. (1994). *Ako: Concepts and learning in the Māori tradition.* Wellington: Te Kōhanga Reo National Trust.

Chapter 33

Zöld Kakas: An Ethos-Oriented Second-Chance High School in Hungary

Mária Molnár, József Braun, and Judit Kováts

Since its opening in 1997, Zöld Kakas (Green Rooster) Líceum and Mental Health Vocational High School in Budapest, Hungary, has been educating students who, despite their academic potential, were unsuccessful in public schools. Without a high school diploma, Hungarian young adults have difficulty finding a job and are unable to pursue higher education. The faculty of Zöld Kakas has been working diligently to find new and innovative ways to work *with* their students to ensure academic and personal growth—not only for the students, but also for the teachers.

Unlike most high schools in Hungary, Zöld Kakas is operated by a non-profit foundation. It gives two hundred fifteen- to twenty-six-year-old students a second chance to complete a four-year, combined vocational educational and college preparatory program, and to prepare for the national college entrance exam. The academic program is supplemented by social and psychological services, vocational education, and after-school activities. While Zöld Kakas' curriculum is based on the national curriculum guidelines that all schools are required to follow, and its students are required to complete the high school exit exam administered in public high schools, the school has a unique structure and innovative educational practices.

The first part of the chapter is dedicated to the new organizational model that was developed based on research and experience at Zöld Kakas. The second part illustrates three inventive practices that the Zöld Kakas community uses to acknowledge a need for, and to foster, students' autonomy, while at the same time helping students and teachers succeed personally and academically.

ETHOS-ORIENTED ORGANIZATION

One of the most innovative aspects of Zöld Kakas is its organizational structure, which is connected to the faculty's distinctive view of students who
did not succeed in public schools. As opposed to using the term *at-risk,* in
Zöld Kakas students are called *young adults in turmoil* or YAITs, because
they often find themselves in difficult situations or turmoil that they did not
cause and cannot control. They are not at risk because they lack something—
knowledge, relationships, or experience—but because they have a surplus
(Kerényi, 2006). They have a need for autonomy, in other words, a trait we
call *autonomy-drive,* of which they are often unaware. It drives YAITs to find
ways to extend their autonomy and spaces to do so. Outside of Zöld Kakas,
this is often perceived as defiance and students get into trouble for it. YAITs
do not respond well to traditional authoritative relationships, but they readily
form partnerships with *congruent* persons (Rogers, 1995) who do not pretend
to be someone they are not and are committed to self-improvement and finding their real selves.

Based on research conducted at Zöld Kakas, one of the authors of this
chapter (Braun, 2008) has developed and written extensively about a new
ethos-oriented educational organizational structure. *The American Heritage
Dictionary* (2006) defines *ethos* as the disposition, character, or fundamental values peculiar to a specific person, people, culture, or movement.

Ethos-oriented organizations are committed to upholding a particular set of values, which are the organizations' basic values—their ethos.
These organizations acknowledge people's autonomy-drive and operate
fundamentally differently than profit-oriented (corporations) or authority-
oriented (city halls, religious groups) organizations. The latter work towards
one specific goal (generating profit or upholding public authority). Ethos-
oriented organizations, for example, foundations organizing volunteer work
or second-chance schools like Zöld Kakas, are not arranged around specific,
outside goals. Their drive is located inside the organization, and is constituted
in the passion of the members who work toward causes they judge worthy.
The organization's ethos is generated as the individual members' drives
interact and magnify each other.

DRIVING PRINCIPLES

Responsibility for change within the organization is dispersed among
its members. This means that any individual or group can influence and
shape the organization's functioning. In ethos-oriented organizations,

these influences cluster around five principles (Braun, 2008; Sencz, 2008):

1. Principle of intentional participation. Because all members of an ethos-oriented organization intend to experience their autonomy to the greatest extent possible, the only way the organization can exist is if its members *choose to participate* in it.
2. Principle of fulfilling the need for autonomy. A person needs a social support network to take advantage of his or her autonomy. People who yearn to increase their autonomy *actively participate in the creation and sustenance* of organizations that allow for this experience.
3. Principle of congruence. A person who yearns for autonomy also yearns for congruence. Congruence or *accepting our real self* (Rogers, 1995) is an integral part of a person's autonomy.
4. Principle of coherence. A person who yearns for autonomy is also committed to live out particular personal values. These values become part of the organization's drive as a series of everyday choices. Commitment to these values forms the organization's dominant (ethos-oriented) structure. Therefore, the basis of the organization's effectiveness is congruence, *alignment of the values, the goals* that are based on these values, and the *processes* aimed to fulfill the goals.
5. Principle of co-evolution. Because the organization's drives are internal, they form an *interconnected web of influences*. Once a drive is in motion, it *forces other drives and influences to evolve*, and it takes on an evolutional quality.

Evolutionary organizational theory, which grew out of research conducted at Zöld Kakas, interprets organization as the space where drives can emerge and develop as opposed to a rigid, goal-oriented structure. If an organization (for example a school) is constructed and operated based on an ethos-oriented structure then young adults in turmoil have a chance to succeed.

THREE KEY INNOVATIONS

Of all the innovative practices at Zöld Kakas, we chose two—student mentoring and restorative conflict resolution—to illustrate ways in which students' autonomy-drive is constantly fostered. In addition, we decided to share the pocket mirror peer-evaluation system to show that innovations at Zöld Kakas are not only focused on students, but also on teachers.

Student Mentoring

Student mentoring is one of the few practices that have been used consistently since the establishment of Zöld Kakas (Bakányi, Kováts, & Lázár, 2008; Sencz, 2008). Mentoring is a complex interaction. Personal support, partnership, and collaboration are all important tools in addressing the need for autonomy. Everyone on the faculty uses the same general framework for mentoring, but the personality of the mentor and the mentee have a great impact on the way mentoring is realized.

Trust is established in a mentoring relationship through choice. Mentor and mentee both choose to establish a partnership with each other. Over time, mentors get to know their mentees, and the connection grows into a deeper bond. Mentors become committed to helping their mentees become successful, well balanced, and happy.

Because mentoring is based on very personal relationships, it is impossible to base it on anything other than the mentors' personal belief system(s). They cannot lie to their students. For example, there is no point preaching about the importance of healthy living if the mentor is a smoker. Mentoring is the role in which mentors reveal themselves the most, in which they need to be most congruent.

Mentor-mentee pairings are *horizontal learning opportunities.* Mentees receive personal support in all areas of their lives. At the same time, mentors, through their mentees, face difficulties they would not otherwise encounter. Pondering these difficulties helps them grow as people and as mentors. In addition, mentees often inspire their mentors to overcome roadblocks in their own personal growth and development.

These mentors' notes give a glimpse into the practical reality of mentoring:

> Mentor 1: I look out the window and there goes Gabi. Away from the school. At the mentoring session he did not show, of course. Then, he comes at the most unexpected moment and smiles at me with that smile of his that also compels his girlfriend to forgive him. There is no doubt, at one point, I will bite his head off. He is failing most subjects, most of them he is taking the second time already, so he is going to have to leave the school. He drives me nuts.
>
> Mentor 2: Kriszti came to see me in every recess today. She poked her head into the teachers' lounge and waved, "I'm here. Don't worry. I'm not ditching." She's been sticking to our mini-contract for almost ten days now. I'm starting to relax. I see that it's hard for her, but maybe she'll hang on this time.

Restorative Conflict Resolution

Young adults in turmoil experience many failures and conflicts and they also face great difficulty solving conflicts successfully. This presents faculty with the challenge of teaching students to resolve conflicts in a way that satisfies all parties while taking into consideration the students' need for autonomy.

The Zöld Kakas community uses restorative conflict resolution (Sentz, 2008), which is based on the belief that all humans are respected, able to accept others, and need acceptance. Conflicts and problems are viewed as part of everyday life and as an opportunity to clarify and untangle relationships. Notably, restorative conflict resolution allows young people to work through the emotional aspects of conflicts in a safe environment. Participants learn to apologize and restore harmony, sometimes in very unconventional ways.

When conflict arises, community members ask for a mediated discussion that continues until a resolution that satisfies all parties is reached. The following four questions guide the discussion:

1. What happened?
2. Who is involved?
3. How are they involved?
4. What should we do?

Zöld Kakas uses restorative conflict resolution techniques to resolve conflicts between students, students and teachers, and colleagues, as well as between employers and employees. Students also transfer the technique outside the school's walls. The following examples illustrate restorative conflict resolution in action:

- The constant bickering of two girls divided the class and disturbed learning. They agreed to discover the positive aspects of each other. The result was unexpected: they became good friends.
- The conflict between the principal and young adults who drew graffiti ev erywhere was resolved by the boys agreeing to paint the hallway and the principal assigning a wall for graffiti.

Peer Evaluation: The Pocket Mirror Process

The teacher evaluation process in Zöld Kakas has been evolving. Over time, teachers realized that they did not want an evaluation system that was based on outside standards. They also became aware that this uneasiness with outside expectations caused previous systems to become ineffective. This led to a large-scale overhaul of the evaluation process and the creation of an unusual system that provides a more desired opportunity for feedback, reflection, and personal attention. Since the process of receiving feedback is similar to looking in a mirror, it was nicknamed *pocket mirror* (Iszlai, 2008; Sentz, 2008).

Each faculty and staff member in the school is randomly paired with a *pocket mirror,* a person who is responsible for providing them with feedback. The role of the *pocket mirror* is to hold a mirror to his or her partner. *Pocket mirrors* observe their partners for a predetermined number of times without any formal observational guidelines. They can be as subjective as they wish to be. The observed partners may suggest topics they want to know more about, or seek assistance with, or they may choose to give the *mirror* free rein to reflect whatever he or she notices. The process ends with a moderated discussion during which the *mirror* shares his or her impressions and the observed responds to this sharing.

During the initial implementation, faculty members were excited to discover that the emerging reflection revealed just as much about the *mirror* as it did about the observed. After participating in the process, faculty members rated the pocket mirror evaluation process as a valuable experience. They received individual attention and personalized feedback throughout the process that they had not received before. Many of them thought that the observation process was just as—or perhaps even more—valuable than the impressions shared at the final discussion.

As a result, the quality and quantity of personal attention has increased within the organization. This attention is not unidirectional as in traditional evaluations, but multi-directional, connecting all participants. Its aim is not to evaluate in the traditional sense, but to get to know another person at a deeper level. This attention has also raised the level of trust within the organization, including in teacher-student relationships. One teacher said:

> During our first discussion, I wanted to know what Ágnes was interested in knowing about herself but there was nothing specific. We decided that I'll observe, we'll talk, and hopefully her particular interest will emerge. But it didn't. We just enjoyed the discussions. I thought that the information and data I collected was coming together into one portrait. So I decided that this is what I will share with her, knowing that it reflected who I, the *pocket mirror* was, just as much as it did her. As a result, some of its parts are exaggerated and others are omitted. Therefore, Ágnes is not like this, but this is the way I see her.

CONCLUSION

Zöld Kakas is an example of an ethos-oriented organization that acknowledges values such as the need for autonomy and support for personal growth. Through mentoring and restorative conflict resolution, it redefines the hierarchical student-teacher relationship. Through the *pocket mirror* peer evaluation process, it offers an alternative to traditional teacher evaluation. The shared samples of Zöld Kakas' ever changing and developing practices may offer new ideas to others in search of innovative ways to reach and teach YAITs who do not make it in public schools.

REFERENCES

Bakányi, L., Kováts, J., & Lázár, A. (2008). *Mentorálás a* Zöld Kakas *Líceumban* [Mentoring at Zöld Kakas Lyceum]. Retrieved on February 17, 2009 from http://hogu.hu/eredmenyek/mentoralasZK.html

Braun, J. (2008). *Második esély iskola, mint segítő szervezet: Szervezeti modell-leírás.* [The organizational structural description of second-chance schools as helping organizations]. Retrieved on February 17, 2009, from http://hogu.hu/eredmenyek/modell.html

Ethos. (n.d.). *The American Heritage® Dictionary of the English Language (4th ed.).* Retrieved March 12, 2009 from http://dictionary.reference.com/browse/ethos

Kerényi, M. (2006). A paprikakoszorú mint alternatív [The pepper wreath as an alternative]. In T. Vekerdi (ed.), *Van más megoldás* [There is another solution]. Budapest: Sulinova.

Rogers, K. (1995). *On becoming a person* (2nd ed.). New York: Houghton Mifflin.

Sencz, J. (2008). *Sikeresen alkalmazható eszközök értékorientált szervezetben* [Tools successfully used in an ethos-oriented organization]. Retrieved on February 17, 2009, from http://hogu.hu/sikeres_eszkozok.html

Chapter 34

Providing Students with Uninterrupted Learning Experiences: A Success Story from Iceland

Ingvar Sigurgeirsson

Laugar Comprehensive is one of the smallest high schools in Iceland, with one hundred and twenty students (grades 11–15). The school is situated in a rural community in the northern part of the country, not far from Lake Myvatn, a natural reserve famous for its exceptional birdlife, hot springs, lava formations, and volcanoes.

Until four years ago, Laugar Comprehensive was a rather traditional boarding school that offered four different programs: social science, natural science, athletics, and sports, and a *general program,* more aptly termed *a special education unit,* designed for students with learning difficulties. The students in the regular programs were mainly taught through whole-class, direct instruction, whereas the teachers in the special education unit had for some years been experimenting with more flexible methods, allowing students to work individually according to their own pace. This flexible approach seemed to work quite well.

Four years ago, the Icelandic Ministry of Education initiated policies that abridged the Icelandic high school graduation requirement from four to three academic years. There were massive debates about these policies. The teachers at Laugar wondered whether there was a real need for *a one size fits all* program and whether an alternative might be preferable. Perhaps an individualized program, allowing students to decide for themselves the time needed to finish their schooling.

Some of the teachers at Laugar had been reconsidering their teaching methods, in light of the fact that in an ordinary classroom few students really participate in the teaching-learning process. These teachers speculated whether they might be standing in the way of their students' learning. As one teacher put it, "It seemed to some of us that we were often interrupting students in their learning, and we were discussing ways to provide them with more uninterrupted learning experiences."

In the spring of 2006, the Laugar staff agreed to start developing a whole-school learning environment based on the experience in the special education unit. They decided to launch a curriculum development project labeled: *A Flexible Learning Environment: A Personalized Program.* The core of the change was simple: cut in half the number of formal lessons in each course and, instead, offer *workshop time* during which students could learn according to their own pace. Further, the program placed emphasis on the application of a greater variety of teaching methods; project-based learning, and closer student-teacher relationships, as well as redefining school routines.

The author of this chapter has been an adviser to the project from the outset, visiting the school regularly, observing lessons and workshops, interviewing students and staff, as well as participating in meetings where the project has been discussed and assessed. This short account will offer a vivid portrayal of this interesting and promising project, arguably one of the most successful innovations in Iceland.

This change was accelerated by many factors. Icelandic high schools have had a prevalent dropout problem, a continuous dropout rate of 20–30 percent (Statistics Iceland, 2004). The teachers at Laugar hoped that by adapting and enhancing the individualized program it would make the school a more attractive and meaningful place to their students. Also, there was pressure on the school staff because of governmental cost-saving measures that questioned the financial effectiveness of small schools. The aim was to strengthen the foundation of the school and make it a more plausible alternative to the regular schools.

THE SCHOOL AS A WORKPLACE

Each school day at Laugar starts at 8:30 A.M. with a thirty-minute workshop. A few students may already have started their studies. Most students will use this first workshop to make a plan for the day or the week. After breakfast, the program continues until 3:30 P.M with a mixture of workshops, formal lessons, and tutorials. Thereafter, students are on their own and can continue their studies or attend to other duties or interests.

The main workshop areas are in two open space environments. Students from all programs attend the same workshops, which are mixed age. Students can also decide to work in the library, the computer lab, or in smaller rooms available for group work, seminars, or quiet work. Care has been

Photo 34 1   Learning in a Relaxed Environment, courtesy of Konráð Erlendsson.

taken to make all workspaces attractive, with books, computers, flowers, pictures, and posters. Students can decide to work together in groups, but individual desks are also available. If students have a book to read, they can also decide to lie down in one of the big leather sofas placed in the open space environments or in the adjoining corridors. A couch is also an ideal meeting place if you need to have a quiet chat with a teacher or a fellow student.

The number of students attending each workshop varies from ten or fifteen to all one hundred and twenty students at the school. This arrangement has increased collaboration across age groups, thus students often seek assistance from their peers. Students are frequently observed helping each other. The author observed a girl, a senior student, helping a first-year student, a newcomer to Iceland from Poland, with her math skills for over half an hour. When the senior student was asked if she had been making good use of her own study time, she responded: "Well, to tell you the truth, you learn most when you teach another person!"

The students decide what assignments to attend to in each workshop. Students know in advance which teachers are present and may decide to work on assignments related to the courses taught by the teachers on duty. Strangely enough, one of the problems with the workshop arrangement has been that the teachers at times feel that they have very little to do!

Most students make good use of their workshop time; the atmosphere is busy, but relaxed, very much like an effective workplace. Occasionally students will attend to personal e-mail, browse the Internet, even close their eyes and daydream for a minute or two, but these are exceptions. The author has observed thousands of classes in Icelandic schools and can state that he has never witnessed such a high level of on-task engagement.

Most students are content with the workshop arrangement, but of course, there are students who are not. Some have complained about the workshop assignments being too monotonous and have suggested more variability during the school day.

STRENGTHENING STUDENT-TEACHER RELATIONSHIPS

One of the main aims of the Laugar project was to strengthen the relationships between teachers and students, providing the latter with more guidance and closer adult attention than before. Students are assigned to mixed-age mentor groups of ten to twelve students. During the week, the mentors keep an eye on their students in the workshops. Once a week each mentor has all of the students in his or her group in the same workshop space, which provides various opportunities, such as having a discussion with the whole group or going through matters with smaller groups or individual students. Since the groups are mixed-age, there is also a chance for peer consultation. The senior students can often help the juniors as they have already taken the courses and may know the teachers better.

The effort to strengthen student-teacher relationships seems to have been successful at Laugar. Many of the students have attended other high schools and can make informed comparisons. Here are some student comments when asked about the positive aspects of the Laugar environment:

- "The teachers here help you much more than teachers in other schools where I have been and they know your work much better. . . . The teachers also show good understanding of your weaknesses and they don't use them against you."
- "The teachers know every single student quite well and what is unique about each person."
- "The teachers are very good and they do not approach me as an object, but as a person."

A VARIETY OF TEACHING METHODS

The teachers have consistently been looking for ways to provide more active and meaningful learning experiences. Because teachers only teach half of the formal classes they used to, many of them place emphasis on developing independent projects. They have also been looking for ways to add creative components to the assignments. Here are some examples of what has come out of these efforts:

- In psychology, in a unit on child development, the teacher used a multiple intelligences approach (Armstrong, 2001). The students took a test revealing their strongest intelligences, and then were grouped accordingly. Each group had to find a way to build on their strengths and to demonstrate what they had learned about their topics. As an example, the music-smart group formed a band and wrote and performed a song on their main conclusions.
- Science course students wrote short stories about Newton's law of motion.
- In social studies, the students wrote and performed plays to show their understanding of public policies regarding children's social welfare.

Most Icelandic high schools arrange courses within a mastery-learning framework. Each program is based on a series of courses, and the courses have to be taken in a prescribed order. In a small school such as Laugar, there are limits to the number of courses offered because a certain number of students are needed to run a course. To overcome this obstacle, teachers have been experimenting with individualized approaches, which means that a single class can include students who are taking different courses. This flexibility also provides possibilities of abandoning end-of-term assessments. The student completes the course when he or she is ready. To maintain peer support, this is often arranged so that two to four students are on similar schedules.

BREAKING UP THE ROUTINE

Each term at Laugar is broken up with a variety of events and projects. There are Short Course Days, Problem-Based Learning Weeks, Open-Days, and Thematic Days. During the annual Short Course Days, students can select courses from a wide range of offerings based on a survey of their preferences. There is emphasis on practical courses of various natures, for example: working with glass, mask making, karate for beginners, ice fishing, highland hiking, rescue work, horse riding, oral presentations, first aid, and cosmetic care. One further option during the Short Course Days is working on the team responsible for organizing an open song contest, arranged by the students at Laugar, and open to students from all other schools in the region. The highlight of this effort is the production and marketing of a CD with all of the music performed by the students.

Another event is the Problem-Based Learning (PBL) Week, when students work on individual or group projects. In one PBL Week, the students had more or less complete freedom to develop their projects, the only criteria being that there had to be a creative component, and the results were to be shown at the Annual Open-Day Exhibition. One group studied fashion, compared modern clothing to Victorian times, and set up an exhibition in the campus cinema.

Another group decided to study cake recipes from around the world. They baked the cakes and offered them with background information during the Open-Day Exhibition. The Open-Day guests also saw an art exhibition, an outdoor installation with an ecological message, music performances and electronic models. Students explained their work and findings to the hundreds of guests attending, including community members, parents, former students, and politicians. The role of the Open Day is to strengthen the bonds with the community. It is held on the First Day of Summer, a holiday that has been celebrated by Icelanders for centuries.

One effort that was aimed at making the curriculum more meaningful was an end-of-term project where the students had to integrate learning objectives and content from two to three different courses. These were individual projects and students had four days to complete them. After a struggling beginning, all kinds of products came to fruition: An exhibition about life in Viking times, a computer game about mythology, a model of the solar system, and another model comparing the geology of Iceland with the geology of Germany were some of the results. A lecture about economic development in China was offered and various children's books were written in Icelandic, Danish, and German.

Creativity at Laugar takes different forms. On the yearly Drug Prevention Day, students decided to go on a rally to the waterfall Godafoss—Waterfall of the Gods—in the neighboring valley. On a snowy day, fifty students and staff walked over a moor carrying banners celebrating peace, healthy living, love, safe sex, education, trust, justice, hope, and empathy. In Viking times, when Icelanders adopted Christianity, one of their spiritual leaders threw the statues of the pagan Nordic gods, Odin, Thor and Freyr, into the waterfall. When the students from Laugar finally arrived at the riverbank near the waterfall, they made snowballs—symbolizing all bad thoughts and feelings—and threw them into the stream!

WHY IS LAUGAR SUCCESSFUL?

The reasons for the success at Laugar seem to go hand in hand with characteristics of successful school improvement efforts that are research-based. (Fullan, 2007). The project was a grassroots effort and it is collaborative; all members of staff participated from the beginning. Most of them have become committed to the project—not only the teachers, but also other members of staff; the chef and the janitor equally share the vision behind the project. A steering committee has carefully monitored the project from the outset, made action plans for consideration and revised them when needed. The steering group members and the principal have understood the complexities of educational change, they have understood that setbacks and frustrations are a part of school development, and they have kept their perseverance and shown the necessary flexibility.

A strong component in the success of the Laugar project has been the emphasis put on continuous evaluation measures. Members of the staff have met regularly to discuss the advantages and disadvantages of each proceeding, and joint decisions have been made about each step taken. Similar forums have been provided for students. The quality of learning and life at Laugar has been scrutinized in weekly meetings, focus groups, and evaluations circles. What may have been essential in the success of the program is the fact that students' opinions have been taken into account and have been used to improve their learning environment. Listening to students' voices may have been the magic key!

REFERENCES

Armstrong, T. (2000). *Multiple intelligences in the classroom.* Alexandria, VA: Association for Supervision and Curriculum Development.

Fullan, M. (2007). *The new meaning of educational change* (4th ed.). New York: Teachers College Press.

Statistics Iceland. (2004). Dropouts from upper secondary schools 2002–2003. *Statistical Series 89*(3). Retrieved February 26, 2009 from http://www.hagstofa. is/lisalib/getfile.aspx?ItemID=954

Conclusion

Audrey Cohan and Andrea Honigsfeld

When we first envisioned writing this book, we wanted to create a book that educators would read cover to cover (perhaps a novel idea . . . pun intended) and not just another book that readers were more likely to skim. It was for this reason that we selected best practices from authors of diverse experiences and backgrounds. We chose educators who capitalized on opportunities for learning and created new ways to address students' diverse needs. We believe the stories from well-established, as well as first-time authors, offer authentic accomplishments and compelling examples of innovative and successful practices. Our authors shared narratives of real-life, genuine innovations so the ideas for change would be inspiring to others.

As we now reflect on the voices of innovation for the twenty-first century—brought together in this volume—the patterns for success and similar positive themes emerge. We encourage our readers to engage in collaborative reflections to discover those patterns and themes for themselves. To get you started, consider the following questions:

- Can teachers nurture a special *journey* for an individual child so that child feels valued and unique? Compare the journey of Martín (Brown) to that of Dalila (Wolsey et al.) in terms of interaction between teachers and students.
- Can teachers create a special *journey* for themselves that will lead to cooperation and successful co-teaching strategies (Dove)?
- Can original ideas and new tools change the learning opportunities of students? Consider the use of the Internet for teaching (Langer de Ramirez) or for collaboration (Powell et al.)
- How can seemingly insurmountable difficulties be overcome to bring a dog or other nontraditional instructional tools to class? (Bostic Frederick).

- What is the link between accountability and collaboration in schools? Consider how infrastructure changes can impact instructional delivery systems (Murphy).
- How can visionary leadership improve the quality of schools? (Daly, Ferris, Fretz, Merz) What qualities, dispositions, and attributes do these leaders demonstrate?
- How can leaders foster the development of shared leadership in schools? (multiple chapters)
- What are key elements to redesigning schools academically? (Freeley et al., Ginsberg, Holzer et al., Hyland et al., Legakes et al.)
- What are the key elements in redesigning the physical structure of schools to meet the needs of all learners? (Capolupo et al., Malone, Parsons)
- How does the physical learning space impact academic achievement? (multiple chapters)
- How can schools interact with the larger community? Can we respond to the community from birth through stages of adulthood? What role do parents play in the learning process? (Binkley, Gomez et al., Howlett, Poinelli, Sanders, Tazi)
- How can an enhanced understanding of learning styles benefit schools? (Cooper, Favre et al., Nigaglioni)
- How can we innovatively meet the needs of all student learners? (Molnár et al., Sigurgeirsson, multiple chapters)
- How can we nurture students for a multicultural or global society? (Bajaj, Harris, Pezone et al., Swerdlow)

In sum, we urge you, our readers to consider the key challenges school leaders, teachers, and communities face in the twenty-first century. Try to deliberate as to which innovations would best address your challenges. Share and celebrate the successes of our authors with your colleagues (all chapters).

Contributors

Monisha Bajaj, Ed.D., is Assistant Professor of International and Comparative Education at Teachers College, Columbia University. Her research has examined peace and human rights education in diverse international contexts, including the Dominican Republic, Zambia, Tanzania, India, and the United States.

Nadine Binkley, Ph.D., is currently Superintendent of the Leominster, Massachusetts public schools. Previously, she taught in the education faculty at the University of British Columbia. She has presented at numerous educational conferences and has written for several educational journals.

Nancy Boxler, B.A., is currently the Assistant Network Director of Alaska Educational Innovations Network at the University of Alaska, Anchorage. She facilitates professional networks that create the conditions for educators to examine their practice as well as give back to their profession by being a resource to others.

József Braun, M.S., is the president of the MH Líceum Foundation the organization that operates Zöld Kakas Líceum in Budapest, Hungary. He has published on the topics of alternative education, second-chance schools, and the ethos-oriented organizational structural model.

Furman Brown, B.A., is the founder and executive director of Generation Schools Network. He taught in South Central Los Angeles and then worked for various non-profit educational organizations in New York City for many years, supporting school reform innovations. He received an Echoing Green Prize for Social Innovation for his work to develop the Generation Schools model.

Sally Brown, Ph.D. is an assistant professor of Reading in the College of Education at Georgia Southern University. Her research interests include classroom discourse, English-language learners, and Latino immigrants.

James Capolupo, D.M.A., is currently the Superintendent of the Springfield School District in Springfield, Pennsylvania. He completed post-doctoral work in Educational Leadership at the University of Pennsylvania and Harvard University. He received the Robert Flynn Distinguished Service Award from the Pennsylvania Association of Supervision and Curriculum Development.

Douglas Carney, M.B.A, is an Architect in Pennsylvania, and is NCARB and LEED AP certified. He has led the Springfield School District Capital Program Committee for sixteen years, which is constructing the first K-12 building designed specifically to reflect differentiated literacy instruction, advancing the nationally recognized literacy program begun in 2000 when he was Board President.

Patricia Chesbro, M.S., is director of the Alaska Educational Innovations Network at the University of Alaska Anchorage College of Education. Though she comes to the College from roles as a high school teacher, principal, and district superintendent, she has had the opportunity to learn much about Alaska and Alaskans in her work with educators from nine diverse districts from around the state.

J. Alan Cooper, B.A., B.Ed., ANZIM, has taught at all levels of New Zealand education from primary to college level. During his twenty years as a primary principal, his school became the first in New Zealand to introduce both Learning Styles (Dunn and Dunn model) and Thinking Maps (Hyerle) school wide. He contributed more than fifty articles for educational magazines in several countries and newsletters including the ASCD's Multiple Intelligences Newsletter, and more regularly in The New Zealand Principal.

Alan J. Daly, Ph.D., is a professor of educational leadership at the University of California, San Diego. Most recently, he was the Program Director for the Center for Educational Leadership and Effective Schools, at the University of California, in Santa Barbara. His research interests include the intersection of trust and leadership and the application of social network analysis to leadership and organizations.

Maria G. Dove, M.A., is assistant professor of the Division of Education at Molloy College, in Rockville Centre, New York. She was as an ESL teacher for 25 years in Valley Stream District 30, New York. Her research interests include co-teaching and English language learners.

Lois Favre, Ed.D., is Assistant Superintendent of Instruction and Curriculum for the Lakeland Central School District, the largest suburban school district in Westchester County, New York. She is an international staff developer presenting on such topics as leadership, change theory, inclusion, collaboration, implementation of differentiated instruction through learning styles, co-teaching, and behavior management in classrooms.

Marc Ferris, M.A., taught Social Studies at H. Frank Carey High School in Franklin Square, New York, prior to becoming the assistant principal and then principal of North Shore Middle School in Glen Head, NY. He is currently a doctoral student at Hofstra University in the department of Foundations, Leadership, and Policy Studies.

Douglas Fisher, Ph.D., is a Professor of Language and Literacy Education in the School of Teacher Education at San Diego State University and a classroom teacher at Health Sciences High and Middle College. He is a recipient of the Celebrate Literacy Award from the International Reading Association.

Karen Bostic Frederick, Ph.D., is an Assistant Professor of Special Education at the University of Nebraska–Kearney. Her research interests include middle-level content area reading, self-management techniques for secondary students with behavioral disorders, and the use of dogs as an educational methodology in the classroom.

Mary Ellen Freeley, Ed.D., is Associate Professor at St. John's University in Queens, NY and Past President of ASCD. In her forty years as an educator, Dr. Freeley has been a superintendent of schools for twelve years as well as a teacher, principal, and professor.

Joan R. Fretz, M.S., P.D., is the Director of Fine and Performing Arts in the Huntington School District and the Chairperson for the Long Island Social Emotional Literacy Forum. As a co-founder of LI SELF, she spearheaded the development of this organization, which facilitates the sharing of information related to Social Emotional Learning and Supportive Learning Environments.

Alice E. Ginsberg, Ph.D., is educational consultant and author or editor of three books and numerous other publications on equity issues, urban school reform, educational philanthropy, and gender studies. She is currently co-editing an anthology of diverse, male K-12 teachers whose work is focused on exploring gender roles or promoting gender equity in the classroom and school-wide.

Diane W. Gómez, Ph.D., is Assistant Professor of Teaching English to Speakers of Other Languages (TESOL) and special education at Manhanttanville College in Purchase, New York. Her research interests include heritage speakers of Spanish, differentiated instruction, teacher training, and multicultural education.

Richard Hanzelka, Ph.D., is Professor at St. Ambrose University in Davenport, IA and Past President of ASCD. In his forty-eight years in education, Dr. Hanzelka has been an elementary and secondary teacher, language arts consultant, division director for an intermediate service agency, and professor, in addition to his international work with ASCD.

Fleur Harris, Ph.D., is a lecturer in the Institute of Early Childhood at Macquarie University, Sydney, Australia, prior to which she was a lecturer at the College of Education, University of Canterbury, New Zealand. She has thirty years of experience in education, including speech-language therapy, early childhood education, and tertiary teaching.

Madeleine F. Holzer, Ed.D., is the Educational Development Director at Lincoln Center Institute for the Arts in Education, responsible for the Institute's work in the New York City metropolitan area. She has numerous publications, including academic articles, essays, poetry, and CD-ROMS, as well as a co-edited book with Scott Noppe-Brandon.

Charles F. Howlett, Ph.D., is an Associate Professor in the Division of Education at Molloy College, New York. He is author of several seminal publications on Peace Education and Peace History. He is the recipient of numerous awards in the fields of history and education. Presently, he is investigating a history of bubble gum cards and the "Horrors of War" series.

Nora E. Hyland, Ph.D., is an assistant professor of elementary and early childhood education at Rutgers University, New Jersey. Her areas of research and teaching interests are: critical multicultural education, teacher education, social justice in schooling, and action ethnography in schools. She is also a founding board member of Generation Schools.

Judit Kováts, M.A, is a teacher and researcher at Zöld Kakas Líceum, Budapest, Hungary. She is one of the coordinators of the Pocket Mirror teacher peer-evaluation program.

Diane E. Lang, Ph.D., is Assistant Professor of early childhood and childhood education at Manhanttanville College in Purchase, New York. Her research interests include field-based teacher education, play and learning, educational anthropology, and bilingual language socialization.

Lori Langer de Ramirez, Ed.D., is the Chairperson of the ESL and World Language Department for Herricks Public Schools. Her areas of research and curriculum development are multicultural and diversity education, folktales in the language classroom, and technology in language teaching. Her interactive Web site (www.miscositas.com) offers teachers over forty virtual picture books and other curricular materials for teaching Chinese, English, French, Italian, and Spanish.

Diane Lapp, Ed.D., is a Distinguished Professor of Education at San Diego State University. Also a teacher at Health Science High and Middle College, she is a member of The International Reading Association's Hall of Fame.

Suzanne M. Lasser, M.S., is a National Board Certified English as Second Language (ESL) teacher and Director of K-12 English Language Learners (ELLs) Programs for the White Plains City School District in New York. Her interests include newcomer centers, dual language programs, and innovative program models designed to support the diverse needs of ELLs.

Anastasia Legakes, M.Ed., in addition to her present assignments as an Advanced Placement English teacher and Department Chair in the St. Lucie County School District in the Florida Public school system, is currently working on her Organizational Leadership doctorate at Argosy University in order to pursue development of innovative curriculum and programs and assist districts and educational institutions in transforming to thrive in twenty-first-century learning.

Michael A. Malone, AIA, NCARB, is the managing partner of PARTNERS in Architecture, PLC located in Mount Clemens, Michigan. His full service architectural design firm specializes in the creation of educational space. He is a member of the American Institute of Architects, the Council of Educational Facility Planners International and the National Council of Architectural Registration Boards.

Judith R. Merz, Ed.D., is a retired superintendent of a K-12 district in New Jersey. She was a recipient of Nova Southeastern University 1996 Kathleen Cooper Wright School Improvement Award and, in that same year, was recognized with the Teacher Educator in a Democracy Award by the New Jersey Network for Educational Renewal. Her interests include leadership, staff development, technology, and school reform.

Mária Molnár, M.A., is a special educator and a doctoral student at Teachers College, Columbia University, New York. Her interests include inclusive education, alternative educational practices, disability studies, and learning disabilities.

Suzanne D. Morgan, M.Ed., is currently working in the St. Lucie County School District. She received the Florida Senate's Medallion of Excellence in 2008. Future endeavors are to build innovative curriculum and programs and assist districts and educational institutions in transforming to thrive in twenty-first-century learning.

Audrey F. Murphy, Ed.D., is currently an Assistant Professor in the TESOL department at St. John's University, New York. She has been an ESL educator and administrator for over twenty years. She worked with schools in the New York City area as a Network Leader, supporting principals in their instructional decisions and day-to-day operations.

Irene Nigaglioni, AIA, REFP, is an architect and partner at PBK, in Texas. Her expertise is in aligning the latest in instructional delivery at the secondary level. She frequently lectures across the United States and serves as an At-Large Representative on CEFPI's International Board of Directors.

Stephen M. Noonan, M.S., M.A., is the founding principal of the High School for Arts, Imagination and Inquiry (HSAII) in Manhattan. The school was created in 2005 through a partnership between The New York City Department of Education, New Visions for Public Schools, and Lincoln Center Institute for the Arts in Education (LCI). He has received awards for his Social Studies teaching.

Scott Noppe-Brandon, ABD, executive director of Lincoln Center Institute, has spent the past fourteen years leading the arts and education branch of Lincoln Center for the Performing Arts. He is known internationally as a speaker, writer, and advocate for education in and through the arts and has helped start and revitalize numerous public schools, as well as author or edit books and articles on the arts and education.

Margaret (Meg) S. Parsons, AIA, REFP, LEED® A.P., is a Principal at Cuningham Group Architecture, P.A., in Minneapolis, Minnesota. She is an expert at assisting schools and districts with facility planning and community engagement.

Michael Pezone, M.S., is a social studies teacher at Law, Government and Community Service Magnet High School in Cambria Heights, Queens, New York. He is also an adjunct instructor and doctoral student at Hofstra University, Hempstead, New York.

Robert Pillar, AIA, LEED AP, is an architect and principal in charge of K-12 design at Burt Hill, in Butler, Pennsylvania. He is currently pursuing and Advanced Certificate in Educational Planning through San Diego State University and is expected to complete these studies in December 2009.

Philip J. Poinelli, AIA, LEED AP, is an architect and principal of Symmes Maini & McKee Associates in Cambridge, Massachusetts, where he specializes in K-12 master planning and educational programming. Former chairman of the Town of Lexington MA Permanent Building Committee and member of the Boston Society of Architects, Education Facilities Committee, Mr. Poinelli applies his knowledge as Principal-In-Charge of many SMMA K-12 school projects.

James H. Powell, Ph.D., is the Chair for the Department of Teaching and Learning and teaches ESL methods, language and culture, and curriculum theory courses in the College of Education at University of Alaska Anchorage. His research focus is on the professional development issues faced by experienced teachers. He has spent the last two years participating in the Language Acquisition Network.

Susan Rundle, B.S., is CEO of Performance Concepts International and Director of the International Learning Styles Network. She is a frequent national and international presenter on learning styles in collaboration with Professor Rita Dunn.

Mavis G. Sanders, Ph.D., holds a joint appointment as senior research scientist at the Center on School, Family, and Community Partnerships and professor in the School of Education at Johns Hopkins University, Baltimore, Maryland.

Ingvar Sigurgeirsson, Ph.D., is Professor at the school of education, university of Iceland in Reykjavík. As a leading scholar of education in Iceland, his current research interests are curriculum and instruction, teaching methods, differentiated curriculum, classroom management, and the use of educational games. His current projects are focused on teaching and learning in Icelandic classrooms and school-based curriculum development.

Alan Singer, Ph.D., is Professor of Secondary Education at Hofstra University and author of numerous publications including *New York and Slavery: Time to Teach the Truth* (SUNY Press, 2008).

Linda Kantor Swerdlow, Ph.D., is an Associate Professor and the Founding Director of the Master of Arts in Teaching program (MAT) at Drew University. Her research focuses upon Global Child Advocacy and the development of leadership, and civic and global awareness in Youth Civic Engagement Programs.

Zoila Tazi, M.S.W., is a Principal in the Ossining Schools serving a student population of approximately 1,000 children from birth through kindergarten. She is currently a doctoral student in Urban Education at the City Universityof New York Graduate Center, New York.

Thomas DeVere Wolsey, Ed.D., is course lead in the literacy and learning graduate degree program at Walden University. He previously taught English, social studies, and elective courses for more than twenty years in public schools.